To What Ends and By What Means?

The Social Justice Implications of Contemporary
School Finance Theory and Policy

EDITED BY

Gloria M. Rodriguez and R. Anthony Rolle

Routledge
Taylor & Francis Group
New York   London

Routledge
Taylor & Francis Group
270 Madison Avenue
New York, NY 10016

Routledge
Taylor & Francis Group
2 Park Square
Milton Park, Abingdon
Oxon OX14 4RN

© 2007 by Taylor & Francis Group, LLC
Routledge is an imprint of Taylor & Francis Group, an Informa business

Printed in the United States of America on acid-free paper
10 9 8 7 6 5 4 3 2 1

International Standard Book Number-10: 0-415-95483-5 (Softcover) 0-415-95482-7 (Hardcover)
International Standard Book Number-13: 978-0-415-95483-9 (Softcover) 978-0-415-95482-2 (Hardcover)

Library of Congress Cataloging-in-Publication Data

To what ends and by what means : the social justice implications of contemporary
    school finance theory and policy / edited by Gloria Rodriguez and R. Anthony Rolle.
        p. cm.
    ISBN 978-0-415-95482-2 (hb) -- ISBN 978-0-415-95483-9 (pb)
        1. Education--Social aspects--United States. 2. Education--Finance--Social
aspects--United States. 3. Education--Economic aspects--United States. 4. Social
justice--United States. I. Rodriguez, Gloria M. (Gloria Mari) II. Rolle, R. Anthony.

    LC66.T6 2006
    306.43--dc22   2006031592

Visit the Taylor & Francis Web site at
http://www.taylorandfrancis.com

and the Routledge Web site at
http://www.routledge.com

DEDICATION

In loving memory of my father, Antonio G. Rodriguez, and in honor of my family, Pascuala (Peggy) S., Tony S., Sheryl Smith, and Casey S. Rodriguez, who have nurtured me with love, laughter, music, prayers, an enduring pride in our people, and the belief that education is a right and a responsibility.

—Gloria M. Rodriguez

In honor of my wife and daughter, Amanda Talley Rolle and Sydney Alexandra Rolle, whose loving spirits endow me with the strength to cry when I am weak, the courage to retreat when I am frightened, and the wisdom to seek counsel when I am in doubt.

—R. Anthony Rolle

CONTENTS

FOREWORD

Patricia Gándara

University of California—Los Angeles

Having spent a good part of the last couple decades researching the social and educational inequalities that result in so many low-income students and students of color failing in school or leaving school altogether, I was immediately excited when I heard of the project that Gloria Rodriguez and Anthony Rolle were conceptualizing. School finance has been mired in paradigmatic dead ends for decades. Ever since the landmark *San Antonio Unified School District v Rodriguez* decision in 1973, which held that education was not a fundamental right protected by the U.S. Constitution, lawyers have been debating about how to extend state constitutional protections to better serve poor children in public schools. But there have been as many losses as wins in the courts. Economists largely abandoned the notion of educational equity, an "equal education for all," in favor of educational adequacy, "a basic education for all," because of the problem of gaining agreement about what constituted equity when children begin life in such different circumstances. Should all children be given the same resources, even if they have very different needs? When are resources sufficient to produce equity in schooling or in opportunity? How much equity is the taxpayer willing to pay for? But, adequacy, too, has proven to be a blunt tool. What constitutes an *adequate* education—sufficient educational resources to make it possible to get a job? Or, sufficient educational resources to *ensure* the ability to get a job? What kind of job—a minimum wage job? Or perhaps a chance to go to college and have a brighter future? School finance cases have dragged on through the courts in most states for years without resolution because there is no consensus about the answers to those questions. And, because even when consensus can be found, the process of finding ways to pay for those solutions nearly always unravels the consensus. But, Rodriguez and Rolle are talking about a different paradigm, a social justice perspective on school finance; that is, what are we morally and ethically bound to do as a society to make good on the social contract that is at the base of these United States? And how shall we understand the circumstances and aspirations of low-income people and people of color from their perspective, rather than from the perspective of those who would interpret their circumstances for them? What should be the role of communities to determine what constitutes an equitable, and socially just, education for their children?

I was so intrigued by Rodriguez's and Rolle's nascent project that I suggested we meet in Santa Fe, New Mexico, for a couple of days to think through the possibilities for such a volume. The conversation was stimulating, sometimes unsettling; all of us at the table attempting to tease out the unique perspective that has come to be represented in this book. And it's about time—beyond time, really. While we have struggled with definitions of equity and adequacy, using the tools of lawyers and economists, we have missed the critical perspectives of philosophers, educational thinkers, and those served by schools about the texture of equality and the human side of the numbers.

More recently, I have been engaged with my colleague, Russell Rumberger, in a major project in California involving some 30-odd scholars in attempting to specify the cost of providing an adequate education to California's K–12 students. Rumberger and I have been charged with conceptualizing what an adequate education for a student who does not speak English—or does not speak it well enough to survive in the mainstream—would look like. We have pored over the literature, examined the models and the data that others have gathered to answer this question about students in general, or poor children, or disabled children. Perhaps most important, though, we have interviewed principals, other administrators, and teachers in schools that are struggling to answer that question every day in their practice. We have asked them how they make decisions about on what to spend money, and what are the things that need to be done that the funds simply do not cover. What we have heard affirms, in many ways, David Berliner's chapter in this volume: there is much that schools can and should do, and much that is beyond their reach, within the present paradigm of schooling. But it is this very paradigm that the authors in this volume question, and challenge.

What impressed us most, however, in the interviews we conducted is the extent to which all of the interviewees mentioned intangible qualities of schools and school personnel as being critical in the achievement of their students. As one principal said in response to a question about how he decides which teachers to hire, "It isn't so much how much they know, it's about who they are. They need to be empathetic and really care about the kids. They have to *really* want them to succeed." Many teachers attributed their achievements to deep collaboration among their fellow teachers; a caring for each other and for their students that extended beyond the routine; and a willingness to find the time to meet, discuss, and thereby improve their pedagogy. Successful schools, we heard from these educational leaders, are schools that care about students, and understand them. Knowing the communities from which the students come is a critical piece of knowing the students themselves. As Rodriguez and Rolle point out, in order to create truly just schools, we must enter into partnership with families and communities to understand how those families and communities define a socially just education. And then we must reflect those values in practice and organization, and in the way that schools advocate for and use their funds.

We also often heard teachers and principals refer to intangible qualities—such as persistence, motivation, and hopefulness—as critical characteristics of students who succeed. Notably, we found that personnel in schools that are successful in the face of challenging circumstances believe that schools can and should nurture these critical characteristics. One principal told us his school dedicated itself to, "as much as we can in addition to literacy skills, behavior, character development, the motivation of students … politeness, knowing how to work and talk to the opposite gender. All of those kinds of things are also part of our responsibilities…." People who work daily with youth and care about them come to understand that a good education—*una buena educación*—is more than just teaching academic subjects, and it is delivered by teachers who are more than just individuals with the appropriate credentials and by administrators who are more than just chief executive officers. A good education, the kind of education that all our students deserve, is one rooted in democracy and reflective of the values of the community it serves. The school finance literature, until this book came along, largely ignored these intangible characteristics of successful schools, teachers, and students, and had not questioned the role that communities can and do play in defining those characteristics. But it has done so to its own detriment. The answer to equitable schools will not be found in simply summing up the costs of X number of teachers or books, or even counselors and nurses (as critical as all of these are), but in understanding what *about* these elements of schooling make them a good fit for the communities they serve. Nor will it be founded on a premise that schools must simply be funded at a level that allows them to address the deficits inherent in the communities they serve. Equitable funding of just schools will start with a critical understanding of the role and purpose of schools in particular communities and the resources necessary to realize the aspirations of those communities, including those "intangible" resources inherent in individuals who bring a particular understanding and empathy to the schools in which they work. In our own work, we have struggled to devise models of community aspirations that reflect the variation that exists across community types. This requires a completely new and different orientation for models of school finance, but this book begins to point the way.

ACKNOWLEDGMENTS

We take this opportunity to express our gratitude to several individuals who have supported and guided this book over the past two years of its development. We wish to thank Dr. Patricia Gándara, whose encouragement of our ideas included sponsorship of a magical retreat outside of Santa Fe, New Mexico, where our contributors first came together to launch this book project. Dr. Daniel Solórzano is warmly thanked and acknowledged for his incisive and inspiring work, which has greatly influenced this volume. Also warmly thanked are Drs. Linda Loubert and Jorge Ruiz-de-Velasco for their input and perspectives during the initial formulations of this volume. We also express deep gratitude to Dr. Richard Valencia, whose early endorsement of our book proposal led to our relationship with Routledge, and whose scholarship served as a model for us as the book came to fruition. Drs. Luis Fraga, Maricela Oliva, Ernesto (Ernie) Chávez, and Eugene García are also sincerely thanked for their mentorship and professional guidance throughout the writing process. Extreme gratitude is expressed to Dr. Julie López Figueroa, who became the "midwife" of this volume with her eleventh-hour heroics as an editor and contributor. We also must acknowledge that the sacrifices of writing this book included missed birthdays and family time, so we express our deep thanks to our families and friends for their enduring support and hope that the book proves worthy of that price. Finally, Gloria wishes to thank Anthony and all the contributors, Barry, Enrique, Art, Nicola, Sarah, James, David, Steve, and Julie, for embracing her dream to engage in a collaborative, critical analysis of school finance on behalf of communities whose voices and presence are conspicuously missing.

We also express special thanks to our editor at Routledge, Catherine Bernard, for her patience, understanding, and support throughout the entire process from proposal to final production. Thank you for your efforts at demystifying and organizing this process and facilitating a dream come true.

WHY A SOCIAL JUSTICE FRAMING OF SCHOOL FINANCE—AND WHY NOW?

Gloria M. Rodriguez

University of California–Davis

R. Anthony Rolle

Texas A&M University

We present this volume as our contribution to a growing dialogue in the field of education regarding the social justice aims of public schools in the United States. To launch this endeavor, we begin with two premises: (1) there is a well-documented and long-standing inequity in the distribution of opportunities for individuals and communities to pursue economic, political, and social self-determination; and (2) one role of educational policy is to intervene in situations where inequities exist and facilitate improvements that better serve the democratic principles of access, participation, and enhanced life chances. Based upon these premises, we offer a rather widely shared definition of social justice as using the means available to us as members of society and as scholars to strive toward the elimination of bias and oppression based on race, class, gender, sexual orientation, and all other forms of subordination and to actively work toward securing full, democratic participation for all members of society (Bell, 1997; Yosso, 2005; Yosso, 2006). In many ways, the impetus for this book was our frustration with contemporary theoretical models in the field of school finance that often omitted any systematic race or class analysis, thus rendering the perspectives of diverse communities completely absent from the discourse. Despite this frustration, however, we also believe that the possibilities introduced by our book can infuse a greater optimism for what communities can do as critical, self-determined participants in a society still challenged by injustice.

We further believe that, given the recent energy surrounding the pursuit of "adequacy" in education finance, our book is a well-timed invitation to channel the wisdom of those who contributed before us and to insert our perspectives among those forging the future of the field of school finance. On the one hand, this book represents a return to the past—to the initial commitments to positive social change that fueled the grassroots efforts to demand reforms in all aspects of education (Gittell, 1998). Yet, challenging ourselves to think about the implications of school finance theory and policy for advancing broader social justice is also, on the other hand, a step toward the future with increased analytical sophistication. For example, the movement to determine adequate funding schemes in more recent challenges to state finance systems does not attend to the root causes of inequity in our society; rather, inequity is repeatedly taken as a "given" of any society: there are haves and there are have-nots. To the degree that we take our professed commitment to democratic principles and democratizing processes within school systems seriously, there appears to be a need to critically examine our operating assumptions and objectives in school finance—including a consideration of what low-income communities and communities of color expect from the school system—to embrace an accountability that is seldom considered. Instead, even with the appropriate steps taken to clearly link financial and human inputs to high expectations for achievement, the communities on whose behalf such energy is spent are rarely if ever consulted in the determination of their children's futures.

Many possibilities still exist for revisiting commitments to democratizing schooling and learning opportunities, which means also identifying the strengths of children of color and low-income children that are not captured by standardized tests; making sure communities continue to develop voices in their schools; and working toward more comprehensive policy analyses that enable school finance policy to be considered in combination with other social policies to make all of our social institutions significantly more responsive to children and families throughout our society. To these formidable goals we dedicate ourselves in the chapters contained in this volume.

ENACTING A SOCIAL JUSTICE METHODOLOGY: SURFACING ASSUMPTIONS AND DEMYSTIFYING SYSTEMS

To the extent that this book can draw upon the endeavors of scholars who seek to establish a social justice methodology for education, we believe that one key process is that of demystification. We suggest that this is an important starting point in developing a social justice framework and agenda for school finance, as well. This objective requires that we make every effort to:

- Surface patterns of participation, exclusion, treatment, and outcomes
- Surface assumptions and value judgments embedded in policy and reform
- Reframe issues for a more critical understanding of the intended and unintended impact of policy and reforms
- Engage in a process of continual questioning/inquiry that ensures greater levels of transparency and open participation in policy-making systems

Thus, readers will find these methodological strategies woven throughout the chapters of our book, which together enable us to explore and interrogate the heretofore taken-for-granted elements of contemporary school finance theory and policy. With that said, we invite readers to engage with us in this, our initial step toward envisioning new possibilities for social justice frameworks in school finance.

The book is organized into two sections. Part 1 focuses on the social justice implications of contemporary school finance theory. Philosopher Barry L. Bull starts us off in this endeavor in Chapter 1, "A Political Theory of Social Justice in American Schools." In this chapter, Bull weaves for us a theoretical rationale for pursuing social justice goals via school finance by considering the key philosophical tenets of liberty, democracy, equal opportunity, and economic growth. His work thus provides a theoretical lens through which we might view the work of school finance researchers and policy analysts to better comprehend the underlying assumptions of policy proposals and anticipate the impact relative to broader social outcomes. In Chapter 2, "Critical Race Theory and Human Capital Theory: Framing the Discourse on the Nexus of Social Justice and Education Finance," Enrique Alemán, Jr. presents his dual consideration of two prominent theories applied to a variety of educational situations. He considers the limitations of the enduring human capital theory in light of critical race theory analysis, while also exploring the possibilities that these two theories might coexist to enhance our understanding of school finance policies as they particularly affect communities of color. R. Anthony Rolle and Arthur X. Fuller provide Chapter 3, "Measuring Educational Productivity in the Face of Social Justice Influences: A Discussion of the Efficacy of Relative Economic Efficiency for Determining School Improvement Factors," in which they assert that contemporary formulations of productivity theories applied to school organizations are premised on inaccurate characterizations of both their behavior and public—particularly, social justice pursuits. This is followed by Nicola A. Alexander's Chapter 4, "Adequacy Revisited: A Critique of Prominent Conceptualizations of School Finance Standards," which is a review of the key assumptions and conceptualizations that currently influence the application of adequacy in school finance to consider how this theory might be further enhanced by the incorporation of social justice perspectives on the role of education to support commitments to social change. These first four chapters thus represent our examination of several prominent school finance theories and their social justice implications.

Part 2 of the book attends to the social justice implications of contemporary school finance policy. The first contributor in this section is Gloria M. Rodriguez, with Chapter 5, "Cycling On in Cultural Deficit Thinking: California School Finance and the Possibilities of Critical Policy Analysis," which explores the use of a combined standard school finance equity framework and a critical policy analysis framework to reveal how such expanded analyses might enable us to produce school finance policies that resist the overreliance on cultural deficit explanations for persistent disparities in educational resources and outcomes. Next, Sarah A. Gonzales and James L. Rodriguez offer their insights on problematic federal policies affecting state and local school systems in Chapter 6, "The Resource Implications of NCLB for the Recruitment, Preparation, and Retention of Highly Qualified Teachers for English Learners in California." David C. Berliner reminds readers in Chapter 7, "Investing in Student Lives Outside of School to Increase Achievement Inside Schools," of the limitations of relying solely upon educational policy to accomplish sustained improvements in social inequality. He asserts that the impact of poverty on communities is manifested in a variety of social indicators representing severe disparities that likewise prevent us in education from reliably predicting the impact of our efforts via school finance policy alone. In similar spirit, Stephen P. Heyneman explores the global context in order to situate our work within a still broader consideration of the role and impact of American investments in education worldwide. His Chapter 8, "On the International Dimension of Education and Social Justice," calls our attention to global considerations of education as a basic human right.

REFERENCES

Bell, L. A. (1997). Theoretical foundations for social justice education. In M. Adams, L.A. Bell, & P. Griffin (Eds.), *Teaching for diversity and social justice: A sourcebook* (pp. 3-15). New York & London: Routledge.

Gittell, M. J. (1998). *Strategies for school equity: Creating productive schools in a just society.* New Haven, CT: Yale University Press.

Yosso, T. J. (2005). Whose culture has capital? A critical race theory discussion of community cultural wealth. *Race, Ethnicity, and Education,* 8(1), pp. 69-91.

Yosso, T. J. (2006). *Critical race counterstories along the Chicana/Chicano educational pipeline.* New York: Routledge.

Part I
The Social Justice Implications of Contemporary School Finance Theory

1

A POLITICAL THEORY OF SOCIAL JUSTICE IN AMERICAN SCHOOLS

Barry L. Bull

Indiana University–Bloomington

FOR GOOD REASON, SOCIAL JUSTICE has become a major theme of recent critiques of American public education and of numerous proposals for reforming a whole array of educational policies and practices. After all, public schooling is one of this country's major social institutions, one that—like few others—significantly, continuously, and inescapably affects all citizens, whether as students, parents, workers, or taxpayers. If we do not expect this institution to treat citizens fairly in these various roles, the hopes that we will be able to achieve anything like a just society are significantly undermined. However, in these recent analyses social justice often is narrowly construed, as dealing with the fair treatment of only one segment of the population (e.g., children or employers) or as involving a single value (e.g., equal opportunity or economic competitiveness). Therefore, the proposals that result from such analyses often do not consider their wider consequences for achieving the complex ideal that social justice represents. This limited focus is particularly troubling when policies for financing the system are at issue precisely because such policies have potentially significant consequences for all of the system's clients, functions, and effects. The wide ramifications of school finance policies make social justice the premier normative criterion for their evaluation, and those ramifications make it imperative that the fullest meaning of social justice be brought to bear in this evaluation. This chapter attempts to articulate and to argue for a set of principles that capture this full meaning and then to consider briefly their implications for two of the most general desiderata of school financing systems, namely equity and adequacy.

There are many approaches to assessing the normative consequences of policy. John Rawls (1999), America's most distinguished 20th-century political philosopher, has differentiated two basic types of normative analysis—those that he labels *metaphysical* and those that he labels *political*. Metaphysical analyses are based on comprehensive ethical theories, those that speak to the full range of human experience and are founded on systematic religious or philosophical premises. Political analyses, by contrast, emerge from an effort to identify what Rawls calls an overlapping consensus among the normative beliefs of those who hold differing comprehensive ethical doctrines within a particular society. Such analyses are a matter not only of collecting together the political principles and judgments about which a wide consensus actually exists, but also of submitting those agreements to a process of reflective equilibrium in which good reasons are sought for maintaining or modifying the agreements and for resolving, at least temporarily, any inconsistencies among them.

In this chapter I will attempt to construct a normative political theory from what seem to be Americans' widely shared beliefs about the purposes of their society, the constraints upon how those purposes can legitimately be pursued, and public schools' role in both achieving those purposes and establishing those constraints. This approach, if successful, promises to provide a broadly appealing basis from which to conduct the normative analysis of school policies in general and school finance policies in particular. I will construct this normative political theory for American public schooling based on four values that are prominent in Americans' discussions of public schooling—liberty, democracy, equality of opportunity, and economic growth (see Bull, 2002).

EDUCATION FOR PERSONAL LIBERTY

Liberty can be understood as the freedom to decide matters that affect our lives (Bull, 1984; 2000b). Americans tend to treat liberty as a set of individual freedoms of self-determination, many of which are protected by the U.S. Constitution's Bill of Rights—freedoms of religious belief, association, and expression, for example. Thus, one aspect of liberty—personal liberty—implies one's control over a sphere of actions and decisions of particular consequence to oneself.

Of course, much—and perhaps most—of what we want to do has potential significant effect on others' lives. Here, liberty is not simply

the freedom to make these decisions entirely on our own but rather to participate fairly in these decisions with others whom they affect. Thus, liberty theoretically encompasses not only individual rights but also political rights—that is, rights to be involved in making the collective decisions that affect us. I will consider political liberties only briefly in this section, but because they are intimately involved with the political value of democracy, I will reserve full treatment of them for the next section, which is devoted to that topic.

An expansive conception of personal and political liberty leaves no room for the application of other political values. After all, every human action, no matter how momentous or trivial, can be understood as the result of some person's or group's decision. If the right to make that decision without interference is reserved to the individual or group primarily affected by it, it will be impossible to regulate any decision, and therefore any action, even in the interests of achieving other political values. But the presence of equal opportunity and economic growth in the constellation of Americans' political values suggests that we do not hold such an expansive view. Americans' conception of politically significant liberty must, in other words, be restricted in some way. The Constitution and its Bill of Rights provide some guidance about how Americans formulate this restriction. On the one hand, the Constitution provides for the protection of certain fundamental individual liberties—the freedoms of speech, religion, and association, for example. On the other hand, it provides a framework for what has been called the rule of law—for example, rights to the due process of law and against unwarranted searches and seizures.

Rawls suggests that what makes certain types of decisions and actions fundamentally important to individuals and, therefore, deserving of political protection is *their centrality to individuals' personhood*—that is, their playing a significant role in an individual's holding a conception of the good that she regards as personally meaningful and in having a reasonable chance to live a life governed by that conception. Thus, the freedoms of conscience and expression, for example, are politically significant in that they enable individuals to learn about the possibilities for, to formulate and revise, and ultimately to embrace conceptions of the good that have personal significance for them. Some freedoms, however, that do not have such an important effect on one's personhood—such as the freedom to keep everything that one earns—are not fundamental in this way and may be regulated by an appropriately constituted government. However, such regulation must still respect the rule of law. Thus, the protections of the rule of law, while allowing for the regulation of many individual decisions and actions that are not fundamental to personhood, are politically significant in that they ensure that such regulations are publicly known in advance, explicitly formulated, and universally rather than capriciously enforced, so that people can, within known limits, confidently formulate and carry out life plans in accordance with their own conceptions of the good.

Now, even if the politically significant and therefore protected personal liberties are limited to those that have a central role in one's personhood, it is still possible for those liberties to come into conflict when individuals attempt to exercise them. At least two cases of conflict are possible. First, one person's exercise of a protected liberty can diminish the chances that others have to exercise that same liberty. For example, one's exercise of the freedom of conscience might lead him to adopt an intolerant religious view that implies that he should restrict the religious views that others may adopt. Acting on such a view would, in turn, require him to attempt to limit others' freedom of conscience. Second, one person's exercising one sort of protected liberty can diminish others' chances to exercise a different protected liberty. For example, the exercise of one's freedom of conscience might lead one to adopt a sexist social doctrine that implies that women should not be allowed to fraternize with men under certain circumstances or for certain purposes. Acting on such a view would require one to attempt to limit others' freedom of association. Rawls also provides guidance about the political resolution of such conflicts by suggesting that the aim should be to maintain a system of personal liberties that is equal for all. A system that protects the equal freedom of conscience or association may thus permit the restriction of even fundamental liberties in the interest of everyone's enjoying the same liberties. This arrangement does not necessarily mean that one is forbidden, for instance, from holding views that conflict with others' protected liberties (by authorizing, for example, the incarceration or brainwashing of those who hold such views), but it does imply that one who holds such views may be prevented from or punished for acting on those views in a way that would effectively diminish others' protected liberties.

A compulsory school system might seem at first blush to restrict personal liberty inappropriately. On the one hand, it prevents children from pursuing the activities they prefer under their current conceptions of the good. On the other, such a school system may interfere with some parents' efforts to raise their children in accordance with the parents' conception of the good. However, it is improbable to say that young children, while they clearly have desires and preferences, are guided by a deliberatively chosen and consciously formulated conception of the good. Thus, restrictions placed on children's current actions do not necessarily violate their fundamental liberties because those actions are not yet expressions of their fundamental personhood. And the younger children are, the less likely it is that such restrictions will be forbidden by a commitment to their personal liberty. In fact, this circumstance is what renders parental authority over children acceptable in a society committed to the protection of fundamental personal liberties, a form of authority that would not be permitted among adults.

Parents, however, do have a protected liberty interest in the raising of their children; that is, they have conceptions of the good that usually have implications for how they exercise their authority over their children. Nevertheless, two considerations suggest that they may not exercise this authority in just any way that their conceptions of the good might imply. First, children are not simply parts of the environment that can be used willy-nilly as instruments for the fulfillment of their parents' conceptions of the good. Rather, they are nascent persons who can come to hold and pursue their own conceptions of the good, and thus children have liberty-related interests in the development of those conceptions (Bull, 1990). Second, children are also members of the community whose aspirations and actions may affect the liberty interests of current adults other than their parents—as, for example, future citizens or work associates. Thus, other adults also have a liberty interest in how children are raised. Constraints on parents' protected liberties in raising their children must be justified on the basis that such constraints are necessary to maintain an equal system of liberty for all—for the parents themselves, the adults the children will become, and other adults outside the family (Bull, Fruehling, and Chattergy, 1992).

A compulsory public school system governed by appropriate purposes and conducted in appropriate ways can be seen as one attempt to maintain such an equal system of politically significant personal liberties; for such a system may foster young adults who are both their own persons in that they personally have meaningful conceptions of the good and are capable of pursuing them, and responsible members of their families and the larger community in that their conceptions of the good and their consequent activities are reasonably compatible with the scheme of activities dictated by the various conceptions of the good held by their parents and fellow citizens. It is unlikely, however, that a school system that takes exclusive direction from the liberty interests of either parents or other adults in the community at large will have such a result, for individual children's interests and emerging conceptions of the good must also be taken into account (compare Gutmann, 1999). The details of the governance and operation of such a system need not preoccupy us here, but based on this analysis, we are able to formulate one general principle of the normative political theory for education that we seek: *Conduct public schooling in a way that allows children to develop both as their own persons—that is, to come to hold personally meaningful conceptions of the good and to acquire the reasonable capacities to pursue them—and as responsible members of their families and communities who respect and support others' politically significant personal liberties and the other political commitments of their society.* By following this principle, a compulsory public school system recognizes and respects the politically legitimate personal liberty interests of children, parents, and other adults simultaneously.

EDUCATION FOR DEMOCRACY

The discussion of personal liberty and its significance to the personhood of individuals implies that political liberties must be restricted to prevent others from exercising an illegitimate influence on the conceptions of the good that individuals develop and embrace, and on the capacities they develop in order to pursue those conceptions. After all, if others have an unlimited power to control the values we come to hold and the activities in which we engage, personal liberties would be meaningless, even if that power were exercised by means of participatory decision-making procedures.

Of course, this restriction of political liberties in the interests of personhood does not mean that others cannot have any influence on our conceptions of the good and their pursuit. As we have seen, others can legitimately constrain such pursuit and even the conceptions themselves in the interest of maintaining an equal system of personal liberty. These constraints provide others the opportunity of informing us about possibilities for our conceptions of the good that they have found compelling, and they give us the chance to develop a conception of the good that acknowledges and respects others' conceptions and therefore to coordinate our activities with others in a way that allows mutual fulfillment of our conceptions. Despite these legitimate constraints, however, others cannot have the final say over individuals' conceptions of the good and their consequent life plans; that ultimate authority is reserved to individuals themselves.

Thus, the politically significant political liberties are limited by the politically significant personal liberties. Moreover, three considerations suggest that the legitimate political liberties are even more limited in scope. First, as already noted, Americans may have allegiances to political values beyond personal and political liberty—namely, to equality of opportunity and economic growth. Thus, the range of decisions that fall within the scope of political liberty must be constrained so as to permit the realization of these other political values. Second, some fully participatory decisions made today can undermine political liberty in the future (Gutmann, 1999). One obvious example is that a majority of citizens today might vote that some current citizens—perhaps the poorest, those who do not speak English, or those who espouse particular political views—will not have franchise tomorrow. Less obviously, citizens might adopt a policy that, while it technically does not exclude others from participation in political decisions, seriously reduces the likelihood that they will do so—perhaps a poll tax or a requirement that all political debate is to be conducted only in English. Clearly, to maintain the value of democracy and therefore of political liberty, such decisions must be placed beyond the reach of democratic decision making.

A third, more complicated but related consideration, is that democratic decision procedures can be used to make decisions that undermine the culture necessary for the practice of democracy itself. Among such decisions might be to adopt what I have called *authoritarian democracy* (Bull, 2000a, 2000b). Briefly, the authoritarian account of democracy holds that a popular government can and indeed should make all of its decisions in light of a robust and fully specified conception of the good for the entire society, a conception of the ends that the society seeks to achieve. In arriving at this conception, procedures of universal participation and thoughtful deliberation are to be followed. Of course, the social conception of the good may also be revised by following democratic procedures. In this sense, then, the decision making is democratic. However, once a conception of the good for the society has been adopted, all subsequent decisions about social policy and institutions are to be made in light of that conception; these subsequent decisions are interpreted simply as judgments about the most effective social means to the social ends specified in the conception. In this sense, this view is authoritarian in that the conception of the social good becomes the sole authority for making subsequent decisions.

This view of democracy is appealing for several different reasons. First, it embodies a common understanding of instrumental rationality—namely, that one is rational by choosing coherent ends and then determining one's actions in order to accomplish those ends. Second, it forbids the use of the instruments of public authority for any purpose except for those articulated by the conception of social good that has been adopted democratically, so that no one will be permitted to use the power of the government exclusively for private ends. Finally, it provides a straightforward basis for determining and judging public policy—namely, by telling us to develop the material, intellectual, and practical capabilities of the society in ways that will allow us to accomplish our collective purposes as reflected in the authoritative conception of the social good.

However, by focusing exclusively on the ends that the society is to achieve, authoritarian democracy seems to ignore political values that place restrictions on the means that may legitimately be taken in pursuit of our ends. One such value is liberty—both personal and political. A society committed to this value, as we have seen, cannot pursue its ends by violating the rights necessary to developing and maintaining the personhood of individuals or the universal participation of citizens. Another such value is equality of opportunity. As we shall see in the next section of this chapter, a society committed to this value cannot pursue its ends by, for example, relegating some of its citizens to a permanently inferior social status based on characteristics that are irrelevant to their potential and achievements. This objection, however, simply requires us to constrain authoritarian democracy in appropriate ways but not necessarily to abandon it entirely. In ruling out the choice of means that entail a violation of protected liberties or of equality of opportunity, an authoritarian democracy may in some instances be forced to adopt means that are not the most efficient for attaining its ends. It may also turn out that some conceptions of the social good cannot be pursued at all because any means available to pursue them would violate these political values. Nevertheless, with these restrictions, a version of authoritarian democracy still seems attractive on the grounds already mentioned—its instrumental rationality, its forbidding public power to be used for exclusively private purposes, and its providing a clear criterion for the development of public policy.

For all its superficial appeal, however, democratic authoritarianism is a deeply flawed conception of political organization. In large part, these flaws stem from the empirical implausibility of its account of the connection between political will and social capacity. This doctrine essentially tells us to imagine the preferred future state of American society and then to engineer Americans' social capacities to achieve that state of affairs. However, this view does not recognize fully the extent to which our ability to imagine our future and, thus, our current choices of social ends are dependent upon our current social capacities. To be sure, it does recognize that our existing social capacities can serve as a reality check on our imaginations by telling us either that some visions of our future might be unattainable because of seemingly intractable limitations in our capacities or that some visions might have to be delayed while we develop capacities that we do not currently possess. But it does not recognize two other important truths about the relationship between political will and social capacity: (1) initially, what we want or can imagine at any particular time depends upon what we can do; and (2) subsequently, what we will want in the future depends upon changes that have taken place in what we can do. Thus, the relationship between political will and social capacity is interactive and not simply hierarchical, as democratic authoritarianism seems to assume. In other words, the supposition that we can come to a permanent collective agreement about a vision of our desired social future—no matter how participatory and deliberative the procedures used to reach that agreement—and then simply change our capacities in order to achieve that vision must be false. After all, the subsequent changes we make in our capacities in order to achieve the original social vision will, in turn, change the social vision of the future that we deem to be desirable.

Yet perhaps this problem can be overcome by simply accepting that our current aspirations are likely to change in the future. In other words, we might simply change our capacities today in order to achieve what we think we want tomorrow in the full recognition that what we will actually want tomorrow may be different and thus may require us to change our capacities in yet other ways. But even this adjustment in democratic authoritarianism is inadequate. Indeed, it reveals an even more fundamental flaw in that conception of democracy, for this revised version of democratic authoritarianism is essentially a recipe for an unplanned, deeply irrational future. From a wider perspective, we can see such a society as profoundly schizophrenic, both believing that it should pursue a particular vision of its future and knowing that attaining that vision will inevitably prove unsatisfactory in entirely unpredictable ways.

In this way, decisions to pursue even a constrained form of authoritarian democracy, though made in a fully participatory manner, can make democracy seem frustratingly pointless, condemning the society to an endless cycle of choosing a social good only to have that good lose its apparent value when we have attained the capacities necessary to achieve it. In this sense, a choice to adopt such a scheme of political organization in the long run undermines citizens' very motivation to act democratically. And to avoid this result, a democratic society must be constrained not just from making decisions that will undermine other significant political values and the future participation of some citizens in democratic decision making, but also from implementing democracy in the centralized, instrumentally rational but inevitably unsatisfactory manner envisioned under the authoritarian conception.

To this end, citizens should be encouraged to understand democracy not as the formulation of a unified and abstract national democratic will and its pursuit by engineering the nation's social capacity appropriately, but instead as a set of more localized experiments in which a variety of competing, incomplete, and concrete hypotheses about the democratic will and social capacity are tested simultaneously. Some of these experiments may indeed take the form of attempts to attain particular goals by modifying social capacities to those ends in order to discover whether those goals still seem valuable to and attainable by citizens who have had their capacities thus modified. Others, however, may assert the putative value of a particular new configuration of social capacities in order to discover whether the goals that citizens come to have as they acquire those capacities seem worthy and attainable. Some of these experiments will succeed and some will fail, but the communities that attempt them can learn from one another's experience about how to formulate more successful and satisfying subsequent experiments (compare Dewey, 1927). And because of this experimental attitude toward the decision-making processes in their own society and the widespread availability of knowledge about the results of the variety of political experiments that continue to take place, citizens' motivation to be involved in democratic politics will remain robust.

It has been assumed, since at least the time of Thomas Jefferson, that democracy requires the operation of a public school system. In light of this analysis, we can see the connection between democracy and public schooling not merely as a way of giving future citizens the information and skills that they need to participate in the established decision-making processes or to carry out its resulting decisions, but also as an attempt to create and maintain a culture that ensures that the various limitations on political liberty I have argued to be necessary are implemented and respected. Understood in this way, a normative political theory includes an ambitious principle that should govern public education in society committed to the value of democracy: *Conduct public schooling in a way that fosters children's ability and willingness to participate in public decision-making processes so as to acknowledge and respect the other political commitments of their society and to make constructive contributions to, to learn from, and to act on the results of those processes in both their own and others' communities.*

A public school system that follows this principle will encourage its students to exercise their political liberties in ways that respect the commitments to personal liberty, to their own and others' political liberty over time, to equality of opportunity, and to economic growth. At the same time, it will develop and maintain a democratic culture in which learning from one's own and others' political successes and mistakes is expected and valued.

EDUCATION FOR EQUALITY OF OPPORTUNITY

In a sense, considerations about the contribution of education to personal liberty and democracy speak to the quality of educational opportunity available within a society (Bull, 2000a). Educational opportunity seen from these perspectives must be of the right kind to enable individuals to lead lives that they find fulfilling and to contribute to the fulfillment of others' lives. And, therefore, decisions about the educational opportunities available in a society must ultimately be made in light of their members' interests in personhood and citizenship.

Beyond this, however, Americans also care about how these opportunities are distributed among citizens. If, for example, citizens decide that making a certain kind of educational opportunity available would be beneficial to them collectively, the chance to take advantage of that opportunity should be made fairly available to all. In part, a fair chance to take advantage of an educational opportunity means that citizens should be allowed to qualify for that opportunity based upon their demonstrated abilities. But it also means that citizens should also be given a fair chance to acquire the abilities that would allow them to qualify.

These two elements of fair equality of opportunity in education—a chance to acquire abilities and a chance to qualify for opportunities based on demonstrated ability—are the basis for a conceptual distinction within a society's educational institutions. To some extent, these institutions are to be universal, giving all citizens a chance to develop their abilities, and to some extent they are competitive, giving all a chance to use their developed abilities to qualify for further education (Gutmann, 1999). Very roughly, public schools are the institutions that Americans expect to provide for universal learning opportunities; colleges and universities are to provide for competitive learning opportunities.

It might seem natural to assume that public schools, in having a universal clientele and a mission to develop all children's abilities, are to generate equal educational outcomes for all or at least outcomes that meet some uniform threshold of performance. Gutmann (1999) has argued that the achievement of absolutely equal school outcomes is not only practically difficult to attain but also, and more importantly, normatively unacceptable. Although she bases her argument on a primary commitment to democracy, a reasonable approximation of it can be stated for the more eclectic political theory being developed here. She notes that differential student achievement derives, in large part, from the widely divergent educational resources to which families and communities have access and that they choose to devote to the learning of their children. Completely correcting for these differences would require massive collective intervention in the lives of these families and communities, which, as a practical matter, is difficult. Of course, perhaps a society should undertake this difficult task if persuasive normative arguments lead to that conclusion.

To the extent that these differences in student achievement depend on differences in their families' and communities' access to resources or differences in the allocation of educational resources to marginalized communities, they represent a genuine injustice that should be corrected. After all, these children have done nothing to deserve the educational differences they experience. But those differences may have a significant influence on the conceptions of the good that those children develop and are able to pursue, and to the extent that children are differentially affected in developing as their own persons, their liberty interests are affected by these educational differences. However, to the extent that these differences derive from choices that families and communities make based on their individual and collective conceptions of the good, they are normatively more acceptable. Beyond the unjust educational differences created by families' lack of resources or government decisions to restrict public resources, some marginalized families' and communities' educational choices are also an expression of their members' conceptions of the good, which, within limits, are protected by their personal and political liberties. Thus, the educational differences that children currently experience can be seen to result, in part, from politically illegitimate violations of children's personal liberties and from, in part, the politically legitimate exercise of families' and communities' personal and political liberties.

As we have seen, the personal liberties of parents can to an extent be overridden in the interests of protecting the future personal liberties of their children. In other words, parents can be compelled to send their children to school in order to provide those children with a chance to become their own persons. However, even under a compulsory school system, parents still retain the right to make a contribution to the education of their children and, thus, to exercise, to a limited degree at least, their personal liberties in this regard. To produce absolute equality of student achievement, the society would have to deny altogether parents' rights to affect the education of their children, which would completely ignore parents' personal liberties in regard to the education of their children. A similar argument about the political liberties of community members also could be constructed that would conclude that equalization of student achievement also denies communities the right to influence the education of the children who live in them.

On the basis of a similar analysis, Gutmann suggests that a justi-fied conception of equal educational opportunity, rather than aiming for absolute equality of student achievement, requires us collectively to ensure that every educable child meets a minimum threshold of school achievement. Such a threshold would to an extent recognize the inter-ests of children in their future personal liberties. But beyond the thresh-old, parents and the members of communities would have the right to determine the education of their children, which would to an extent also recognize their personal and political rights.

I find this argument to be powerful, based as it is on certain realities of American social life and on Americans' commitments to personal and political liberties. However, I believe that two considerations lead to the conclusion that Gutmann does not follow the implications of these realities and commitments to their full logical conclusions.

Let us examine first the ramifications of the pursuit of equal school outcomes up to a specified threshold, which I will call *basic education*, for the lives of children while they attend school and as adults thereafter. Some children will have more difficulty in reaching this threshold than others. In part, this implies that the society will have to devote more and more focused resources to the basic education of these children than will be necessary for others. But it also means that these children will have to devote more of their time and energy to attaining a basic educa-tion than will other children. Moreover, based on current sociological realities, the children who have difficulty in meeting a politically speci-fied threshold will come disproportionately from economically and culturally marginalized communities and families. Unless we assume that all children will be required to leave the public school system when they meet the threshold (and Gutmann argues against this assumption), some other children, by contrast, will have the time, energy, and public resources to pursue their education beyond the threshold. On top of that, these children also will tend to have disproportionate access to the additional resources that their parents can afford to devote to the education of their children beyond the threshold.

American children live in a competitive society and economy in which their chances to fulfill as adults their own conceptions of the good depend significantly on any comparative advantage they may come to have over their peers. Achieving up to the threshold will not confer a competitive advantage on anyone since it is assumed that all chil-dren will reach this level. Thus, any educationally relevant comparative advantage that children attain will depend entirely on their achievement beyond the threshold. However, children from marginalized commu-nities will find it difficult to achieve such a comparative advantage for two reasons—they will be required to spend more of their time and energy in attaining the threshold—which, as we have said, confers no comparative advantage—and they will have less time and may have fewer resources, both public and private, for their education beyond the threshold, which does confer such an advantage. Ironically, then, establishing a threshold of school achievement that all children are to meet may well create barriers for children from marginalized communities in developing and realizing their conceptions of the good, and the higher the threshold is set, the greater the barriers that these children face (Bull, 1996). To be sure, these children will be ostensibly assured that they can achieve at the threshold level in that their society will provide the resources to make such achievement possible, but achieving at that level does not enhance their chances of self-defined success in a competitive social and economic system. Of course, on Gutmann's interpretation of equal opportunity, there is no normative reason to be disturbed by this result, since all children have been provided with an educational start in life that takes them at least to the threshold level.

That leads us to the second consideration—whether we should be satisfied with Gutmann's interpretation, especially given the formulation of Americans' political commitments that we have developed thus far. Gutmann's reasoning for the satisfactoriness of her interpretation seems to rest on one of two assumptions—either that the normative adequacy of an education is to be judged entirely on its own merits and not for any effect that education may have on children's cultural, social, or economic future, or that although an education's adequacy is to be judged at least partly on its subsequent social effects, an education up to the threshold can provide children with a reasonable platform from which to pursue achievements that will enable them to pursue their conceptions of the good. While the first assumption has a certain academic appeal in that it portrays education as having inherent rather than instrumental value, it goes too far in this direction by suggesting that the political value ought to rest entirely on the former. Moreover, in the context of the political values that we have formulated thus far, judgments about inherent value are to be made from the standpoint of individuals and communities—based on their own conceptions of the good—rather than by the political structures of the society at large. To the extent that education or any other good is a legitimate *political* concern of the society, it must therefore be understood as instrumental to the satisfaction of individuals' or communities' self-determined conceptions of the good, not as realizing any inherent good that the society deems to be authoritative. It is not that education must be viewed as bereft of inherent value, but that society at large must not be the judge of such value. Therefore, the first assumption on which the argument for the normative satisfactoriness of Gutmann's interpretation of equality of educational opportunity may rest simply cannot hold for a society that is committed to the political values we have been formulating.

Perhaps the second assumption will prove more robust. It asserts, on the one hand, that there is a common set of learnings that everyone must achieve in order to have a fair chance of trying to develop the comparative advantages that will enable the pursuit of their and their communities' conceptions of the good and, on the other, that the threshold guarantees everyone a reasonable chance to attain these common learnings. Of course, this is partly an empirical proposition in that it asserts, first, that there are certain common skills and knowledge upon which everyone's self-defined success depends and, second, that we know what they are. I find the first assertion to be wildly improbable for the sort of open and diverse society that is consistent with the political values we have described thus far—namely, a society in which success is defined as the ability to pursue one's own conception of the good. Be that as it may, however, the second assertion must surely be false. The course of social, cultural, scientific, technological, and economic development is an inherently unpredictable affair. As such, the claim that we know the prerequisites for such development with any precision must be delusory. In light of the improbability of the empirical content of this assertion, its normative content also seems inadequate. It asserts that the society's educational obligations to its citizens have been satisfied when it has provided the bare prerequisites for success according to some particular conception of the good held by a political majority. Beyond that, any educational provision must be entirely a matter of individual luck—say, whether the family or community into which a child is born values or has the resources for education beyond the threshold. This arrangement is problematic on two grounds. First, it asserts that a society need only provide an education that meets the prerequisites of a particular conception of the good that some children and communities may not share. This assertion clearly violates the principles of personal liberty and democracy. Second, it asserts that the society has no educational obligations beyond these prerequisites. This assertion denies educational resources to those who hold a conception of the good that is different than that of the political majority, and it also violates the equality of personal and political liberty. On both empirical and normative grounds, therefore, the second assertion on which the defense of Gutmann's interpretation of equal opportunity may rest seems as dubious as the first.

This result could lead us to the uncomfortable conclusion that equality of educational opportunity can have no legitimate place in a society committed to the values of personal and political liberty. After all, neither the absolute equality of learning outcomes nor the uniformity of learning outcomes up to a threshold level is consistent with those values. However, it may be that both of these interpretations are seeking equality in the wrong place—that is, in terms of learning outcomes. Rather than equalizing the opportunities that all children have to attain the same educational outcomes, we might equalize the opportunities that all children have to become different in ways that advantage them in the competition for further educational and employment opportunities that they find meaningful (Bull, 2000b). As long as the determinants of these educational differences come from children's emerging personal and collective conceptions of the good, a society that pursues this sort of equality will not unfairly diminish children's future liberties. And as long as the differences that we permit and support lead them to respect others' rights to develop and pursue their conceptions of the good, we also will not violate the existing liberties of adults. Since the principles governing education for personal liberty and democracy already limit the conceptions of the good that children are encouraged to develop to those that are consistent with others' personal and political liberties, the principle of equality of opportunity in schooling becomes: *Conduct public schooling so that children have an equal chance to develop the differential abilities required for success under their emerging individual and collective conceptions of the good.*

A public school system that acts on this principle will give those children who aspire to one conception of the good as good a start in that direction as it gives to those aspiring to another. This principle requires, in effect, a society to exert something like equal educational effort on behalf of the self-defined success of each child as that society endeavors to meet the requirements of the first two principles. Indeed, as Foley, Levinson, and Hurtwig (2001) explain, this is what various scholars of color have been emphasizing recently as they identify and document the very real advantages that children from marginalized communities bring to their education. Moreover, public schooling that supports a wide range of children's aspirations is more likely to lead to a more broadly based form of social equality than a narrow focus on an authoritative threshold of skills and knowledge, for, although different children will be enabled to do different things in their adult lives, they will be supported in developing the talents of greatest meaning to them. In a very real sense, a society's enforcing a single pathway to success and the public schools' complicity in doing so makes social inequality incorrigible both by narrowing the aspirations and talents that children can develop and utilize in their search for individually and socially fulfilling lives and by allowing those who have current advantages to focus their resources on maintaining that advantage (Bull, 2000a).

EDUCATION FOR ECONOMIC GROWTH

The most traditional and straightforward justification of the political value of economic growth is based on utilitarian ethical theory: the idea that a society should seek to maximize its citizens' happiness (Rawls, 1999). The utilitarian argument for the value of economic growth runs something like this: Because humans are at least in part material beings, material resources play an important role in the attainment of human happiness by, for instance, directly satisfying human desires or realizing inherent value or by establishing the conditions under which the satisfaction of desire or the realization of inherent values can be pursued. Thus, the attainment of happiness depends significantly, although by no means entirely, on the material well-being of a society's members—that is, the material resources they have at their disposal. In general, then, the greater the supply of material resources that is under human control, the greater the chances for happiness. Because economic growth expands this supply of material resources, it is valuable as an instrument for maximizing human happiness.

Of course, there are significant variations among utilitarians about such matters as the distribution of economic resources and the social conditions under which those resources can best be developed, but one conclusion about this argument for economic growth is unavoidable—namely, that it cannot be used in its original form as a *political* justification for economic growth in the sense intended here, as an appeal to a consensus that can be maintained among those with differing fundamental metaphysical commitments. After all, utilitarianism's assertion that human happiness, however it is interpreted, is the highest human value is itself a metaphysical commitment, and a highly controversial one at that; for Americans can and do disagree about whether or the extent to which happiness is the fundamental value in life, committing themselves to a wide variety of alternative accounts of ultimate value, such as obedience to the will of God, the development of human reason, the maintenance of caring relationships, and so on. Beyond this, such a justification is inconsistent with the accounts that we have formulated of the commitments to personal and political liberties and with equality of opportunity. To be sure, various utilitarians have argued that liberty, equality of opportunity, or both are instrumental to the achievement of human happiness. For example, Mill (1978) has argued that since individuals are the best judges of what makes them happy, a society that aims to maximize happiness must allow individuals to make their own choices in life and to pursue the courses of action to which those choices lead. Similarly, a utilitarian might argue that equality of opportunity improves social efficiency by allocating citizens to the social positions for which they are most qualified and productive, and such efficiency permits the society to produce the most happiness with its available stock of resources. However, these utilitarian arguments are not entirely consistent with our formulation of the values of liberty and equal opportunity. For instance, the principle of personal liberty we have developed implies that individual commitments to fundamental values are largely matters of personal conscience, but the utilitarian arguments for liberty imply that a society must be committed to assigning the highest and most fundamental value to human happiness regardless of what its citizens happen to think. Similarly, the principle of equal educational opportunity we have developed specifies that the various educational opportunities that a society is to make available are to be guided by individuals' own conceptions of the good, but the utilitarian arguments for equality of opportunity do not respect such a specification because they assume that the allocation of citizens to social and economic opportunities is to be made so as to maximize human happiness regardless of whether they happen to aspire to that end.

The principles of personal and political liberty imply a concern with both the quality and quantity of opportunity that is available within a society. Being our own persons requires, in part, having adequate resources to select or develop our own conceptions of the good, but it also requires the resources to develop plans to achieve those conceptions and to carry them out to the extent that they do not unduly interfere with others having the resources to do so as well. To some extent, the resources required for personal and political liberty are the protections of our freedoms of conscience, expression, and association and the guarantees that the society will make decisions democratically and be bound by the rule of law in making and implementing those decisions. These resources, as we have seen, are also educational in that individuals require the chance to learn about the personal and collective conceptions of the good that they may find fulfilling, to gain the skills necessary to make good decisions about the adequacy of those conceptions, and to develop the abilities to construct plans to realize those conceptions and carry them out. But beyond this, we also need appropriate opportunities to enact those plans. In other words, the opportunities available within American society should ideally be sufficiently numerous and of the right kind to give its citizens a reasonable chance to live their lives as their conceptions of the good dictate.

In any real society, of course, these opportunities are inevitably inadequate to allow all citizens the luxury of realizing their conceptions completely. Thus, we will have to negotiate and compete with one another over who will have access to these scarce opportunities. We want this negotiation and competition to be fair, and it is the purpose of the principle of equal opportunity to ensure that they are—by, on the one hand, giving citizens a chance to develop abilities that are in line with their conceptions of the good and, on the other, guaranteeing that the decisions about the allocation of opportunities to use those developed abilities are made according to citizens' potential to take advantage of them.

A society's economy is relevant to these concerns in two ways. First, it supplies the resources necessary to enforce citizens' liberties and to provide the educational opportunities that the exercise of those liberties require. Second, the economy generates many of the opportunities that citizens have to realize their conceptions of the good either by supplying the material prerequisites of the pursuits those conceptions imply or by creating types of employment that themselves realize their citizens' aspirations. Thus, for instance, for someone whose conception of the good requires climbing mountains, such employment may allow the accumulation of the resources needed to accomplish that feat. And, for someone whose conception of the good requires conducting scientific experiments, employment may be available in that very line of work.

Growth of the economy is an expansion of the productive capacity of a society. In part, such growth can make it possible for a society to provide more adequately for the protection of liberties and for the education needed to realize those liberties and to equalize opportunities. Economic growth can also enhance citizens' concrete opportunities to realize their conceptions of the good (Bull, 1996). An expansion of the economy takes place in one of two ways, either by increasing the number of available jobs or by enhancing the productivity of existing jobs. When the number of jobs increases, there is more opportunity available for work in the society. When the productivity of jobs increases, the quality of opportunity in the society may be improved. In either case, the quality of life for the members of the society may be enhanced, not only because there is more disposable income available to them for the realization of their conceptions of the good, but also because the opportunity to engage in personally rewarding activity may be expanded either to include more people or to enhance the work experience of those who are employed. In other words, economic growth can be socially valuable because it transforms the quantity and quality of inherently or instrumentally satisfying work within a society.

This argument for the social value of economic growth definitely is not an unqualified endorsement of that phenomenon, as the utilitarian argument tends to be, for a society's economy may expand without increasing the resources available for the enforcement of freedom or the provision of education. Indeed, some mechanisms of growth may actually diminish those resources, either by making citizens less willing to pay taxes to support these things or by, for example, requiring child labor that displaces education. Moreover, either of the mechanisms described for the enhancement of productivity may not have the desired effect on citizens' ability to realize their conceptions of the good. That is, the jobs added to the economy may displace some higher paying jobs, or changes in the quality of jobs may make them less likely to satisfy the requirements of those conceptions. When, however, economic growth results in more public resources for the protection of liberties, the enhancement of education, or the equalization of opportunity and when it produces higher paying jobs or more fulfilling work, it is of genuine value within the normative political theory we have been developing.

Any justified principle of public education for economic growth must be framed within this account of the political value of economic growth. Of course, it may well be that beyond education for liberty, democracy, and equal opportunity, public schools have no additional role in enhancing politically desirable economic growth as we have defined it. These forms of education already make important contributions to the realization of this type of economic growth. Education for liberty enables children to become their own persons, which in turn makes it less likely that they will accept forms of employment that do not help them advance their conceptions of the good. Education for democracy enables children to understand their obligations within the society at large, which makes it less likely that they will use their political liberty to authorize forms of employment that obstruct their fellow citizens' chances to realize their conceptions of the good. And education for equal opportunity develops children's abilities in line with their emerging conceptions of the good, which helps to ensure that the paths most readily available for economic growth in their society are consistent with those conceptions. Despite these contributions, though, a society may neglect the opportunities available to encourage legitimate forms of economic growth. Moreover, it still seems possible for economic growth to take forms that are antithetical to Americans' most central political values, and society may legitimately take action to protect itself from this possibility. The crucial issue is whether schools, beyond meeting the responsibilities we have identified, can be reasonably expected to be involved further in the actions necessary to encourage constructive economic growth or to discourage economic growth that is destructive to Americans' basic political commitments.

In the past several decades, economists have developed what has come to be called *human capital theory* (see, for example, Thurow, 1970). This theory notes that human capabilities are just as important factors of production as raw materials and labor, for example. Thus, improving economic productivity may require changes in the economic capabilities of citizens as much as it requires, say, enhanced access to natural resources. In fact, such capabilities can lead to improvements in our access to and use of the other factors of production. Human ingenuity can develop novel products or streamline production processes and resource extraction in ways that render the economy more productive. Indeed, this line of thinking lies behind many of the efforts to reform the public schools in America since the 1980s, for schooling has become thought of as an important social means of changing future workers' capabilities and thus of encouraging economic growth. On this theory, then, schools have a definite economic role in developing their students' motivations and abilities in line with the present and future needs of the economy.

However, our analysis of the legitimate political value of economic growth implies that Americans should be cautious about adopting human capital theory in its entirety, in large part because the normative justification of contemporary economics appeals straightforwardly to utilitarian ethical theory, which we have found to be at least partially inconsistent with Americans' other political values. For example, human capital theory might direct public schools to develop certain work skills among students even though their emerging conceptions of the good might lead them in quite different directions. Even worse, this theory might authorize schools to engineer students' personal and social conceptions of the good in particular ways that are deemed necessary to encourage economic growth. Finally, this theory might, on the grounds of efficiency, direct schools to neglect or minimize the education of certain segments of the student population—for example, students with disabilities—and to emphasize the education of other segments. These possibilities demonstrate that the normative grounding of the theory of human capital is at odds with the normative political theory that we have been developing here.

Nevertheless, when appropriately qualified, human capital theory can help clarify the economic role that schools are to play in the lives of their students. The schools' commitments to education for personal liberty, democracy, and equal opportunity are their highest priorities. But, as these responsibilities are being accomplished, schools have an obligation to inform students about the economic value of various developed capabilities, to help them develop life plans that take into account the role that such capabilities may have in pursuing their own emerging personal and social conceptions of the good, and to provide opportunities for developing any economically valuable capabilities that their life plans may include. Thus, a principle emerges for the public schools' politically legitimate role in enhancing a society's economic growth: *Conduct public schooling in a way that allows children to understand the role that economically valued capabilities may have in formulating and pursuing their emerging personal and social conceptions of the good and that helps them develop the economic capabilities included in their life plans.*

This principle allows public schools to make a contribution to their society's economic growth by honestly representing to students the personal and social economic consequences of their decisions and by fostering the economically valued capabilities that are of meaning in their students' lives. But it does not permit the schools or their political leadership to become the ultimate decision makers about which paths toward economic growth are to be followed. That right is retained by the students themselves. Of course, in following this principle, a society's economic growth may be less than maximal in that its citizens are likely to hold conceptions of the good that differ from utilitarianism, but it will be constructive growth in the sense of making a contribution to the achievement of its citizens' aspirations.

SOME CONCEPTUAL IMPLICATIONS FOR SCHOOL FINANCE

The theory of social justice in education developed here makes judgments about the normative acceptability of school finance systems more complex than allowed by the usual terms in which such assessments are frequently made. For example, equality is a central concern of this theory in that equal liberties and opportunities are to be among the social results to which the school system contributes. However, simple equality of resources between schools or school districts, or horizontal equity, is probably not able to provide an acceptable measure of the system's contribution to these results, for both the material and cultural conditions under which children are raised are likely to affect schools' social outcomes in these matters, and such conditions vary by school and geographic region. Thus, social justice in school finance is significantly a matter of vertical equity—that is, of providing the unequal distribution of resources to enable schools to meet these varying conditions of children and their families. We are familiar with the idea that the school may have to compensate for poorer families' inability to allocate sufficient resources to the education of their children, but these principles suggest that other forms of educational compensation in the interests of social justice can place legitimate demands on school resources as well. For example, the more insular the family culture is or the more isolated particular cultures are within the society, the more difficult it will be to enable children to gain a respectful regard for at least some other cultures in their society, and the more resources that schools with children from such families will have to allocate so that the children can achieve their own personhood, respect others' personal liberties, and become citizens who are willing to teach about their own communities' political endeavors and to learn from those of other communities. Thus, in addition to challenging the moral and political relevance of horizontal equity as defined in the school finance literature, this theory suggests an amplification of the conditions that can create educational inequity and, therefore, an expansion of the meaning of the goal of vertical equity.

On this revised definition of vertical equity, however, neither equal school achievement nor all children's attaining a uniform minimum standard of achievement—often called *educational adequacy* in the school finance literature—provides a reasonable measure of the system's realizing a socially just state of affairs. First, as we have seen, personal and political liberty imply that any such measures of whether a system of schools has been adequately funded are unsatisfactory. To be sure, these principles imply common goals of education for personal and political liberties, namely, personhood and citizenship. However, the attainment of these goals is consistent with a wide range of specific school achievements because those outcomes are to depend upon maturing children's own judgments about the individual and collective conceptions of the good to which their lives will be devoted. For example, one can imagine a circumstance in which all children attain a specific standard of reading achievement but none develops the independence of judgment needed to achieve his own personhood. Similarly, we can imagine a circumstance in which children attain very different levels of reading achievement but nevertheless achieve the ability to make genuinely independent judgments about their conceptions of the good. Thus, equal or minimum uniform achievement is neither a necessary nor a sufficient condition of social justice in the interests of liberty. Here we need instead to attend to the quality of the processes by which children learn and to the purposes to which they apply their learning to decide whether the education they have received is adequate and thus whether their education has been adequately funded.

Second, as we also have seen, equality of opportunity within the sort of diverse society that such liberties produce is not likely to be achieved when vertical equity is measured in such uniform ways; for equal learning is a realization of equal opportunity only when children's aspirations are the same. Of course, maturing children can in one sense be said to have common aspirations in a just society in that they all want to succeed according to the conceptions of the individual and collective conceptions of the good that they adopt. The specific school achievements that are relevant to fulfilling this common aspiration, however, may be very different for different children and different communities. That is, what an aspiring electrical engineer and an aspiring ballet dancer need to know to have an equal chance to achieve their aspirations are quite distinct. Thus, the school achievements of individuals need to be measured against children's own conceptions of the good. And to the extent that children's conceptions of the good vary systematically with their geographic, ethnic, and cultural backgrounds, different types and levels of school achievement are perfectly consistent with their enjoying an equal opportunity to succeed. As noted before, the relevant measure of equal educational opportunity is equal effort by school authorities to assist children to achieve their diverse aspirations rather than equal learning outcomes. And thus the measure of an adequately funded school system is whether it permits such equal if distinctive efforts to be made.

Finally, the improvement or the equalization of incomes is not necessarily an accurate measure of the achievement of a socially just educational system. Here, too, the adequacy of income is to be defined in terms of its relevance for achieving one's personal and collective conception of the good, not in terms of its meeting some uniform minimum level, its increase over past levels, or its equalization; for, as we have seen, the relevance of economic growth to the principles of social justice for schooling lies in whether such growth realizes or supports the activities required by those conceptions. Thus, a socially just school system may contribute to a stable or even declining economy, and it may produce significant or even increasing economic inequalities as long as it allows its future citizens to make judgments about the economic skills that they develop on the basis of their relevance to those individuals' emerging conceptions of the good—both personal and collective.

Of course, in many circumstances inequality of learning, learning resources, or income may signal a violation of these principles of social justice. If, in fact, two large populations of children (with, it can be assumed, collectively similar talents) have similar or similarly distributed aspirations, such inequalities indicate that the educational system does not serve them as the principles indicate and that a redistribution of educational resources is required on the basis of social justice in schooling. However, the real injustice does not lie inherently in the inequality of outcome itself but in the failure of the educational system to respond to the self-determined aspirations of the two populations. Thus, even in such a case, the redistribution should aim not at achieving mere equality of results, but instead at improved responsiveness of the educational system to children's emerging conceptions of the good. If after that redistribution the children's aspirations remain the same, then equality of results will follow as a matter of course. If, however, the redistribution changes children's aspirations, as may very well happen in a diverse society in which additional educational resources can call forth different conceptions of the good, inequalities may very well result; but such inequalities do not represent an injustice if the redistribution has ensured that the system is equally and adequately responsive to children's revised aspirations. Indeed, under these changed circumstances, an enforced equality of outcomes would itself represent a social injustice. Thus, adequacy in funding reflects whether the resources available to the schools are sufficient to permit them to be responsive to children's aspirations.

REFERENCES

Bull, B. (1984). Liberty and the new localism: Toward an evaluation of the tradeoff between educational equity and local control of schools. *Educational Theory, 34*(1), 75–94.

Bull, B. (1990). The limits of teacher professionalization. In J. Goodlad, R. Soder, & K. Sirotnik. (Eds.), *The moral dimensions of teaching* (pp. 87–129). San Francisco: Jossey-Bass.

Bull, B. (1996). Is systemic reform in education morally justified? *Studies in Philosophy and Education, 15*(1), 13–23.

Bull, B. (2000a). National standards in local context: A philosophical and policy analysis. In B. A. Jones (Ed.), *Educational leadership: Policy dimensions in the 21st century* (pp. 107–121). Stamford, CT: Ablex.

Bull, B. (2000b). Political philosophy and the balance between central and local control of schools. In N. Theobald & B. Malen (Eds.), *Balancing local control and state responsibility for K–12 education: 2000 yearbook of the American Educational Finance Association* (pp. 21–46). Larchmont, NY: Eye on Education.

Bull, B. (2002). A political theory for the normative assessment of school reform in the U.S. In T. Kvernbekk & B. Nordtug (Eds.), *The many faces of philosophy of education: Traditions, problems and challenges* (pp. 72–89). Oslo: University of Oslo Institute of Educational Research.

Bull, B., Fruehling, R., & Chattergy, V. (1992). *The ethics of multicultural and bilingual education.* New York: Teachers College Press.

Dewey, J. (1927). *The public and its problems.* New York: Henry Holt.

Foley, D. A., Levinson, B. A., & Hurtwig, J. (2001). Anthropology goes inside: The new educational ethnography. In W. G. Secada (Ed.), *Review of research in education, 25, 2000–2001* (pp. 37–98). Washington, DC: American Educational Association.

Gutmann, A. (1999). *Democratic education* (Rev. ed.). Princeton, NJ: Princeton University Press.

Mill, J. S. (1978) *On liberty.* Indianapolis: Hackett. (Original work published 1859)

Nozick, R. (1974). *Anarchy, state, and utopia.* New York: Basic Books.

Rawls, J. (1999). *A theory of justice* (Rev. ed). Cambridge, MA: Harvard University Press.

Thurow, L. C. (1970). *Investment in human capital.* Belmont, CA: Wadsworth.

2

CRITICAL RACE THEORY AND HUMAN CAPITAL THEORY

Framing the Discourse on the Nexus of Social Justice and Education Finance

Enrique Alemán, Jr.

University of Utah

MANY AUTHORITIES IN THE PUBLIC SPHERE—including educational leaders, policy makers, and elected officials[1]—utilize the language of human capital theory (HCT) to discuss the merits of issues such as equalized state funding, high-stakes testing, accountability systems, and performance incentives in teacher pay. Public policy debates often include rationalizations of how increased public investment in education will yield increased efficiency or productivity in the U.S. economic system. Although Levin (1989) issued a critique of educational researchers as lacking the technical expertise to carry out economic analyses of critical problems in education, the field of school finance has developed quite extensively in this realm, with ever-increasing sophistication in quantitative analysis and modeling (see also Rolle & Fuller, this volume). The purpose of this chapter is thus not to refute HCT or to call for the abandonment of economic analysis. Rather, it is to outline a supplementary theoretical framework—critical race theory (CRT)—from which to evaluate, analyze, and interrogate the impact of human investments via educational finance in the quest for socially just educational opportunities.

BACKGROUND

Dantley and Tillman (2006) provide a starting point for discussing and conceptualizing social justice. Their definition emphasizes "moral values, justice, equity, care, and respect and the imperative for investigating the impact of race, ethnicity, class, gender, sexual orientation, and disability on the educational outcomes of students" (p. 19). As they state, "social justice focuses on marginalized groups—those groups that are most often underserved and underrepresented and who face various forms of oppression in schools" (p. 19). Marshall (2004) discusses how social justice researchers and educational leaders challenge power inequities by providing alterative "truths and voices" (p. 5) to research communities and fields of practice. Marshall and Gerstl-Pepin (2005) further describe how conceptualizations of social justice and equity are no longer relegated to fighting for individual rights. Rather, scholars investigate how "social justice is relational and distributive" (p. 72), researching power differentials, marginalization of student groups, and the institutionalization of inequitable outcomes in student success (Marshall & Oliva, 2006; Valenzuela, 2004) and access to educational opportunities, such as in higher education (Villalpando, 2003; Yosso, 2006).

As was done in a special issue of the *Educational Administration Quarterly* in 2004, this chapter centers social justice and equity as tantamount to closing educational achievement gaps—whether they are disproportionate dropout rates, graduation rates, access to advanced placement courses, participation and scoring on the Scholastic Aptitude Test (SAT) and the American College Test (ACT), and so on—and providing equal educational opportunities (through access to equitable resources and quality educational programs). In addition, the goal is, as Marshall has stated, to discuss "how we can use our research, status, and power to transform our profession to take leadership for social justice in schools and even in society" and to make scholarship and research "useful for transforming our policies and practices" (2004, p. 3). Likewise, I take an openly critical, progressive, and action-oriented stance in laying out my social justice arguments. This chapter seeks to address the historically crippling effects of unjust and unfair educational policies in general (Bell, 2004; Donato, 1997; McNeil, 2000; San Miguel, 1987; Spring, 1997; Takaki, 2000; Valencia, 2002; Valenzuela, 1999) and morally bankrupt educational finance policies specifically (Anyon, 1997; Cardenas, 1997; Kozol, 1991, 2005).

Economic analysis may play a central role in the evaluation of educational programs and policies, but it should not be the only framework informing policy and driving educational decision making. In addition, an understanding of the educational finance should not be devoid of an analysis of politics, race, and power. The human factor—policy effects on students' lives and their ramifications for communities—should not be neglected simply by preferencing HCT principles above other paradigms. Some scholars agree, stating that the "school part" of education has been neglected in educational research and political debate. For example, Harris, Handel, and Mishel (2004) offer a detailed quantitative analysis that challenges the findings in the U.S. Department of Education National Commission on Excellence in Education's *Nation at Risk* report (1983). While acknowledging that education of the nation's future workforce affects the national economy and refuting the negative policy and economic assertions assigned to educational systems by *A Nation at Risk*, they point out the centrality of economic arguments embedded in school reform policy discourse. They question the implications that public educational institutions have failed to meet the competitive demand of the global workplace market. Pointing to the utmost importance that the economy played on a report about schools, they further critique the absence of a broader discussion about schools, students, and communities:

> Yet, the words "school" and "education" are nowhere to be seen in the report's first sentence. Rather, the scope is clearly fixed on the economy—"commerce," "industry," "technological innovation," and later, "exports," "training," and "employment." Indeed, there are more economic terms than educational ones throughout the report. The title could very well have been *An Economy at Risk*. (Harris et al., 2004, p. 37)

The utilization of economic rationales, arguments, and frameworks in the political discourse and in policy arena is nothing but omnipresent. Similar to Levin's (1989) statement that "virtually all of the recent calls for national educational reform predicate their arguments on the urgent need for the U.S. to be economically competitive with other nations" (p. 13) and Harris et al.'s contention that the *Nation at Risk* authors were misguided in their blaming public education for the economic downturn of the 1970s, policy makers, community activists, and parents have employed economic and/or human capital arguments in calling for educational reform, increased funding, voucher programs, charter schools, and a myriad of other policies. The conceptual argument laid out in this chapter is that the prevalent human capital rationales proffered by numerous policy actors, researchers, and politicians neglect to critically understand the role that HCT has on maintaining a state of inequity in the nation's public schools. Educational decision making necessitates a grounding of equity discourses and analyses via a CRT framework, rather than relying solely on HCT frameworks, which continue to pervade both educational practice and political rhetoric to the detriment of equity.

DEFINING AND CONCEPTUALIZING
HUMAN CAPITAL THEORY

Gary S. Becker and Theodore W. Schultz, economists awarded the Nobel Prize for the formulation and development of HCT, have theorized that education is an investment in individual human beings that yields benefits to economies and individual earnings. The concept of human capital has been described as the "know-how" that individuals possess (Langelett, 2002, p. 1), the knowledge, training, values, or talents that cannot be separated from an individual "the way it is possible to move financial and physical assets" (Becker, 1992, p. 85). The core premise of HCT is "that individuals and society derive economic benefits from investments in people" (Sweetland, 1996, p. 341) and "assumes that schooling endows an individual with knowledge and skills that enable him or her to be more productive and thereby to receive higher earnings" (King, Swanson, & Sweetland, 2003, p. 39). Individuals benefit in their increased capacity to produce and consume more, which in turn benefits their community and boosts society's capabilities in generating goods and higher tax yields.

Schultz is credited with having initialized the formal development of HCT during a 1960 speech to the American Economic Association (Baptiste, 2001; Kiker, 1966). In his speech, he argued that economists generally "treat education as an investment in man" and "treat its consequences as a form of capital" (1961, p. 571). Schultz affirmed this notion as well:

> Since education becomes a part of the person receiving it, I shall refer to it as human capital. Since it becomes an integral part of a person, it cannot be bought or sold or treated as property under our institutions. Nevertheless, it is a form of capital if it renders a productive service of value to the economy. (p. 571)

Although HCT was formalized by Becker and Schultz, Kiker (1966) notes how the concept of human capital—valuing human beings or human skill—has been theorized and written about since the late 17th century. He identifies many scholars who prior to Becker and Schultz's work conceptualized human capital, quantifying human value monetarily because they wanted to measure national strength; to evaluate the benefits of education, medical care, or migration; to examine taxing proposals; to estimate the cost of war; and to provide estimates of compensation and worth for personal injury litigation.

Kiker (1966, p. 485) also states that economists who believed in valuing human beings did so because of assumptions that real costs of education exist, that worker productivity increases national wealth, and that increasing investment in human beings benefits national wealth. He also states,

> Although some economists included man himself as capital, most of them included only human skill... Whether or not we define skills and/or the acquirer of them as capital is relatively unimportant. The distinction between skills and the person is important however. (p. 496)

Given that economists were formulating theories and influencing policies by valuing humans as capital during the 17th, 18th, and 19th centuries—a time period when many Africans and African-Americans were actually being bought and sold as property and bred like livestock (Takaki, 2000)—is troubling and runs counter to any social justice or equity notion of analysis. Yet this point is central to understanding how HCT arguments influence the political debate in the way that U.S. history of racial discrimination and violence has all but been eliminated from policy debate.

Becker admits to initially balking at the titling of his seminal work, *Human Capital* (Becker, 1975), because of the implication that "it treated people like slaves or machines" (1992, p. 85), a criticism subsequently charged after its publication. Yet at the time of his lecture to the American Philosophical Society in 1991, he seemed to have fewer misgivings with the term, citing widespread application and acceptance by many in the social sciences and media. Previous to Becker's speech and book publication, Schultz (1960) addresses this "moral issue," with his response to those who "view the very idea of human capital" as "repugnant" (p. 572). The study of human capital does not deny "cultural purposes" of education, such as providing opportunities for individuals to develop into democratic citizens who appreciate art, music, and literature, he claims. Further, this understanding of human capital does not denigrate or prevent the goals of cultural education.

Rather, HCT actually augments the cultural purposes of education by analyzing how educational investments add to personal or national wealth in addition to individual productivity. As Schultz states,

My treatment of education will in no way detract from, or disparage, the cultural contributions of education. It takes these contributions for granted and proceeds to the task of determining whether there are also some economic benefits from education that may appropriately be treated as capital that can be identified and estimated. (p. 572)

The "task of determining" productivity by Becker, Schultz, Kiker, and others (Hy, 2000; Jorgenson & Fraumeni, 1989; Mincer, 1989; Owings & Kaplan, 2004) is not at issue in this chapter. Rather, it is how the use of a HCT discourse in the political arena precludes legitimate challenges to the assumptions, beliefs, and principles at the heart of the theory. In essence, its unquestioned prevalence does "detract" and "disparage" the arguments of those attempting to achieve some measure of social justice and equity. If public educational systems are to be considered a public good, as many already claim, alternative frameworks must be utilized in determining access and opportunities for success.

APPLICATIONS OF THE HCT FRAMEWORK

Educational institutions and systems historically have provided one of society's core functions—educating, training, and preparing the nation's workforce and its political, community, and business leadership (Spring, 1997). Brimley and Garfield (2005) point to the growing expenditures and investment in educational institutions and systems as evidence of HCT usefulness as a theoretical framework. They argue that the "importance of education to the growth of the national economy is no longer challenged" (p. 15). Langelett (2002) also notes that increased educational funding has benefited the national economy. In addition, Brimley and Garfield indicate that the educational system in the U.S. has served as the one of the nation's "biggest businesses, when viewed in terms of the numbers of people and dollars of income involved in its operation" (2005, p. 15).

Numerous research benefits have been attributed to the application of HCT and its study of educational investment. Langelett (2002) outlines some of the major findings that have contributed to an understanding of how investment benefits individuals generally and the economy:

Changing perceptions and expectations that individuals have of themselves and society;

Developing "complimentary resources" that may act as substitutes to scarce resources simultaneous to the efficient use of these resources;

Promoting high literacy and life expectancy rates;

Increasing research in new technological innovations;

Developing of the workforce and the creation of the next generation of leaders;

Increasing worker adaptability to change, therefore increasing efficiency and productivity; and,

Increasing labor participation rates and reducing fertility, meaning additional access for women in the workplace. (pp. 17–18)

While Langelett takes a more macroeconomic focus, Schultz (1961) addresses the effects of investment on individuals. Although students may forgo earnings while they attend school or invest in on-the-job training opportunities, he writes, "such investment in human capital accounts for most of the impressive rise in the real earnings per worker" (p. 1). Becker (1960), however, has found little evidence to link individual productivity, economic growth, and military progress to the results of investment in college attendance and completion. He states that "limited available evidence did not reveal any significant discrepancy between the direct returns to college education and business capital, and thus direct returns alone do not seem to justify increased college expenditures" (p. 354).

Baptiste (2001) demonstrates that divergent views on human capital actually have benefited the economy since the 1980s. He notes that the "mediating effect of technology" pushed scholars to refine their preliminary conceptualizations and theoretical framework of the theory. Whereas some found earlier iterations of HCT to be "too simplistic" in theorizing educational effectiveness and its influence on the economy (p. 188), incorporation of other variables such as technology, creativity, and flexibility enhanced the appeal of HCT, and it soon earned the endorsement of such groups as the Organization for Economic Cooperation and Development. One variable that economists enveloped into the updated version of HCT included individual choices to private investment in higher education. For instance, if after weighing anticipated costs and benefits an individual decides to attend college— willingly forgoing earnings and accepting the possibility of incurring debt—then that person would reap the benefit of higher earnings. However, if the same person chose otherwise, then that person would forgo the "risk" of securing higher earnings (Baptiste, 2001).

HCT SOCIAL JUSTICE WEAKNESSES

In his critique of HCT, Baptiste (2001) attempts to "alert educators to the social bankruptcy of human capital theory" (p. 198), deconstructing two foundational assumptions human capital theorists support that run contrary to social justice aims. The first assumption is that "there is an unqualified, causal effect of human capital on economic productivity," and the second is "that differences in workers' earnings are due entirely to differences in their human capital investments" (p. 189). Although Schultz (1961) acknowledges that "racial discrimination and religious discrimination are widespread" (p. 14), he consistently asserts that human capital investment will inevitably bring about increased productivity and individual earnings:

> Low earnings of many Negroes [*sic*], Puerto Ricans, Mexican nationals, indigenous migratory farm workers, poor farm people and some of our older workers, reflects this failure to have invested in their health and education. Past mistakes are, of course, bygones, but for the sake of the next generation we can ill afford to continue making the same mistakes again. (p. 14)

While many scholars would disagree that these "past mistakes" are, in fact, in our past (Bell, 2004; Darder, Torres, & Gutiérrez, 1997; Kozol, 2005; Ladson-Billings, 1998; Valencia, 2002; Valenzuela, 2004; Villalpando, 2003; Yosso, 2006), Schultz contends that simply increasing human capital investments will address individual productivity, yet he never speaks to the effects of the institutionalized group marginalization that has stained the historical background of the United States.

Becker (1992) also contends that increased investment in human capital would rectify the state of economic inequity for certain groups, however he is more pointed in his assertion. Rather than implicate failing systems or policies that institute inequity, he lays blame on individuals or families for choosing to ignore the benefits of placing a higher value on human capital investment:

> Differences among ethnic groups in the United States in the relation between number of children and spending per child are fascinating. Groups with small families generally spend much on each child's education and training, while those with big families spend much less. The Japanese, Chinese, and Cubans have few children who become well-educated, while Mexicans, Puerto Ricans, and blacks have big families, and the education of children suffers. I should add that the Mormons are an interesting

exception, for they have both very large families and high levels of achievement. (p. 90)

As such, Becker and other human capital theorists promote a decontextualized and ahistoric perspective of economic and educational reality.

And, ignoring countless scholarly attempts to think and write about more critical understandings of educational underachievement (Foley, 1997; Valenzuela, 1999; Yosso, 2006) and economic inequity (Anyon, 1997; Kozol, 1991), as well as more radical attempts at describing the nature of and linkages among power, politics and race (Carmichael & Hamilton, 1967; Gutiérrez, 1998; Ross, 1989), human capital theorists are, as Baptiste stated, promoting a "social bankruptcy" (p. 198), with its philosophical understandings, political ramifications, and policy proposals. Baptiste (2001) alerts those who are proponents of social justice in educational opportunities, such as increasing students of color in higher education (Delgado Bernal, 2002; Villalpando, 2004; Yosso, 2006) or improving educational leadership programs (Brown, 2004; Marshall & Oliva, 2006) in order to not minimize the effects of institutionalized or systemic forms of discrimination and racism. Warning that education and training are not the "cure-all," Baptiste states that "the next time you hear someone explain and justify differences in earnings simply on the basis of differences in educational attainment, beware!" (p. 198).

DEFINING AND CONCEPTUALIZING CRITICAL RACE THEORY

Relative to human capital theory, critical race theory is a newer theoretical framework. Although scholars have been discussing the intersections of institutional and systemic racism, power, and education in the United States for some time (Du Bois, 1903/1994; Omi & Winant, 1994; West, 2001; Woodson, 1933/1998), formalized theories of racism and their application to legal, educational, and societal institutions have emerged in the analysis of legal studies (Crenshaw, 2002; Delgado & Stefancic, 2001; Omi & Winant, 1994) during the last two decades. Utilized more frequently in educational research over the last decade, the examination of educational administration and politics (Alemán, 2006; López, 2003; Morfin, Perez, Parker, Lynn, & Arrona, 2006), K–12 educational policy (Ladson-Billings & Tate, 1997), and higher education policy and practice (Parker, 2003; Solórzano, 1998; Solórzano & Delgado Bernal, 2001; Villalpando & Delgado Bernal, 2002), its prevalence in economics of education or school finance literature, aside from one notable exception (Brady, Eatman, & Parker, 2000), has been scant.

Critical race theorists place the study of race and racism at the center of their scholarship, but they also understand how race and racism intersect with, among other things, class, gender, and sexual orientation. In addition, CRT researchers consider the multidimensional levels that race and racism exist within, pervading educational institutions, systems, social norms, and practices at institutional, structural, and societal levels. At the federal institutional level, CRT scholars posit that the property rights that the U.S. Constitution is grounded upon create tension with the human rights it purports to protect (Crenshaw, Gotanda, Peller, & Thomas, 1995; Ladson-Billings & Tate, 1997; Valdés, Culp, & Harris, 2002). For example, history scholars point to how Africans were property to be legally sold and used as commodities in the U.S. economic structure, while Native Americans were treated like expendable "savages" who possessed land necessary for European expansion and profit (Spring, 1997; Takaki, 2000). While extensive analysis of state constitutions is yet to be completed—and given that all state educational finance systems are codified in particular state laws—the next step for critical race researchers is to conduct analyses at the subfederal level.

Although slavery has been outlawed since the 19th century, legalized Jim Crow segregation, discrimination, and violence toward African-Americans continued well into the 20th century (Williams, 1987). Other communities and students of color were also affected by the remnants of a foundationally racist American history.[2] Mexican Americans in the Southwest were murdered and systematically denied their rights under law (Johnson, 2003; Montejano, 1987; Paredes, 2004), while Native Americans and Asian Americans continued to endure harsh working and living conditions (Blauner, 1987; Takaki, 2000, 2002). Today, America's legacy of unjust institutions and policies, such as discriminatory housing covenants, criminal statutes, and university admissions criteria, continue to disadvantage citizens and students of color. In K–12 education, various scholars have studied how curriculum, testing mechanisms, attendance policies, and school funding structures have contributed to this continued legacy of inequity and marginalization of students and communities of color (Lugg, 2003; Spring, 1997; Takaki, 2000; Valenzuela, 1999). Although not CRT scholars specifically, they study and understand inequity in education using some of the same tenets held by CRT research.

The current CRT movement began as an outgrowth of critical legal studies (CLS) and radical feminism (Delgado & Stefancic, 2001). Crenshaw (2002) notes in her reflective essay that the movement was incited by the refusal of white critical legal theorists to consider their own white privilege as they examined and wrote about hegemonic practices and the power differentials inherent in legal doctrine. The CLS group, dominated by white men, was challenged by a core group of legal scholars seeking to situate race at the center of the discourse. Among those leading this burgeoning form of scholarship was Harvard law professor Derrick Bell (Crenshaw, 2002), known to many as the "movement's intellectual father figure" (Delgado & Stefancic, 2001). Bell was a law professor at Harvard Law School until the early 1980s, when his departure and the refusal of the school's administration to hire another professor of color to teach his class on race and constitutional law sparked students to question hiring practices (Crenshaw, 2002).

Taylor (1998) describes CRT as "a form of oppositional scholarship" that "challenges the experience of whites as the normative standard and grounds its conceptual framework in the distinctive experiences of people of color" (p. 122). Delgado and Stefancic (2001) describe CRT as a "movement" and a "collection of activists and scholars interested in studying and transforming the relationship among race, racism, and power" (p. 2). In describing the evolution of race and critical scholarship into the CRT movement, Crenshaw (2002) notes that CRT is now used "interchangeably for race scholarship as Kleenex is used for tissue, was basically made up, fused together to mark a possibility" (p. 1363). This "possibility" is further utilized by scholars in education, sociology, ethnic studies and women's studies.

Still, with all the social justice benefits that CRT brings to analysis of educational finance phenomenon, researchers employing the framework have major weaknesses in communicating their message and promoting social change. Critics state that CRT scholarship lacks rigor, essentializes communities and persons of color, is not applicable to practice, and focuses too much on race and racism, to the detriment of other "isms," like classism, that deserve study. Convincing researchers, politicians, and citizens to embrace CRT concepts and the pervasiveness of racism will perhaps be the most difficult challenge to address in affecting changes to normative conceptual and analytical frameworks.

CRT A PRIORI HCT: IMPLICATIONS FOR RESEARCH, PRACTICE, AND SOCIAL JUSTICE

Even after the weaknesses that have been described, a CRT analysis should occur a priori an HCT analysis, if social justice concerns are the primary reason for analyzing policy or evaluating effectiveness of programs. If the primary concern is for efficiency to be achieved, then one could continue to focus on HCT as its central frame of analysis. Because educational leadership programs are aiming to better prepare leaders to contend with the varying educational issues, policies, and research from social justice perspectives, it is critical that educational finance scholars and professors also begin to think of introducing more progressive modes of inquiry. Understanding the practice of school finance—for example, local budgeting, tax rate policy, bond elections—is vital; however, not having the ability to understand and advocate for proposals beneficial to one's district at the state and local levels could potentially endanger current and/or future funding, especially for those leaders who advocate for more equitable funding or socially just systems of finance. An HCT framework, discourse, or methodology would not help to embrace social justice and equity goals.

The use of a CRT analytical framework has implications for a broadening of the current traditional forms of research that limit findings, proposals for, and solutions to the problems of marginalized groups, and students and communities of color (Brady et al., 2000). This chapter discusses implications for an increased use of qualitative research in the courts and legislative process (Parker, 2003). Narrative data—which could provide "voice" to communities of color—could assist in highlighting inequities and serve to organize leaders and activists in their advocacy efforts. Educational finance is one of the most contentious areas of research and practice, a terrain that educational leaders, policy analysts, and researchers must learn to navigate.

Placing CRT a priori HCT also has implications for researching, teaching, and practicing educational finance in a different light. While CRT research has implications for approaching an often technical subject matter from a qualitative perspective, it also argues that all educational policy—that at the state and local levels, for instance—should attempt to explain and describe policy effects in a similar methodological manner. The methods provide an alternative to the traditional frameworks of conducting "policy analysis" and add practice-oriented interpretations to the research field. As already indicated, policy research has rarely been conducted using a CRT framework of analysis, and the instances in which educational finance has been researched from this perspective are also lacking. Opportunities to broaden the scope of this conceptual argument abound.

Revisionist Historical Analysis

CRT scholarship calls for challenging and reinterpreting many of the landmark events, legislation, and court cases deemed as groundbreaking during the civil rights era of the 1950s and '60s. This type of research would also include critically reanalyzing state court decisions and state funding equalization plans implemented over the last 40 years. Delgado and Stefancic state that "revisionist history reexamines America's historical record, replacing comforting majoritarian interpretations of events with ones that square more accurately with minorities' experiences" (2000, p. 20). For example, some educational scholars have begun to explore how "equitable" (Brady et al., 2000) or "substantially equal" (Alemán, in press) finance systems do, in fact, continue to financially disadvantage districts or campuses with a predominant number of students of color. This principle of CRT calls for the critical interrogation of the racial hierarchies created by policies and institutions of education, how the policies were adopted, and who influenced their implementation.

While HCT only allows for ahistoric and decontextualized analysis, CRT specifically calls for researchers to analyze history from a revisionist viewpoint (Delgado & Stefancic, 2001). Even during the time when scholars like Becker (1960, 1962, 1975), Schultz (1960, 1961), and Kiker (1966) were writing about and pushing their area of inquiry into new and exciting directions, the state of black and brown America was in the midst of extreme inequity, legalized racial segregation, brutality, and unpunished murder (Acuña, 1988; Carmichael & Hamilton, 1967; Donato, 1997; Gutiérrez, 1998; Ross, 1989; San Miguel, 1987; Williams, 1987; X & Haley, 1964). CRT research enables scholars and leaders to illuminate how power and privilege were doled out to the dominant group during these years. Either through polices and politics, educational programs, or narrow research methodologies that deemphasized equity and social justice, communities and students of color were disadvantaged (Bell, 2004; Donato, 1997; Farr & Trachtenberg, 1999; San Miguel & Valencia, 1998).

Challenging Concepts of Neutrality, Objectivity, and Meritocracy

CRT scholars challenge notions of neutrality, objectivity, and meritocracy and in fact argue that belief in the concepts is a barrier to social justice (Crenshaw et al., 1995; Delgado & Stefancic, 2001). Delgado and Stefancic define merit as "individual worthiness" and state that CRT scholars "question the view that people may be ranked by merit and that distribution of benefits is rational and just" (2001, p. 150). One need only observe participation and achievement on standardized tests (i.e., the SAT and ACT) to see how students of color, namely African-American and Latina/o students, are disproportionately affected by a so-called merit-based test. The authors add that CRT opponents also often criticize CRT theorists' stance on objective truth. They counter that for "the critical race theorist, objective truth, like merit, does not exist, at least in social science and politics ... truth is a social construct created to suit the purposes of the dominant group" (Delgado & Stefancic, 2001, p. 92). Neutrality also fits within the same purview; they are simply concepts and standards that cannot be achieved in the highly contested world that we live in.

In regard to educational finance, CRT provides a framework from which to analyze the effects of "neutral" formulas common in many state school finance systems. Equalized formulas, performance-based compensation, and concepts such as school finance equity and adequacy are all suspect in terms of their actual contribution to social justice efforts. Baptiste (2001) notes that human capital theorists assume that society operates under a perfect "educational meritocracy in which a person's socioeconomic status is limited, presumably, only by his or her educational investment" (p. 195). A person is most productive when she chooses to invest with education; inequalities in income are the result of education, not the result of institutional or systemic racism. Rather, inequities are "natural and inevitable outcomes of a competitive, free market ... (it) is the most (if not the only) legitimate social institution; that is, it is the only institution that can adequately and justly govern, regulate, and explain human behaviors and achievements" (p. 195). Applying a CRT framework centers challenges to so-called objective, neutral, and merit-based standards of educational finance and measurement of student success.

Giving Voice to Marginalized People

Solórzano, Yosso, and others (Solórzano & Yosso, 2001; Yosso, 2006) consider experiential knowledge to be a linchpin to a CRT methodology. Because students and communities of color are very often left out of the policy or the political process, understanding and valuing the centrality of their experiences is an aspect that HCT does not recognize as legitimate, which in turn advantages those from the dominant group. HCT is not designed to allow for analysis or evaluation to consider the "voice" of those that are marginalized. However, Yosso (2006) states that "CRT finds the experiential knowledge of People of Color legitimate, appropriate, and critical.... Critical race research in education views this knowledge as a strength and draws explicitly" (p. 7) from their words, lives, traditions, and realities. HCT considers the effect to the national economy or individual earnings to be the sole measurement of a human capital investment. Anything else is outside the scope of study or analysis. The "counter–story telling" method that Delgado (2001) and others write about attempts to counter the dominant perspective, inserting a critical retelling of the realities that are often left out.

Anyon (1997), Bell (2004), Cardenas (1997), Kozol (1991, 2005), and San Miguel and Valencia (1998) all demonstrate analysis and provide examples of how understanding an educational finance phenomenon from a critical perspective can look much different from a human capital or purely economic perspective. For example, in speaking with high school students in an impoverished and unequal school—made up predominantly of students of color—Kozol (1991) asks the students if differences in facilities, resources, and opportunities exist between their urban school and other predominantly white schools.

> "Let me answer that," says Israel, a small wiry Puerto Rican boy. "If you threw us all into some different place, some ugly land, and put white children in this building in our place, this school would start to shine. No question. The parents would say: 'This building sucks. It's ugly. Fix it up.' They'd fix it fast—no question. People on the outside," he goes on, "may think that we don't know what it is like for other students, but we visit other schools and we have eyes and we have brains. You cannot hide the differences. You see it and compare...." (p. 104)

Because HCT is not meant to provide multiple perspectives, its success in hearing the dominated voices is ineffective relative to CRT.

Commitment to Social Justice

Solórzano (1998) adds commitment to social justice and an interdisciplinary perspective to these CRT tenets. He notes that CRT challenges the dominant education theory, discourse, policy, and practice and adds that CRT is significant in the way "it challenges the traditional paradigms, texts, and related discourse on race, gender and class" (p. 123). Delgado and Stefancic (2001) state that "critical race contains an activist dimension" and that it attempts to not only understand racist social phenomenon but "to transform it for the better" (p. 3). This type of activism is evident in the way that segregation policies, school finance systems, funding formulas, and state taxing structures have been reformed through the tireless, grassroots efforts of communities of color, activists, and progressive attorneys (Acuña, 1988; Alemán, 2004; Bell, 2004; Cardenas, 1997; Darder et al., 1997; Donato, 1997; Farr &

Trachtenberg, 1999; Gutiérrez, 1998; San Miguel, 1987; San Miguel & Valencia, 1998; Valencia, 2005; Williams, 1987).

As implied, HCT does not allow for social justice projects. Becker (1992) notes, "Whether because of school problems, family instability, or other forces, young people without a college education are not being adequately prepared for work in modern economies" (p. 86). He and other HCT scholars do not consider the role of institutions, systems, and policies as barriers to success. Rather, they treat "school problems, family instability, or other forces" to be outside their purview of analytical concern. CRT scholars believe the opposite to be true. If social inequality is to be addressed and remedied, students and their families must not be looked upon as the "problem"; rather, the systems and institutions that the students are educated in must be looked upon as the greatest culprits of inequity. Scholarship and theorizing interact with and inform the practice of social justice activism.

THE CONTINUING NEED FOR CRT IN EDUCATION FINANCE RESEARCH

Given the history of the United States mentioned previously, racism continues to be a major factor leading to social injustice and inequity in society in general and education in particular. Bell (1992) discusses structural racism present in society by describing how white power brokers bargain, negotiate, and deal black citizens to fictional "aliens" in an effort to ensure their own survival. This illustrates how black citizens are characterized as inferior and expendable to the dominant group. Similar to Bell, Delgado and Stefancic (2001) state that "racism is ordinary, not aberrational—'normal science,' the usual way society does business, the common, everyday experience of most people of color in this country" (p. 7). Lawrence (1987) further develops this principle with his introduction of unconscious racism to the discourse noting,

> Americans share a common historical and cultural heritage in which racism has played and still plays a dominant role. Because of this shared experience, we also inevitably share many ideas, attitudes, and beliefs that attach significance to an individual's race and induce negative feelings and opinions about nonwhites. To the extent that this cultural belief system has influenced all of us, we are all racists. At the same time, most of us are unaware of our racism. (p. 322)

CRT scholarship provides opportunities for study of systemic, institutional, and epistemological racism. Scheurich and Young (2002) argue that "epistemological racism means that our current range of epistemologies—positivism to postmodernisms/poststructuralisms— arise out of the social history and culture of the dominant race, that these epistemologies logically reflect and reinforce that social history and that racial group..." (p. 8). HCT represents one of these epistemologies, or ways of knowing, that reflects the dominant race and keeps other types of epistemologies from gaining any traction in the policy or political arena. In her review of educational policy areas to be studied, Ladson-Billings (1998) states, "Perhaps no area of schooling underscores inequity and racism better than school funding" (p. 20), meaning that the systems, policies, and research methodologies used to study finance equity contribute to social injustice. She argues for a critical analysis of the systematic and institutional racism perpetuated by systems that rely primarily on property as their means of revenue generation, including state school finance systems.

CRT differs from HCT in that it clearly does align itself with an analysis of systems and institutions. As Langelett (2002) states, "Economists generally assume that individuals, whether rich or poor, are rational in their decision-making." As they see it, if the individual rationalizes that the costs are greater in acquiring additional education than the benefits, the individual will not pursue education. If, however, the individual surmises that the benefits of on-the-job training or investing in a college education outweigh the costs, then pursing the training will soon follow. Baptiste (2001) critiques human capital theorists who characterize individuals as "*homo economica:* radically isolated, pleasure-seeking materialists who are born free of social constraints or responsibility, who possess no intrinsic sociability, and who are driven, ultimately, by the desire for material happiness and bodily security" (p. 195). The fact that HCT scholars view and study the world through this paradigm advantages the dominant group, disallowing political debate or policy analysis to inform decision makers of their sense of reality. CRT calls for applying research methods and techniques that analyze the pervasiveness of racism in society, which is perpetuated through policies and systems including those in educational finance.

CONCLUSIONS

In both the research community and the political arena, the silencing of divergent arguments effectively stops change, controls marginalized communities, and eliminates hope (Bachrach & Baratz, 1962). Given the many ways that states have failed to move into the 21st century with educational reform—ignoring issues of educational achievement gaps, equal educational opportunities and access, and equitable educational policy implementation (Alemán & Rorrer, 2006; Carey, 2004; Valenzuela, 2004)—the research field is ripe for inquiry, particularly in the field of educational finance.

Many have borrowed the arguments of human capital theorists, arguing that increased funding will benefit the state's economy. However, the HCT framework dehumanizes students—especially students of color. It ignores their voices, histories, cultures, and languages, their narratives of success, family, and educational experience. HCT discourse and analysis blocks any attempt to contextualize the policy issues, relying on majoritarian perspectives of history. It fails to promote a social justice or transformative projects, ensuring the continuance of inequity and inadequacy in the form of low teacher salaries, high class sizes, and low per-pupil expenditures.

Applying a CRT analytical and policy framework to the educational finance moves research agendas toward a genuine discussion of inequity and injustice. CRT provides opportunities for policy makers to consider and activists and educators to contextualize the way funding institutions have historically marginalized communities of color. The framework broadens definitions of the term *data* to include the voices and realities of those most affected by educational finance reforms. In short, if social justice efforts are to be successful a CRT framework must be a priori HCT methods, assumptions, and findings. This provides an avenue to insert the "human" back into the educational finance research.

NOTES

1. See, for example, the report issued by president George W. Bush's Domestic Policy Council, Office of Science and Technology Policy (2006) in which the economy's strength is tied to productivity and efficiency. Proposals in science and technology, and workforce training, are delineated in addition to proposals for improving public education. As stated in the document,

    America's economy is strong and getting stronger. My 2007 Budget recognizes the importance of innovation to our economic future—fostering and encouraging all the components that make our economic engine the envy of the world. In partnership with the private sector, State and local governments, and colleges and universities, the *American Competitiveness Initiative* will promote new levels of educational achievement and economic productivity. With the right policies, we will maintain America's competitive edge, we will create more jobs, and we will improve the quality of life and standard of living for generations to come. (p. 3)

2. Examples of this foundation are the fact that five of the first seven U.S. presidents were slave-owning landowners during their presidency. George Washington was the largest slave owner at the time of this death. Thomas Jefferson became the largest slave owner when Washington died. Of the first 18 presidents, 12 were slave owners. In addition, one need not look any further than the original U.S. Constitution to read how certain residents of the United States—Africans and African-Americans—were to be considered three-fifths of a person.

REFERENCES

Acuña, R. (1988). *Occupied America: A history of Chicanos* (3rd ed.). New York: HarperCollins.

Alemán, E. (2004). *Mexican American school leadership in South Texas: Toward a critical race analysis of school finance policy*. Unpublished doctoral dissertation, University of Texas–Austin.

Alemán, E. (2006). Is Robin Hood the "prince of thieves" or a pathway to equity? Applying critical race theory to school finance political discourse. *Educational Policy, 20*(1), 113–142.

Alemán, E. (in press). Situating Texas school finance policy in a CRT framework: How "substantially equal" yields racial inequity. *Educational Administration Quarterly*.

Alemán, E., & Rorrer, A. (2006). *Closing educational achievement gaps for Latina/o students in Utah: Initiating a policy discourse and framework*. Salt Lake City: Utah Education Policy Center.

Anyon, J. (1997). *Ghetto schooling: A political economy of urban educational reform*. New York: Teacher's College Press.

Bachrach, P., & Baratz, M. (1962). Two faces of power. *American Political Science Review, 56*(4), 947–952.

Baptiste, I. (2001). Educating lone wolves: Pedagogical implications of human capital theory. *Adult Education Quarterly, 50*(3), 184–201.

Becker, G. S. (1960). Underinvestment in college education? *American Economic Review, 50*(2), 346–354.

Becker, G. S. (1962). Investment in human capital: A theoretical analysis. *Journal of Political Economy, 70*(5, part 2), 9–49.

Becker, G. S. (1975). *Human capital: A theoretical and empirical analysis, with reference to education* (2nd ed.). New York: National Bureau of Economic Research.

Becker, G. S. (1992). Human capital and the economy. *Proceedings of the American philosophical society, 136*(1), 85–92.

Bell, D. A. (1992). *Faces at the bottom of the well*. New York: Basic Books.

Bell, D. A. (2004). *Silent covenants: Brown v. Board of Education and the unfulfilled hopes for racial reform*. Oxford: Oxford University Press.

Blauner, R. (1987). Colonized and immigrant minorities. In R. Takaki (Ed.), *From different shores: Perspectives on race and ethnicity in America* (pp. 154–173). New York: Oxford University Press.

Brady, K., Eatman, T., & Parker, L. (2000). To have or not to have? A preliminary analysis of higher education funding disparities in the post–*Ayers v. Fordice* era: Evidence from critical race theory. *Journal of Education Finance, 24*(3), 297–322.

Brimley, V., & Garfield, R. R. (2005). *Financing education in a climate of change* (9th ed.). Boston: Pearson Education.

Brown, K. (2004). Leadership for social justice and equity: Weaving a transformative framework and pedagogy. *Educational Administration Quarterly, 40*(1), 77–108.

Cardenas, J. A. (1997). *Texas school finance reform: An IDRA perspective.* San Antonio, TX: Intercultural Development Research Association.

Carey, K. (2004). *The funding gap 2004: Many states still shortchange low-income and minority students.* Washington, DC: Education Trust.

Carmichael, S., & Hamilton, C. V. (1967). *Black power: The politics of liberation in America.* New York: Vintage.

Domestic Policy Council, Office of Science and Technology Policy (2006). American competitiveness initiative: Leading the world in innovation. Washington, DC: Author.

Crenshaw, K. W. (2002). Critical race studies: The first decade—critical reflections, or "a foot in the closing door." *UCLA Law Review, 49*, 1343–1372.

Crenshaw, K. W., Gotanda, N., Peller, G., & Thomas, K. (Eds.). (1995). *Critical race theory: The key writings that formed the movement.* New York: New Press.

Dantley, M. E., & Tillman, L. C. (2006). Social justice and moral transformative leadership. In C. Marshall & M. Oliva (Eds.), *Leadership for social justice: Making revolutions in education* (pp. 16–30). Boston: Pearson.

Darder, A., Torres, R. D., & Gutiérrez, H. (Eds.). (1997). *Latinos and education: A critical reader.* New York: Routledge.

Delgado, R., & Stefancic, J. (2001). *Critical race theory: An introduction.* New York: New York University Press.

Delgado Bernal, D. (2002). Critical race theory, Latino critical theory, and critical raced-gendered epistemologies: Recognizing students of color as holders and creators of knowledge. *Qualitative Inquiry, 8*(1), 105–126.

Donato, R. (1997). *The other struggle for equal schools: Mexican Americans during the civil rights era.* Albany: State University of New York Press.

Du Bois, W. E. B. (1994). *The souls of black folk.* New York: Dover. (Contains unabridged original work published in 1903)

Farr, J. S., & Trachtenberg, M. (1999). The Edgewood drama: An epic quest for educational equity. *Yale Law and Policy Review, 17*, 607–727.

Foley, D. (1997). Deficit thinking models based on culture: The anthropological protest. In R. R. Valencia (Ed.), *The evolution of deficit thinking: Educational thought and practice* (pp. 113–131). London: Falmer Press.

Gutiérrez, J. A. (1998). *The making of a Chicano militant: Lessons from Crystal.* Madison, WI: University of Wisconsin Press.

Harris, D. N., Handel, M. J., & Mishel, L. (2004). Education and the economy revisited: How schools matter. *Peabody Journal of Education, 79*(1), 36–63.

Hy, R. J. (2000). Education is an investment: A case study. *Journal of Education Finance, 26*(2), 209–218.

Johnson, B. H. (2003). *Revolution in Texas: How a forgotten rebellion and its bloody suppression turned Mexicans into Americans.* New Haven, CT: Yale University Press.

Jorgenson, D. W., & Fraumeni, B. M. (1989). Investment in education. *Educational Researcher, 18*(4), 35–44.

Kiker, B. F. (1966). The historical roots of the concept of human capital. *Journal of Political Economy, 74*(5), 481–499.

King, R. A., Swanson, A. D., & Sweetland, S. R. (2003). *School finance: Achieving high standards with equity and efficiency* (3rd ed.). Boston: Pearson Education.

Kozol, J. (1991). *Savage inequalities.* New York: Harper Perennial.

Kozol, J. (2005). *The shame of the nation: The restoration of apartheid schooling in America.* New York: Crown.

Ladson-Billings, G. (1998). Just what is critical race theory and what's it doing in a *nice* field like education? *Qualitative Studies in Education, 11*(1), 7–24.

Ladson-Billings, G., & Tate, W. (1997). Toward a critical race theory in education. *Teachers College Record, 97*(1), 47.

Langelett, G. (2002). Human capital: A summary of the 20th century research. *Journal of Education Finance, 28*(1), 1–24.

Lawrence, C. R. (1987). The id, the ego, and equal protection: Reckoning with unconscious racism. *Stanford Law Review, 39*, 317–388.

Levin, H. M. (1989). Mapping the economics of education. *Educational Researcher, 18*(4), 13–16.

López, G. R. (2003). The (racially neutral) politics of education: A critical race theory perspective. *Educational Administration Quarterly, 39*(1), 69–94.

Lugg, C. A. (2003). Sissies, faggots, lezzies, and dykes: Gender, sexual orientation, and a new politics of education? *Educational Administration Quarterly, 39*(1), 95–104.

Marshall, C. (2004). Social justice challenges to educational administration: Introduction to a special issue. *Educational Administration Quarterly, 40*(1), 3–13.

Marshall, C., & Gerstl-Pepin, C. (2005). *Re-framing educational politics for social justice.* Boston: Pearson Education.

Marshall, C., & Oliva, M. (Eds.). (2006). *Leadership for social justice: Making revolutions in education.* Boston: Pearson Education.

McNeil, L. M. (2000). *Contradictions of school reform: Educational costs of standardized testing.* New York: Routledge.

Mincer, J. (1989). Human capital and the labor market: A review of current research. *Educational Researcher, 18*(4), 27–34.

Montejano, D. (1987). *Anglos and Mexicans in the making of Texas, 1836–1986.* Austin: University of Texas Press.

Morfin, O. J., Perez, V. H., Parker, L., Lynn, M., & Arrona, J. (2006). Hiding the politically obvious: A critical race theory preview of diversity as racial neutrality in higher education. *Educational Policy, 20*(1), 249–270.

Omi, M., & Winant, H. (1994). *Racial formation in the United States: From the 1960s to the 1990s* (2nd ed.). New York: Routledge.

Owings, W. A., & Kaplan, L. S. (2004). School finance as investment in human capital. *NASSP Bulletin, 88*(640), 12–28.

Paredes, A. (2004). *With his pistol in his hand: A border ballad and its hero* (14th ed.). Austin: University of Texas Press.

Parker, L. (2003). Critical race theory and its implications for methodology and policy analysis in higher education desegregation. In G. R. López & L. Parker (Eds.), *Interrogating racism in qualitative research methodology* (pp. 145–180). New York: Peter Lang.

Ross, F. (1989). *Conquering Goliath: Cesar Chávez at the beginning.* Keene, CA: El Taller Grafico Press.

San Miguel, G. (1987). *"Let all of them take heed": Mexican Americans and the campaign for educational equality in Texas, 1910–1981.* Austin, TX: University of Texas Press.

San Miguel, G., & Valencia, R. R. (1998). From the Treaty of Guadalupe Hidalgo to *Hopwood*: The educational plight and struggle of Mexican Americans in the Southwest. *Harvard Educational Review, 68*(3), 353–412.

Scheurich, J. J., & Young, M. D. (2002). Coloring epistemology: Are our research epistemologies racially biased? In J. J. Scheurich (Ed.), *Anti-racist scholarship: An advocacy.* Albany: State University of New York Press.

Schultz, T. W. (1960). Capital formation by education. *Journal of Political Economy, 68*(6), 571–583.

Schultz, T. W. (1961). Investment in human capital. *American Economic Review, L1*(1), 1–17.

Smith-Maddox, R., & Solórzano, D. G. (2002). Using critical race theory, Paulo Freire's problem-posing method, and case study research to confront race and racism in education. *Qualitative Inquiry, 8*(1), 66–84.

Solórzano, D. G. (1998). Critical race theory, racial and gender microaggressions, and the experiences of Chicana and Chicano scholars. *International Journal of Qualitative Studies in Education, 11*(1), 121–136.

Solórzano, D. G., & Delgado Bernal, D. (2001). Examining transformational resistance through a critical race and LatCrit theory framework: Chicana and Chicano students in an urban context. *Urban Education, 36*(3), 308–342.

Solórzano, D. G., & Yosso, T. J. (2001). Critical race and LatCrit theory and method: Counter-storytelling. *Qualitative Studies in Education, 14*(4), 471–495.

Spring, J. (1997). *The American school: 1642–2000* (5th ed.). New York: McGraw-Hill Higher Education.

Sweetland, S. R. (1996). Human capital theory: Foundations of a field of inquiry. *Review of Educational Research, 66*(3), 341–360.

Takaki, R. (2000). *Iron cages: Race and culture in 19th century America* (Rev. ed.). New York: Oxford University Press.

Takaki, R. (Ed.). (2002). *Debating diversity: Clashing perspectives on race and ethnicity in America.* New York: Oxford University Press.

Taylor, E. (1998). A primer on critical race theory. *Journal of Blacks in Higher Education,* (19), 122–124.

U.S. Department of Education, National Commission on Excellence in Education. (1983). *A nation at risk: The imperative for educational reform.* Washington, DC: Author.

Valdés, F., Culp, J. M., & Harris, A. P. (Eds.). (2002). *Crossroads, directions, and a new critical race theory.* Philadelphia: Temple University Press.

Valencia, R. R. (2005). The Mexican American struggle for equal educational opportunity in *Mendez v. Westminster*: Helping to pave the way for *Brown v. Board of Education. Teachers College Record, 107*(3), 389–423.

Valencia, R. R. (Ed.). (2002). *Chicano school failure and success: Past, present, and future* (2nd ed.). New York: Routledge-Falmer.

Valenzuela, A. (1999). *Subtractive schooling: U.S.-Mexican youth and the politics of caring.* Albany: State University of New York Press.

Valenzuela, A. (Ed.). (2004). *Leaving children behind: How Texas-style accountability fails Latino youth.* Albany: State University of New York Press.

Villalpando, O. (2003). Self-segregation or self-preservation? A critical race theory and Latina/o critical theory analysis of a study of Chicana/o college students. *International Journal of Qualitative Studies in Education, 16*(5), 619–646.

Villalpando, O. (2004). Practical considerations of critical race theory and Latino critical theory for Latino college students. *New Directions for Student Services, 105,* 41–50.

Villalpando, O., & Delgado Bernal, D. (2002). An apartheid of knowledge in academia: The struggle over the "legitimate" knowledge of faculty of color. *Equity and Excellence in Education, 35*(2), 169–180.

West, C. (2001). *Race matters* (2nd ed.). New York: Vintage.

Williams, J. (1987). *Eyes on the prize: America's civil rights years, 1954–1965.* New York: Penguin.

Woodson, C. G. (1998). *The mis-education of the negro.* Trenton, NJ: Africa World Press. (Original work published 1933)

X, M., as told to Haley, A. (1964). *The autobiography of Malcolm X.* New York: Ballantine.

Yosso, T. J. (2006). *Critical race counterstories along the Chicana/Chicano educational pipeline.* New York: Routledge.

3

MEASURING EDUCATIONAL PRODUCTIVITY IN THE FACE OF SOCIAL JUSTICE INFLUENCES

A Discussion of the Efficacy of Relative Economic Efficiency for Determining School Improvement Factors

R. Anthony Rolle

Texas A&M University

Arthur X. Fuller

Vanderbilt University

POLICYMAKERS, ADMINISTRATORS, AND RESEARCHERS have spent considerable energy developing educational finance systems and accountability standards—and statistical measures associated with both—designed to increase student learning in public schools. Among these efforts, it is generally accepted that education finance and economics of education researchers tend to investigate three types of efficiency when examining productivity in the schooling process (Rolle, 2005):

1. *Technical efficiency*: maximizing student learning objectives and policy outcomes while minimizing financial and human resource inputs
2. *Allocative efficiency*: maximizing student learning objectives and policy outcomes, given input prices and the effectiveness of management strategies, while utilizing financial and human resources optimally

3. *Total economic efficiency*: maximizing student learning objectives and policy outcomes while pursuing allocative and technical efficiency simultaneously.

When conducting productivity analyses, researchers typically employ the use of statistical formulas called *production functions*. Relying heavily on standard microeconomic theories, these formulations assume that public districts and schools act similarly to private businesses; and accordingly, administrators of public districts and schools pursue cost-minimizing management strategies. However, it is important to acknowledge that public school spending is conducted in sociopolitical environments where both organizations and individuals struggle for legitimacy and the capacity to distribute scarce resources. More specifically, as public organizations charged with meeting the multiple needs and demands of diverse constituents, the ability to negotiate and compromise becomes an essential asset for all actors. The resulting concessions generate a myriad of objectives—many in opposition to one another—that emerge as political, organizational, and individual goals. Nevertheless, school districts are expected to provide a broad-based curriculum, qualified teachers, quality teaching materials, introductions to new technologies, and a wide range of extracurricular activities for all students. Add to this atmosphere the broader equity and social justice principles of advocates seeking to influence the distribution of educational resources and opportunities,[1] and the resulting complexity appears to threaten the assumed rationality of long-established educational productivity theories.

While there already have been considerable and lengthy debates in school finance about whether "money matters" in improving educational outcomes, we do not wish to take up that debate extensively in this chapter.[2] We believe the larger question to be revisited is, *How should educational productivity be measured within the context provided by the principles of social justice?* School administrators have little discretion over determining optimal levels and proportions of input resources, so the utilization of production and cost functions in the measurement of efficiency in public schools may never be fruitful. In fact, it seems inappropriate for a public school's level of productivity to be measured as a pursuit of what could be the unattainable: an absolute mathematical representation of a legislative process that determines and distributes resources to administrators who may or may not direct resources toward desired organization or policy goals.

Given this more pragmatic perspective, and as Deller and Rudnicki (1993) have argued, production function analyses used to measure levels of productivity in educational organizations may be predisposed to show weak statistical relationships in at least three ways:

1. There is an assumption that all students, teachers, and administrators are performing optimally in pursuit of the same educational policy goals; but, no universally accepted determination of this optimality—or its measurement—exists for student effort, teacher effectiveness, or education management.
2. There is a casualness that surrounds the construction of statistical models used to estimate student learning costs; but, no universally accepted pedagogical or curricular—and therefore no statistical—structure exists for the educational production process.
3. There is education policy research that refers to the significant influences of community, household, and peer characteristics; but, no universally accepted definitions for these characteristics—or their measurement.

Therefore, when acknowledging differing rationales and applications of social justice influences on educational productivity, the applicability of normative economic efficiency frameworks—and their cost-minimizing assumptions—to public educational institutions is questionable. As such, the purpose of this chapter is to contribute to our knowledge about linkages between educational productivity and social justice concepts by providing evidence that supports two assertions:

1. Given that differing social justice principles are pursued within various educational contexts, levels of school productivity should be reconceptualized as the amount of technical efficiency generated by combinations of financial and human resources, sociopolitical influences, instructional and management strategies, and levels of student effort that maximize educational outcomes.
2. Given that differing social justice principles are pursued within various educational contexts, the measurement of efficiency in public schools should be reconceptualized to focus on what the highest student learners achieve compared to the lowest student learners—not the best average performances predicted by traditional production function analyses. Accordingly, the measures used should focus on relative comparisons of the best observed performers to the worst.

Specifically, this chapter will provide a brief literature review that (1) describes the "money matters" debate; (2) critiques the appropriateness of normative economic approaches for public schools; and (3) describes the appropriateness of an alternative (i.e., budget-maximizing) economic approach for public schools.[3] The chapter will proceed by describing three methods that determine levels of relative economic efficiency: *modified quadriform, stochastic frontier,* and *distance function* analyses. The conclusion will offer a possible application of relative economic efficiency measures to public educational organizations in determining school improvement factors.

BACKGROUND: A PERSPECTIVE ON THE MONEY MATTERS DEBATE

In *A Nation at Risk* (1983), the U.S. Department of Education National Commission on Excellence in Education claimed that fiscal equity and economic efficiency should be pursued simultaneously:

> We cannot permit [productivity] to yield to [equity] either in principle or practice...To do so would deny young people their chance to learn and live according to their aspirations and abilities. [Granting preference to equity] also would lead to a generalized accommodation to mediocrity in our society on one hand or to the creation of an undemocratic elitism on the other.... (p. 5)

The commission charged that within the equity movement, the traditional measures of academic success (e.g., standardized achievement scores or college admission) came to be seen as compensation that all students deserved regardless of their academic performance. The report noted that "the educational foundations of our society are presently being eroded by a rising tide of mediocrity that threatens our very future as a nation and as a people..." (p. 1).

As disturbing as these findings seemed for students, the commission and the media focused the nation's attention on the economic consequences of a low quality education system, noting, "If only to keep our competitive edge in world markets, we must rededicate ourselves to the reform of our educational system for the benefit of all... Learning is the indispensable investment required for success in the emerging information age..." (p. 2). Ultimately, the politics and publicity surrounding *A Nation at Risk* shifted the focus of education finance researchers away from the issues of fiscal equity (Rodriguez, 2004). Instead, these researchers began to explore new avenues of research designed to support the development of a more demanding curriculum and improving levels of economic efficiency in education.

Educational Excellence Research: Pursuing Educational Efficiency

The ensuing educational excellence movement used *A Nation at Risk* as the political basis for their educational reform efforts. This movement popularized the notion that competent principals and high quality teachers know how to educate students well, but the "administrative blob" of the educational bureaucracy reduces their effectiveness (Toch, 1991). Moreover, these researchers spread the idea that what works in schools does not require additional dollars. What is needed, they argue, is more productive uses of existing resources (Finn, 1983; Hanushek, 1981, 1986, 1989, 1991; Kirst, 1983; Mann & Inman, 1984; Walberg & Fowler, 1987; Walberg & Walberg, 1994). Gains in educational achievement, they proclaimed, can be achieved through increasing efficiencies in the organization, management, and operation of districts and schools.

After the release of *A Nation at Risk*, Finn (1983) asserted that supporters of the educational bureaucracy found it in their best interests to foster the notion that improvements in productivity require increased spending. In direct opposition to this "more money" belief, he claimed that there were revenue neutral policies that educational excellence reformers must reestablish as tenets of the new educational equity standards movement:

- Comprehensive school improvement strategies should be developed
- High academic standards should be established for all students
- The profession of teaching must have rigorous entry qualifications
- Universities should have rigorous entrance requirements

These assertions were supported by both Kirst (1983) and Mann and Inman (1984), who published research pieces claiming that a permanent improvement in educational practices could be accomplished at little or no additional costs. Additionally, Hanushek (1986) asserted that differences in educational productivity exist not because of differences in school expenditures, class sizes, or other school attributes but primarily because of inequities in the distribution of teachers' education and ability. Later, Hanushek (1989) found no consistent statistical relationship between educational expenditures and student performance. In subsequent articles, Hanushek (1995a, 1995b, 1996) claimed that differences among schools come primarily from differences in teacher quality. As a result of these analyses, educational excellence researchers claimed that school districts should support policies that attract and retain experienced teachers who desire to leave schools with low-performing students as their tenure lengthens.

In just over 30 years after the release of *A Nation at Risk*, research detailing the low levels of educational productivity generated by combinations of students, their families, teachers, and school administrations is plentiful and accepted widely (National Center for Education Statistics, 2000). Fittingly, the original education excellence reformers revisited the inequities of American public education in *A Nation Still at Risk* (Bennett et al., 1998). They claimed that the U.S. no longer faces a global danger in terms of economic decline or technological inferiority. Yet, due primarily to an unchanging educational bureaucracy, they assert the state of our children's futures still is at risk in terms of providing equitable academic opportunities for all students. Educational excellence reformers claim that issues at the center of fiscal equity and educational efficiency reforms still have to do with demanding high academic standards for all children and teachers, as well as effectiveness and efficiency from the system as a whole. Changing the public's perception of the nation's education system was their success in the 1980s and early 1990s. Early in the 21st century, the challenge for these reformers is to build on their successes by attempting to improve levels of economic efficiency in educational organizations through the creation of educational service markets in the form of vouchers, charter schools, and tuition tax credits; and, by implementing successfully 2001's No Child Left Behind Act.

Effective Schools Research: Also Pursuing Educational Efficiency

Despite the large number of media, political, and research reports that support the claim that public educational organizations produce outcomes inefficiently, the notion that economically efficient relationships exist between educational expenditures and outcomes also is well supported. Ironically, *A Nation at Risk*'s conclusion that public schools exert little influence on student achievement independently of socioeconomic status not only spawned educational excellence research; it also created what now is known as *effective schools research*, which usually focuses on one of three concepts: educational leadership, effectiveness, and equity. Odden (1986) wrote one of the first notable articles describing possible research agendas in the then new era of educational excellence reform. In this piece, he urges researchers not to avoid equity issues surrounding educational inputs, the outcomes generated, and the quality of schools. Similarly, Murphy and Hallinger (1986) have called for a discussion of *third generation equity issues* that focus on educational processes consisting of teacher quality, uses of school time, and course content as well as their relationships to educational productivity.

Rossmiller (1987) discussed the issues of effective and efficient schools by using concepts of educational equity that were embedded in the seminal educational finance research of Cubberley (1906), Mort (1924), and Strayer and Haig (1923) to discuss the issues of educational efficiency in terms of minimum dollar inputs that generated desired outcomes. Moreover, Rossmiller asserts that fiscal equity and economic efficiency research no longer should imply that spending more money on schools will generate increases in educational outcomes. In fact, he claims that determining how current revenue levels are spent best to improve student learning would be more useful. In economic terms, educational revenues are necessary—but not sufficient—to increase student achievement. In support of Odden and Rossmiller, Murnane (1991) claims it was myopic to conclude that additional funds cannot improve the educational output of schools based solely on weak production function relationships. Murnane also asserts that increasing funds for low-achieving students—a form of vertical equity—will help only some districts due to inefficiencies in their organizational structure and management.

In what has become a classic in the debate over whether money matters in education, Hedges, Laine, and Greenwald (1994)—also continued in Laine, Greenwald, and Hedges (1996)—have reanalyzed Hanushek's earlier meta-analyses detailing the relationship between educational resources and student learning outcomes. Hanushek's research found no significant statistical relationships between educational expenditures and student achievement. However, Hedges et al. (1994) have found that increasing education spending *did* result in higher achievement when using an improved meta-analysis methodology. Moreover, the relationships discovered were large enough to be of statistical and practical significance. As a result, Hedges et al. caution researchers who drew conclusions from Hanushek's previous analyses to use the results carefully.

Cooper (1993)—and later, Cooper and Associates (1994)—have warned that true productivity relationships between educational inputs and student outcomes still are unknown. Even though a production function for education has yet to be discovered, Cooper asserts that understanding how resources are used equitably within schools is an important element in its discovery. Even though traditional economic research methods indicated that the relationship between educational resources and students is unclear, Cooper and Associates (1994) claim that there is some type of economically efficient relationship between educational inputs and student outcomes as long as the resources reach schools, classrooms, and students. Adams (1997) links human and financial resource policy decisions to student outcomes not by asking, Does money matter? or Where does the money go? but by asking, Why was the money allocated in the manner it was? As such, the tenor of the debate regarding fiscal equity and educational productivity changes. Essentially, Adams asserts that it is necessary for education finance policy developers, implementers, and consumers to understand *how* (a reference to equity and efficiency) and why (a reference to accountability) human and financial resources were allocated in any particular manner.

A CRITIQUE ON THE USAGE OF COST-MINIMIZATION ASSUMPTIONS IN THE MEASUREMENT OF EDUCATIONAL PRODUCTIVITY

Regardless of sociopolitical perspective utilized to frame analyses, the fiscal equity and educational efficiency debate has been summarized most appropriately by Coons, Clune, and Sugarman (1970) near its inception:

> Whatever it is that money may be thought to contribute to the education of children, that commodity is something highly prized by those who enjoy the greatest measure of it. If money is inadequate to improve education, the residents of poor districts should at least have an equal opportunity to be disappointed by its failure. (P. 30)

More than 25 years later, Alexander (1998) reiterates the same message, claiming that reasonable and intelligent people almost always will agree that the distribution and management of resources available to public schools affect their level of performance. Despite controversies over research results, economic efficiency analyses have led to generalizations about what levels of resources are appropriate to consistently improve educational outcomes (Hoenack, 1994; King & MacPhail-Wilcox, 1994; Monk, 1990; 1992; Verstegen & King, 1998; Porter, 2003):

Fiscal and physical capacity: expenditures per student, high teacher salaries, and contemporary facilities

Administrative policies: collaborative management, low student-teacher ratios, and small class sizes

Teacher characteristics: teacher training, verbal ability, years of experience, and cultural diversity

Classroom and curriculum content: preschool preparation, student ability groupings, and instructional interventions for students at-risk of failure

More recently, education finance researchers are attempting to improve these conventional education production and cost function approaches by focusing primarily on several areas of interest (Levin, 1997; Rice, 2001; Schwartz & Stiefel, 2001; Verstegen & King, 1998; Stiefel, Schwartz, Rubinstein, and Zabel, 2005):

Improving statistical relationships among purchased school inputs, nonpurchased school inputs, student learning, and organizational policy outcomes

Understanding relationships among human resources allocation, organizational incentives, and the individual preferences of administrators, faculty, and students

Creating incentives that transform individual and institutional productivity efforts into pursuits of increased student learning and organizational policy outcomes

Still, despite the promise of these investigative efforts, major challenges continue to complicate the employment of educational production and cost functions (Rolle, 2004b):

There is a need to expand the traditional two-stage statistical relationship (i.e., dollars purchase educational services, and these services generate outcomes) into more accurate multistage models (e.g., dollars purchase personnel; personnel provide services; services are utilized by students; and, students generate outcomes)

There is a need to analyze distinct subgroups (e.g., by levels of language ability, poverty, or urbanicity)—using the expanded models mentioned above—that accurately represent the educational process for various types of students being educated in multiple contexts

There is a need to investigate the effects of time—and time-lagged effects—on levels of educational productivity and its measurement for various types of students being educated in multiple contexts.

Given the importance of such questions about efficient resource usage by educational organizations, it is unfortunate that traditional economic analyses have not been able to define and measure educational productivity adequately. And, despite the lack of clear evidence in favor of—or against—the existence of a normative economic relationship between educational inputs and outcomes, education finance researchers have been reluctant to investigate alternative analytical paradigms.

BUDGET-MAXIMIZATION THEORY: AN ALTERNATIVE TO THE NORMATIVE EFFICIENCY FRAMEWORK

Budget-maximization theory offers an alternative framework to normative educational productivity analyses by addressing two important features of public sector organizations that are not consistent with the cost-minimizing assumptions of private agencies (Boyd & Hartman, 1988):

Public managers lack property rights and profit motives that can influence the successful performance of the organization
Public organizations receive recurring tax-supplied budgets whose supply is independent of satisfying individual customers

Anchored in these concepts, the productivity levels of public districts and schools that might otherwise appear irrational (i.e., more politically expedient than educationally productive) can be explained (Niskanen, 1971; 1975; 1991; 1994). For instance, in place of salary increases through profit sharing, public education personnel may seek to maximize such items as the sizes of their budgets or the scopes of their activities. As such, with this budget-maximizing approach—a subset of public choice theory—the personal goals of employees in public schools often can take precedence over the stated objectives of district offices and, consequently, may generate outcomes inefficiently.

In fact, seminal research developing economic theories for bureaucratic organizations—and research regarding the behavior of public sector administrators—indicate that it is highly implausible that district and school administrators are cost minimizers (Boyd & Hartman, 1988; Buchanon & Tollison, 1984; Downs, 1967, 1998; Hentschke, 1988; Peacock, 1992; Tullock, 1965). In addition, researchers from Mises (1944) to Levin (1976) to Barnett (1994) assert that educational organizations are structured for bureaucratic management—not for efficient management—strategies that are supported by centralized authorities, hierarchical rule orientations, and external (i.e., economic, political, and social) influences. Therefore, since educational quality is measured primarily by levels of—but not optimal use of—financial and human resource inputs, we assert that educational agencies are much more likely to be budget maximizers (Barnett, 1994; Hayes & Grosskopf, 1993; Niskanen, 1968, 1971; Rolle, 2003).

A large body of research supports the notion that managers of public bureaus systematically request budget increases regardless of the level of organizational output generated. These ideas have been relatively unchallenged since Wildavsky (1964) claimed bureaucrats request moderate annual budget increases in order to maximize long-term budget goals. Still, economic efficiency research on how public schools behave consists mainly of production and cost function studies that assume implicitly that schools are cost-minimizing organizations. A generalized expression for a basic educational algorithm that is designed to predict levels of student learning costs looks an equation

Student learning costs = A combination of (C,H,I,P,S)

in which C represents community characteristics; H represents household characteristics; I represents individual student characteristics; P represents peer influence characteristics; and S represents school resource characteristics. Mathematically, the algorithm described above can be represented as

$$C_i = \alpha + \sum_{p=1}^{p} B_p Y_{pi} + u_i$$

where C_i represents student learning costs; α represents a computational constant; B_p represents the direction and magnitude to which Y_{pi} influences student learning outcomes; Y_i represents numerous characteristics that influence student learning costs; and u_i represents measurement error. However, patterns among education organizations seem to be characterized by annual increases in size, fiscal resources, and constancy—or decreases—in educational outcomes (Sowell, 1993; Walberg & Fowler, 1987; and Walberg & Walberg, 1994). As a result, applying the normative efficiency measures of private industries to public schools is not appropriate.

On the other hand, investigating concepts of economic efficiency in public schools within the context of the theory of budget-maximizing bureaucratic behavior does seem appropriate (Niskanen, 1968, 1971, 1973). This alternative economic framework describes public schools as budget-maximizing agencies—as opposed to cost-minimizing—whose costs are determined by a sociopolitical process that acquires and distributes revenue (Duncombe, Miner, & Ruggiero, 1997; Romer & Rosenthal, 1984; Rolle, 2003; Stevens, 1993). From the vantage point of public education agencies, budget-maximization theory asserts that the preferences of the sponsor (i.e., the collective organization that ultimately determines expenditure levels and designations) can be summarized mathematically by a cost equation called the *budget-output function* (Niskanen, 1971, p. 25). Several types of equations share these two properties, but the theory uses a quadratic function of the following form to represent the concave down budget-output function to reflect that sponsors are reluctant to grant large budget increases to long-standing programs.

$$B_t = aQ_{t-1} - bQ^2_{t-1} \text{ subject to } Q_{t-1}:Q_{t-1} \in [0, {}^a/_{2b}]$$

where B_t represents maximum total budget sponsor is willing to grant to a bureau during a specific time period; Q_{t-1} represents expected level of output by bureau during a specific time period; t represents time in academic years; and a and b represent the coefficients for Q_{t-1} and Q^2_{t-1}, respectively.[4]

Niskanen claims a total budget-output function is a necessary building block for a theory of supply by bureaus because the exchange of promised activities, and expected output for a budget, is conducted "entirely in total" rather than in "unit" terms. The budget-output function, therefore, should be considered to be the product of two relationships (Niskanen, 1971, pp. 25–26): (1) the relationship between budget and level of service (e.g., the relationship between teacher salary and teacher quality); and (2) the relationship between level of service and output (e.g., the relationship between teacher quality and student learning outcomes).

Two arguments are advanced in support of bureaucrats being budget-maximizers: *rationality* and *survival*. According to the theory, either by "predisposition or indoctrination", bureaucrats try to actualize their perception of the public interest. However, a bureaucrat cannot acquire all of the information on individual preferences and production opportunities that is necessary to predict the public interest. In addition, the bureaucrat does not have the managerial authority to order an action that is contrary to the interests—real or perceived—of other bureaucrats or the sponsors of the collective organization. In order to pursue a multiplicity of goals, the bureaucrat has no choice but to maximize budgets. Facing this quandary, Niskanen believes even the most devoted bureaucrats choose to pursue narrower goals that are more feasible politically. Unfortunately, he continues, this response usually leads to the bureaucrat developing expertise in some narrow field—K-12 public school finance for example. This development of "expertise" is what generates the sense of dedication to the public interest with which many bureaucrats are identified (Niskanen, 1971, p. 39).

The survival argument also reinforces the assumption that bureaucrats maximize budgets. Two groups of people influence a bureaucrat's tenure in office significantly: employees of the bureau and sponsors of the collective organization. Employees can be cooperative, responsive, and efficient. Given the proper incentives, they also can deny information to, undermine the directives of, or embarrass the bureaucrat before constituencies or officers of the collective organization. Accordingly, the actions of employees are dependent on their real—and perceived—benefits of employment in the bureau. Therefore, bureau employees' interests in larger budgets are parallel to those of the bureaucrat: greater opportunities to receive promotions, increased job security, and more perquisites (Niskanen, 1971, p. 40).

The power the sponsor organization wields over the bureaucrat's tenure is more obvious than are their interests in the maximization of the budget. Sponsors nominate and confirm the appointments of the bureaucrat or can force resignation; therefore, they have direct control over a bureaucrat's tenure. On the other hand, since the total activities and budget structures of most bureaus are beyond their comprehensive understanding, sponsors also are dependent on bureaucrats to lobby for increased expenditures in old programs as well as develop budgets for new programs. Therefore, at each stage of the program and budget review process, legislative sponsors focus most of their efforts evaluating the proposed budget increases or program changes. Their preferences become revealed by observing which proportions of program and budgets are approved. Depending on the political climate, budget-maximization may not be behavior that is consistent with the maximization of a bureaucrat's personal utility. But, those bureaucrats who do not attempt to maximize the budgets they control will have a relatively short tenure (Niskanen, 1971, pp. 40-41).[5]

As education researchers begin acknowledging economic, financial, and budgeting realities that now are more transparent within the new multicultural and global economy, the need to examine levels of educational productivity from multiple analytical perspectives will emerge prominently. Necessarily, then, alternative frameworks for economic efficiency measures should be explored in tandem with more traditional methods. Regardless of the paradigmatic frameworks preferred by researchers, the ultimate goal of educational finance and economic research is to improve the quantity and quality of educational opportunities provided to all children. Moreover, addressing educational finance and economic productivity issues thoroughly is important because policy makers, administrators, and researchers agree that improvements in educational outcomes are desirable—just not at the expense of efficiency.

THREE METHODOLOGIES FOR MEASURING RELATIVE ECONOMIC EFFICIENCY

Based on the research literature presented, developers and investigators of education finance policy can begin examining issues of educational productivity within more sociopolitically attuned budget-maximizing frameworks rather than the cost-minimizing ones of traditional economic analyses. Furthermore, given the budget-maximizing public policy context within which public schools operate, it seems more appropriate to apply relative measures of economic efficiency—not the absolute measures of typical productivity analyses. Specifically, researchers investigating measures of economic efficiency for public education need to pursue at least three non-traditional forms within public choice paradigms: 1) Modified Quadriform Analysis; 2) Data Envelopment Analysis; and, 3) Stochastic Frontier Analysis. Below are brief descriptions of three methods that are appropriate for measuring levels of relative educational efficiency within this new framework.

Modified Quadriform Analysis

The quadriform was originally an abstract tool devised to allow two-dimensional relationships to be viewed graphically (Genge, 1991, 1992; Hickrod, Liu, Arnold, Chaudhari, Frank, Franklin et al., 1989; Hickrod, Genge, Chaudhari, Liu, Franklin, Arnold, et al., 1990). Typically, student outcomes are measured along the vertical axis, and expenditures are measured across the horizontal axis. The terms *efficient, effective, ineffective,* and *inefficient* define the economic relationships shown by the quadriform (see Figure 3.1).

Efficient public districts and schools are those that generate higher than expected educational outcomes using lower than expected expenditures (quadrant 1). *Effective* public districts and schools are those that generate higher than expected educational outcomes using higher than expected expenditures (quadrant 2). *Ineffective* public districts and schools are those that generate lower than expected educational outcomes using lower than expected expenditures (quadrant 3). Finally, *inefficient* public districts and schools are those that generate lower

Quadrant 1: Efficient Low Input - High Output	Quadrant 2: Effective High Input - High Output
Quadrant 3: Ineffective Low Input - Low Output	Quadrant 4: Inefficient High Input - Low Output

Figure 3.1 Basic Quadriform Diagram

than expected educational outcomes with higher than expected expenditures (quadrant 4).

Later, the *modified quadriform analysis* was used to examine expenditure-output relationships quantitatively and to measure differential levels of economic efficiency between school districts (Anderson, 1996; Rolle, 2003, 2004a; 2004b). Theoretically, the modified quadriform is constructed by using two separate multiple regression (or time series) equations to develop the axes of the quadriform; and the regression residuals are used to determine which of the four quadriform categories a school district is assigned. Mathematically, the two regression equations are of the form

$$Z_i = \alpha + \sum B_i w_{t-i} + u_t$$

where Z_i represents the expected values—expenditure or outcome—for each school "corporation" or district, for our purposes; and W_i represents the unalterable values for each school district. Consequently, the Z_i's forming the expenditure and outcome regressions create the axes of the quadriform. Accordingly, statistically determined best-performing school districts have the highest levels of economic efficiency—the residual organizations are labeled as inefficient (or ineffective or effective) producers in relative comparison to the economically efficient districts.

Stochastic Frontier and Distance Function Analyses

When acknowledging the influences of sociopolitical characteristics on the generation of educational outcomes, the efficiency measurement question to address becomes (Debreu, 1951; Farrell, 1957): When an organizational environment is determined to be nonoptimal economically, is it possible to develop a methodology that consistently measures the difference between relatively efficient and inefficient performers?

Stochastic frontier measures of economic efficiency are used commonly by economic and public finance policy researchers to evaluate levels of technical efficiency present in an organization relative to the "best-performing" organization(s) in the sample investigated (Murillia-Zamarano, 2004; Rolle, 2005; Worthington, 2001). Accordingly, the focal point of the analysis lies in determining statistically the best-performing organization. If the statistically determined best-performing organization has higher levels of economic productivity than the remaining organizations, the residual organizations are labeled as inefficient producers in relative comparison to the best-performing

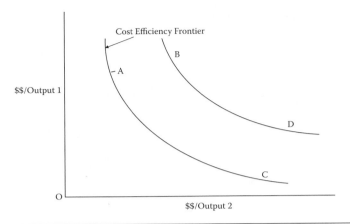

Figure 3.2 Graphical example of stochastic frontier analysis for School B

organization(s) in its comparison group (Coelli, Rao, and Battese, 1998; Cubbin and Zamani, 1996).

Before we present a mathematical example, consider a given cost curve (i.e., this cost curve—also called an *isoquant*—represents combinations of outputs produced at lowest cost when inputs are used in a technically efficient manner); Schools A and C lie on the cost frontier and can be labeled *efficient* (see Figure 3.2). On the other hand, schools B and D lie above the cost curve and are labeled *inefficient*. In this case, the estimated level of inefficiency for Schools B and D can be represented by the efficiency ratio [(BD/AC) – 1]. The ratio gives the extent to which costs are above the estimated level of efficiency denoted by AC (Barrow, 1991; Fare, Grosskopf, and Lovell, 1994; Kumbhakar and Lovell, 2000).

In addition to measuring overall levels of efficiency, stochastic frontier analysis can also allow for the distinct measurements of technical efficiency depending upon its functional form and availability of data.

Mathematically, Aigner, Lovell and Schmidt (1977) are credited with developing stochastic frontier analysis techniques. This method improved the deterministic frontier method by incorporating a technical efficiency term into the regression equation, and by isolating the effects of random error from the effects within the control of organizational managers. For the simplest case, where homogeneity is assumed, the single-output organization can be represented by the stochastic frontier model

$$C_i = \alpha + \sum_{p=1}^{P} A_p Y_{pi} + \sum_{p=1}^{P} B_p Z_{pi} + (u_i + n_i)^*$$

where C_i represents student learning costs; a represents a computational constant; A_p represents the direction and degree to which Y_{pi} influences student learning outcomes; Y_{pi} represents numerous purchased characteristics that influence student learning costs; B_p represents the direction and degree to which Z_{pi} influences student learning outcomes; and Z_{pi} represents numerous nonpurchased characteristics that influence student learning costs (Cooper & Cohn, 1997).

The equation $u_i + n_i$ is a composite error equation in which u_i represents randomness and n_i represents technical inefficiency. The portion of the error equation representing statistical noise, u_i, is assumed to be identically independent and identically distributed. With respect to n_i, it is assumed to be a nonnegative, one-sided error equation that most frequently assumes a half-normal or exponential distribution. If the two error equations are assumed independent of each other, independent of the input variables, and independent of the distributions mentioned above, then either maximum likelihood or corrected ordinary least square estimates can be used to determine the appropriate estimates.

Much like stochastic frontier analyses, *distance function* measures of economic efficiency also are used to evaluate levels of technical efficiency present in an organization relative to the "best-performing" organization(s) in the sample investigated. Here, in lieu of a mathematical example, consider another given cost curve where schools A and C lie on the cost frontier and can be labeled *efficient* (see Figure 3.3). On the other hand, school B lies above the cost curve and is labeled *inefficient*. In this case, the estimated level of inefficiency for school B can be represented by the efficiency ratio [(OB/OB*) – 1]. The ratio gives the

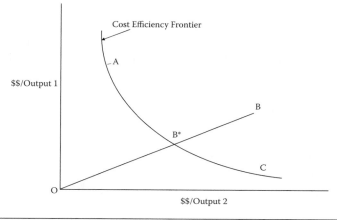

Figure 3.3 Graphical example of distance function analysis for School B

extent to which costs are above the estimated level of efficiency denoted by *AC* (Barrow, 1991; Fare, Grosskopf, and Lovell, 1994; Kumbhakar and Lovell, 2000).

RECOMMENDATIONS: DETERMINING SOCIALLY JUST SCHOOL IMPROVEMENT FACTORS USING RELATIVE MEASURES OF ECONOMIC EFFICIENCY

The purpose of this chapter has been to explore new linkages between educational productivity and social justice by providing evidence that supports the two assertions made at the outset:

1. Given the differential social justice climates existing within various educational contexts, levels of school productivity should be reconceptualized as the amount of technical efficiency generated by combinations of financial and human resources, sociopolitical influences, instructional and management strategies, and levels of student effort that maximize educational outcomes.
2. Given the differential pursuits of social justice objectives within various educational contexts, the measurement of efficiency in public schools should be reconceptualized to focus on what the *highest* student learners achieve compared to the lowest student learners—not the best average performances predicted by traditional production function analyses. Accordingly, the measures used should focus on relative comparisons of the best observed performers to the worst.

And, assuming the arguments made here are salient, sound, and convincing, there is still a need to discuss how using relative measures of economic efficiency (i.e., stochastic frontier, distance function, or modified quadriform analysis) can be used in determining socially just school improvement factors.

Prior to conducting any thorough analysis of economic efficiency, qualitative analytical methods need to be employed. Qualitative methods must be used to describe the historical, political, and socioeconomic context of any multidimensional educational setting. Through analyses of a variety of public documents, public records, and research literatures, the qualitative technique should be used to narrow the scope of the broad concepts into specific emergent themes that provide a sense of the meanings and intentions inherent to the particular situation examined. Only then should quantitative methods—as the ones discussed previously—be used to examine economic efficiency, educational productivity, and social justice relationships.

Given these qualitative suppositions, the overall analytical strategy used to determine socially just school improvement factors should be focused on analyzing three specific research questions.

Question 1: Are financial and human resources utilized efficiently in public school districts?

To answer this question, each relative efficiency measure discussed should be used to analyze an individual state's public school district financial and human resources and student outcome data. In addition to an examination of these resources in the aggregate, the data should also be examined by multiple, stratifying demographic categories to determine if specific subgroups (e.g., low-income or minority populations) are affected in manners inconsistent with total group averages. And, to increase the robustness and stability of the results, all of the aforementioned analyses should be conducted cross-sectionally and longitudinally over a period of at least five years.

Question 2: Across the measures of educational productivity examined, are public school districts categorized similarly based on levels of efficiency?

To answer this question, future research should analyze the efficiency/nonefficiency groupings to determine if differences exist across the relative efficiency measures examined. In addition to an examination of the relationship(s) in the aggregate, the data also should be examined by multiple, stratifying demographic categories to determine if specific subgroups are affected in manners inconsistent with total group averages. Again, all of the aforementioned analyses should be conducted cross-sectionally and longitudinally over a period of at least five years.

Question 3: Are there characteristic differences in public school districts based on levels of efficiency?

In the case(s) that disparities in financial, human resources, and student outcomes are found between efficient and inefficient districts, the research designed above should describe characteristic differences and trends based on differences in levels of economic efficiency and measures and, accordingly, begin to investigate remedies to remove the differences when necessary. In addition to an examination of these resources in the aggregate, the data also should be examined by multiple, stratifying demographic categories to determine if specific subgroups are affected in manners inconsistent with total group averages cross-sectionally and longitudinally over a period of at least five years.

If these tensions between the desires for educational efficiency and socially just outcomes can be reduced by results found in future research, at least a five-criteria examination needs to be implemented before discussing differences in levels of educational productivity between "efficient" and "inefficient" districts:

1. What policy or program goals can be pursued specifically for existing—and proposed—state educational programs?
2. Are the policy or program goals deemed valuable for educational purposes? That is, do the programs increase the learning skills or knowledge base of students?
3. Can the educational objectives of particular programs or policies be measured with specificity?
4. If an educational program's goals are not designed strictly to achieve measurable educational outcomes, what community, state, or societal goals are being met?
5. Should these "noneducational" societal goals be financed—and therefore evaluated—as part of the public education system or by some other state sponsored program?

Without such a reassessment of the purpose of educational programs, the true relationship between education budgets and student outcomes—as well as the level of technical efficiency present in the public school system—will remain coupled loosely at best by analyses utilized within the normative framework. With this increased understanding of educational efficiency within a budget-maximizing framework, legislators, education personnel, parents, and the public can address the complex issue of improving the use of public resources to produce higher levels of educational outcomes with greater awareness of the social justice principles from which education finance policy can be improved and administered.

NOTES

1. For the purposes of this chapter, *social justice* is defined as the pursuit and acquisition of equitable economic, political, and social opportunities without limitation or benefit from observations of—or interpretations of—stereotyped individual or group characteristics.
2. We do offer a brief summary of the "Does money matter?" debate as context for our exploration of productivity and efficiency, particularly for readers who are unfamiliar with the key arguments in this debate.

3. This history of normative efficiency and budget maximizing theories is summarized from Rolle (2000).

4. Rolle (2000, 2003; 2004a) provides evidence to support the existence of concave-up budget-output functions. That is, even though sponsors are reluctant to grant large budget increases, they are more willing to provide multiple small increases over time.

5. Most school districts, however, supply two or more of instructional—and noninstructional—services. Consequently, Niskanen also evaluates the behavior of a multiservice organization to determine if its behavior differs from the summation of individual bureau behavior (1971, pp. 106–111). In this scenario, a school district is assumed to be a monopoly supplier of several different educational services. This district also is assumed to face multiple sponsors (i.e., from the state, local, and federal levels) that provide its total financing and pay competitive prices for factors of production. The model Niskanen develops is specific to organizations that supply only two services, but he claims the results easily are generalizable to public agencies that supply three or more services.

REFERENCES

Adams, J. E. (1997). Organizational context and district revenue allocation: Does the setting matter? *Journal of Education Finance, 23*(2), 234–258.

Aigner, D. J., Lovell, C. A. K., & Schmidt, P. J. (1977). Formulation and estimation of stochastic frontier production function models. *Journal of Econometrics, 6*(1), 21–37.

Alexander, K. (1998). Money matters: Commentary and analyses. *Journal of Education Finance, 24*(4), 237–242.

Anderson, D. M. (1996). Stretching the tax dollar: Increasing efficiency in urban and rural schools. In L. O. Picus and J. L. Wattenbarger (Eds.), *Where does the money go?* (pp. 156–177). Thousand Oaks, CA: Corwin Press.

Barnett, W. S. (1994). Obstacles and opportunities: Some simple economics of school finance reform. *Educational Policy, 8*(4), 436–452.

Barrow, M. M. (1991). Measuring local education authority performance: A frontier approach. *Economics of Education Review, 10*(1), 19–27.

Bennett, W. J., Fair, W., Finn, C. E., Jr., Flake, Rev. F., Hirsch, E. D., Marshall, W., et al. (1998). *A nation still at risk.* Washington, DC: Heritage Foundation.

Boyd, W. L., & Hartman, W. T. (1988). The politics of educational productivity. In D. H. Monk & J. Underwood (Eds.), *Micro-level school finance: Issues and implications for policy* (pp. 271–310). Cambridge, MA: Ballinger.

Buchanon, J. M., & Tollison, R. D. (1984). *The theory of public choice II.* Ann Arbor: University of Michigan Press.

Coelli, T. J., Prasada Rao, D. S., & Battese, G. E. (1998). *An introduction to efficiency and productivity analysis.* Boston, MA: Kluwer Academic Publishers.

Coons, J. E., Clune, W. H., & Sugarman, S. D. (1970). *Private wealth and public education.* Cambridge, MA: Harvard University Press.

Cooper, B. S. (1993). *School-site cost allocations: Testing a micro-financial model in 23 districts in 10 states.* Unpublished manuscript, Fordham University.

Cooper, B. S., & Associates (1994). Making money matter in education: A micro-financial model for determining school-level allocations, efficiency, and productivity. *Journal of Education Finance, 20*(3), 66–87.

Cooper, S. T., & Cohn, E. (1997). Estimation of a frontier production function for the South Carolina educational process. *Economics of Education Review, 16*(3), 313–327.

Cubberley, E. P. (1906). School funds and their apportionment. New York: Teachers College, Columbia University.

Cubbin, J., & Zamani, H. (1996). A comparison of performance indicators for training and enterprise councils in the UK. *Annals of Comparative Economics, 67*(4), 603–632.

Debreu, G. (1951). The coefficient of resource allocation. *Econometrica, 19*(3), 273–292.

Deller, S. C., & Rudnicki, E. (1993). Production efficiency in elementary education: The case of Maine Public Schools. *Economics of Education Review, 12*(1), 45–57.

Downs, A. (1967). *Inside bureaucracy.* Boston: Little, Brown.

Downs, A. (1998). *Political theory and public choice.* Northampton, MA: Edward Elgar.

Duncombe, W., Miner, J., and Ruggiero, J. (1997). Empirical evaluation of bureaucratic models of inefficiency. *Public Choice, 93*(1-2), 1–18.

Fare, R., Grosskopf, S., & Lovell, C. A. K. (1994). *Production frontiers.* New York: Cambridge University Press.

Farrell, M. J. (1957). The measurement of production efficiency. *Journal of the Royal Statistical Society, ser. A, 120*(3), pp. 253-81.

Finn, C. E. (1983). The drive for educational excellence: Moving toward a public consensus. *Change, 15*(3), 14–22.

Genge, F. C. (1991, March). *A further application of the quadriform to the study of economic efficiency in K–12 schools in Illinois.* Paper presented at the annual meeting of the American Education Finance Association, Williamsburg, VA.

Genge, F. C. (1992, March). *Assessing inefficiencies in Illinois school districts.* A paper presented at the annual meeting of the American Education Finance Association, New Orleans.

Hanushek, E. A. (1989). The impact of differential expenditures on school performance. *Educational Researcher, 18*(4), 45–62.

Hanushek, E. A. (1986). The economics of schooling: Production and efficiency in public schools. *Journal of Economic Literature, 24*(3), 1141–1177.

Hanushek, E. A. (1981). Throwing money at schools. *Journal of Policy Analysis and Management, 1*(1), 19–41.

Hanushek, E.A. (1991). When school finance "reform" may not be a good policy. *Harvard Journal on Legislation, 28*(2), 423–456.

Hanushek, E. A. (1995a). Improving school performances while controlling costs. In W. J. Fowler (Ed.), *Developments in school finance, 1995* (pp. 111–122). Washington, DC: National Center for Education Statistics.

Hanushek, E. A. (1995b, November). Moving beyond spending fetishes. *Educational Leadership*, pp. 60–64.

Hanushek, E. A. (1996). The quest for equalized mediocrity. In L. Picus and J. Wattenbarger (Eds.) *Where does the money go?* (pp. 20–43). Thousand Oaks, CA: Corwin Press.

Hayes, K., & Grosskopf, S. (1993). Local public sector bureaucrats and their input choices. *Journal of Urban Economics, 33*(2), 151–166.

Hedges, L. V., Laine, R. D., & Greenwald, R. (1994). Does money matter? A meta-analysis of studies of the effects of differential school inputs on student outcomes. *Educational Researcher, 23*(3), 5–14.

Hentschke, G. C. (1988). Budgetary theory and reality: A micro view. In D. H. Monk & J. Underwood (Eds.) *Micro-level school finance: Issues and implications for policy.* Cambridge, MA: Ballinger Publishing Company, pp. 311–336.

Hickrod, G. A., Genge, F. C., Chaudhari, R. B., Liu, C. C., Franklin, D. L., Arnold, R., et al. (1990). *The biggest bang for the buck: A further investigation of economic efficiency in the public schools of Illinois.* Normal, IL: Center for the Study of Educational Finance.

Hickrod, G. A., Liu, C. C., Arnold, R., Chaudhari, R., Frank, L., Franklin, D., et al. (1989). *The biggest bang for the buck: An initial report on technical economic efficiency in Illinois K–12 schools. With a comment on "Rose v. the Council."* Normal, IL: Center for the Study of Educational Finance.

Hoenack, S. A. (1994). Economics, organizations, and learning: research directions for the economics of education. *Economics of Education Review, 13*(2), 147–162.

King, R. A., & MacPhail–Wilcox, B. (1994). Unraveling the production equation. *Journal of Education Finance, 20*(1), 47–65.

Kirst, M. W. (1983). A new school finance for a new era of fiscal constraint. In A. Odden & L. D. Webb (Eds.), *School finance and school improvement linkages for the 1980s* (pp. 1–15). Cambridge, MA: Ballinger.

Kumbhakar, S. C., & Lovell, C. A. K. (2000). *Stochastic frontier analysis.* New York: Cambridge University Press.

Laine, R. D., Greenwald, R., & Hedges, L. V. (1996). Money does matter: A research synthesis of a new universe of education production function studies. In L. Picus and J. Wattenbarger (Eds.) *Where does the money go?* (pp. 44–70). Thousand Oaks, CA: Corwin Press.

Levin, H. M. (1976). "Concepts of economic efficiency and educational production." In J. T. Froomkin, D. T. Jamison, & R. Radner (Eds.), *Education as an industry.* Cambridge, MA: National Bureau of Economic Research Ballinger, 149–196.

Levin, H. M. (1997). Raising School Productivity. *Economics of Education Review, 16*(3), 303–311.

Mann, D., & Inman, D. (1984). Improving education with existing resources: The instructionally effective schools' approach. *Journal of Education Finance, 10*(2), 259–69.

Mises, L. (1944). *Bureaucracy.* New Haven, CT: Yale University Press.

Monk, D. H. (1990). Efficiency and the use of private markets to produce and distribute educational services. In *Education finance: An economic approach* (pp. 3–11). New York: McGraw-Hill.

Monk, D. H. (1992). Education productivity research: An update and assessment of its role in education finance reform. *Educational Evaluation and Policy Analysis, 14(4),* 307–32.

Mort, P. R. (1924). The measurement of educational need. New York: Columbia University Press.

Murillia-Zamarano, L. R. (2004). Economic efficiency and frontier techniques. *Journal of Economic Surveys, 18*(1), 33–76.

Murnane, R. J. (1991). Interpreting evidence on "Does money matter?" *Harvard Journal on Legislation, 28* (Summer), 457–464.

Murphy, J., & Hallinger, P. (1986, March). Education equity and differential access to knowledge: An analysis. Paper presented at the annual meeting of the American Education Finance Conference, Chicago.

National Center for Education Statistics (2000). *Trends in academic progress: Three decades of student performance, NAEP 1999.* Washington, DC: U.S. Department of Education, Office of Research and Improvement.

Niskanen, W. A. (1968). The peculiar economics of bureaucracy. *American Economic Review, 58*(2), 293–305.

Niskanen, W. A. (1971). Bureaucracy and representative government. Chicago: Aldine-Atherton.

Niskanen, W.A. (1973). Bureaucracy: Servant or master? London, England: The Institute of Economic Affairs.

Niskanen, W. A. (1975). Bureaucrats and politicians. *Journal of Law and Economics, 81*(3), 617–644.

Niskanen, W. A. (1991). A reflection on "Bureaucracy and representative government." In A. Blais and S. Dion (Eds.), *The budget-maximizing bureaucrat: Appraisals and evidence* (pp. 13–32). Pittsburgh: University of Pittsburgh Press.

Niskanen, W. A. (1994). Bureaucracy and public economics. Northampton, MA: Edward Elgar.

Odden, A. (1986). A school finance research agenda for an era of educational reform. *Journal of Education Finance, 12*(3), 49–70.

Peacock, A. T. (1992). Public choice analysis in historical perspective. Cambridge: Press Syndicate of the University of Cambridge, 1–83.

Porter, A. C. (2003, October). Prospects for school reform and closing the achievement gap. Paper presented at Measurement and Research Issues in a New Accountability Era, invitational conference of the Educational Testing Service, New York City.

Rice, J. K. (2001). Illuminating the black box: The evolving role of education productivity research. In S. Chaikind & W.J. Fowler, Jr. (Eds.) *Education finance in the new millennium: 2001 Yearbook of the American Education Finance Association.* Larchmont, NY: Eye on Education, Inc., pp. 121–139.

Rodriguez, G. M. (2004). Vertical equity in school finance and the potential for increasing school responsiveness to student and staff needs. *Peabody Journal of Education, 79* (3): pp. 7–30.

Rolle, R. A. (2000). Marching to the beat of a different drum: An empirical analysis of public school corporations as budget-maximizing bureaus. Unpublished doctoral dissertation, Indiana University.

Rolle, R. A. (2003). Getting the biggest bang for the educational buck: An empirical analysis of public school corporations as budget-maximizing bureaus. In W. J. Fowler, Jr. (Ed.), *Developments in School Finance: 2001–02* (pp. 25–52), Washington, DC: National Center for Education Statistics.

Rolle, R. A. (2004a). An empirical discussion of public school districts as budget-maximizing agencies. *Journal of Education Finance, 29*(4), 277–298.

Rolle, R. A. (2004b). Out with the old and in with the new: Thoughts on the future of educational productivity and efficiency. *Peabody Journal of Education, 79* (3): pp. 31–56.

Rolle, R. A. (2005). Rethinking educational productivity and its measurement: A discussion of stochastic frontier analyses within a budget-maximizing framework. In L. Stiefel, A. E. Schwartz, R. Rubenstein, & J. Zabel (Eds.), *Measuring school performance and efficiency: Implications for practice and research* (pp. 185–201). Larchmont, NY: Eye on Education.

Romer, T., & Rosenthal, H. (1984). Voting Models and Empirical Evidence. *American Scientist, 72* (5), 465–473.

Rossmiller, R. A. (1987). Achieving equity and effectiveness in schooling. *Journal of Education Finance, 12*(4), 561–577.

Schwartz, A. E., & Stiefel, L. (2001). Measuring school efficiency: Lessons from economics, implications for practice. In D.H. Monk, H.J. Walberg, & M.C. Wang (Eds.) *Improving educational productivity.* Greenwich, CT: Information Age Publishing, pp. 115-138.

Sowell, T. (1993). *Inside American education: The decline, the deception, and the dogmas.* New York: Free Press.

Stiefel, L., Schwartz, A. E., Rubenstein, R., & Zabel, J. (2005). *Measuring school performance and efficiency: Implications for practice and research.* Larchmont, NY: Eye on Education.

Stevens, J. B. (1993). The economics of collective choice. Boulder, CO: Westview Press Incorporated, pp. 263-297.

Strayer, G. D., & Haig, R. M. (1923). *The financing of education in the State of New York.* New York: Macmillan.

Toch, T. (1991). *In the name of excellence: The struggle to reform the nation's schools, why it's failing, and what should be done.* New York: Oxford University Press.

Tullock, G. (1965). The politics of bureaucracy. Washington, DC: Public Affairs Press.

U.S. Department of Education National Commission on Excellence in Education (1983). *A nation at risk: The imperative for educational reform.* Washington, D.C.: Author.

Verstegen, D. A., & King, R. A. (1998). The relationship between school spending and student achievement: A review and analysis of 35 years of production function research. *Journal of Education Finance, 24*(4), 243–262.

Walberg, H. J., & Fowler, W. J. (1987). Expenditure and size efficiencies of public school districts. *Educational Researcher, 16*(7), 5–13.

Walberg, H. J., & Walberg, H. (1994). Losing local control. *Educational Researcher, 23*(5), 19–26.

Wildavsky, A. (1964) *The politics of the budgetary process.* Boston, MA: Little, Brown.

Worthington, A. C. (2001). An empirical survey of frontier measurement techniques in education. *Education Economics, 19*(3), 245–268.

4

ADEQUACY REVISITED

A Critique of Prominent Conceptualizations of School Finance Standards

Nicola A. Alexander

University of Minnesota

EDUCATIONAL RESEARCHERS HAVE LONG EMPHASIZED rational approaches to financing schools. Their reliance on economic theory has led to the domination of education finance texts and research that use education production functions and principal-agent theories. While the field has evolved conceptually from an emphasis on equity to a focus on adequacy, the methodology used to measure these values has continued to be entwined with economics. The purpose of this chapter is to offer a different approach to operationalizing adequacy, one that reflects the essence of adequacy but remains a helpful tool for policy makers. This discussion adds to the discourse by injecting institutional and cultural considerations in the operationalization of adequate funding of schools. I argue that adequacy is not merely a rationally derived concept that can be achieved only through rational methods. Rather, adequacy is socially derived and encompasses socially derived notions of what it means to have a just society and equitable schooling.

Because adequacy is a socially derived concept, it cannot be defined in a vacuum. The very term begs the question: Adequate for what and for whom? One problem with the current rational approaches to operationalizing adequacy is the presumption that we as a society have already answered those questions. The field seems to ask us to accept an underlying objectivity that is not real. The notions of adequacy and social justice are wrapped up in the prioritization of shared values— quality, fraternity, liberty, order, efficiency, quality, individuality, and so on (Fowler, 2004). Consequently, one's view of justice, and therefore adequacy, is not shaped simply by the facts, but by one's assembling of those facts. Hartman (1984) writes, for example, "What we bring to the event of seeing is therefore as important as the data at hand, if not more so. For not only is our seeing perspectival in its very essence, but it is also "theory laden" (p. 5).

This chapter focuses on the assembling of the facts regarding adequacy from an institutional and cultural perspective. I examine school funding specifically in the context of social justice. The primary intent of this discussion is to encourage the evolution of the definition of adequacy with its present emphasis on results and efficiency goals to an operationalization that includes cultural and social nuances and makes explicit the givens of the field.

The remainder of this chapter is divided into five sections. The first section broadly explores adequacy and its current conceptualizations in the field of education finance. The second section offers an exploration of the use of adequacy as a vehicle for social change through the provision of established inputs and educational programs. The third section focuses on adequacy as defined by overall student performance. The fourth section explores an operationalization of adequacy using the capacity of schooling organizations to attain the goals established by policy makers. The chapter closes by revisiting the concept of adequacy in school finance and discussing its implications for social justice.

BROAD EXPLORATIONS OF ADEQUACY

Currently, four key strategies have emerged from leaders in education finance on the appropriate operationalization of adequacy. Guthrie and others have argued that professional judgment should be the approach taken to determine the appropriate funding for schools (see, e.g., Guthrie and Rothstein (1999). Odden (2003) and others favor looking at successful schools as a benchmark for determining adequate funding. Hanushek (2006) advocates a cost function approach, which is essentially the inverse of the traditional production function methods. There is also a "state of the art" methodology that is deeply entrenched in using existing evidence and statistical procedures.

These approaches are all grounded in the tenets of economic theory. Because of the domination of an economic perspective in education finance, the essential questions surrounding values have often centered on the perceived dichotomy between efficiency and equity (Okun, 1975); liberty and justice (Friedman, 1963; Rawls, 1999); and excellence and equity (Bennett et al., 1998; Kirst, 1983; U.S. Department of Education National Commission on Excellence in Education, 1983). However, recent conceptualizations of adequacy can serve to dispose of the myth that these values are necessarily in conflict.

In a rational economic analysis of social justice, the notions of property rights and Pareto optimality[1] (efficiency) are crucial. Self-interested behavior is largely thought to be aligned with the common good except under unusual circumstances. According to standard microeconomic theory, an individual's pursuit of her own interests will, by and large, lead to the betterment of society. Relying on an economic paradigm, however, assumes that society is in agreement with the goals of schooling. Critical theory suggests that there is no clear consensus on goals. Before determining how schools can be funded adequately to produce better students, critical theorists challenge us to define what we mean by better students.

In much of the education finance literature, better students are presumed to be those who perform well on standardized tests; better schools are those that produce higher proportions of these students. Social justice would then require us to distribute this good in a fair manner. Economic approaches would take that goal as a given and consider strategies for efficiently achieving these goals as the proper focus of analysis. By contrast, Engel (2000) insists that we should have a public discourse on the purpose of public schools, which he argues should go beyond market ideology and economic considerations. Indeed, Ogawa, Crowson, and Goldring (1999) note that while efficiency is important for the individual, effectiveness is crucial for the collective. That is, "effectiveness is the extent to which an organization attains its goals; efficiency is the extent to which individuals attain theirs" (p. 280). Effectiveness in this context has much in common with attaining an adequate educational system.

By employing any of the four identified strategies used to measure adequacy, a system may be defined as more or less adequate without undergoing fundamental change. While a certain degree of flexibility in definitions is necessary, the continued abstraction of adequacy is problematic. On the one hand, abstract notions of fairness play a big role in how we evaluate resource allocation within and between school systems. On the other hand, policy makers need concrete guidance in assessing whether policies are more or less fair. Garms (1979) and Berne and Stiefel (1984) have added much to the early school finance debate by grounding the abstract concept of equity into measurable terms.

However, focusing largely on statistical methods without sufficient discussion on the ends to which adequacy should be anchored is premature. First and Miron (1999) suggest, for example, that discussion of adequacy is incomplete if they omit the value premises of community, accountability, and responsibility, noting that

> these values should form the framework to understand the social construction of adequacy which is embedded in any legal or "educational" (i.e. technical) discussion. At present, however, educational reform only takes account of two of the three, accountability and responsibility.... Our only hope is that in the search for a legally defensible notion of educational adequacy the pattern of substituting "minimum" for adequate is not repeated. (pp. 443-444)

Guthrie and Rothstein (1999) contend that the national adequacy debate can be seen, in part, as an effort to evaluate "whether ... spending growth [i.e., increased state expenditures on education in response to litigation] has been sufficient [to avoid future litigation] and to ensure that the new money is distributed within states in a fashion that will produce desired outcomes" (p. 211). They characterize the "modern" discourse surrounding adequacy as one that is technically defined and outcome oriented, while historically it was one of politically determined inputs. While I agree with the authors that there has been a shift in the discourse from inputs to outputs, I disagree that that shift is any less political than when the focus was on the level of funding or the type of education treatment that should be offered. Notwithstanding, Guthrie and Rothstein rightly recognize that an important first step in translating adequacy from theory to practice is community and professional dialogue rather than the development of complicated statistical techniques. They note,

> Statistical sophistication has, in this case, outpaced ability to explain the relationship between spending and school performance ... the precision implied by statistical modeling may be misleading because each of the definitions of data used in these equations, and rationales for their use, requires assumptions and judgments that are not necessarily more precise than those professionals operating without statistical models ... the seemingly precise results of the models reflect the imprecision of the assumptions.... We prefer the professional judgment approach, not because we believe it is more precise than statistical or inferential methods (it may not be more precise) but rather because its imprecision is more transparent. (1999, pp. 221–223, 231)

Definitions of Adequacy Using Expenditure
Categories and Cost Approaches

Miner (1983) argues that definitions of adequacy are best derived for each of the major expenditure categories for elementary and secondary schools, highlighting seven such categories: (1) instruction; (2) plant operations and maintenance; (3) administration; (4) transportation; (5) food; (6) attendance, health, and other; and (7) fixed charges. He assumes that the national average of the units used in each category is an appropriate measure of the units needed, but allows expenditures to vary by state for each category. As with other transactions, the costs of the services will influence the number and quality that may be purchased. Consequently, it is important for policy makers to distinguish between "basic" and "luxury" brands of schooling components. The work on cost indexes is crucial as policy makers assess how much they need to spend to obtain an adequate level of resources.

To that end, Chambers, Levin, and Parrish (2006) and Reschovsky and Imazeki (2001) have developed cost indexes that allow policy makers to take into account the cost differentials that may occur in hiring teachers. One limitation with the cost-estimation approach is the assumption that differences in costs are largely reflective of differences in efficiencies rather than simply differences in tastes. Cultural theorists would argue that the choice imposed on a school district and system is largely reflective of the dominant culture. Therefore, when policy makers allocate budgets to reflect "efficiency defined" cost differentials, they may unwittingly be rewarding a particular taste for education.

Exploring Adequacy As a Vehicle of Social Change

Policymakers often perceive education as a means of shaping society, and schools a mechanism for developing an educated human being (Sadovnik, Cookson, Jr., and Semel, 2001). In this pursuit, there are three important pieces in the educative (or production) process: (1) the inputs that are invested; (2) the pedagogical and organizational strategies that are employed; and the (3) outcomes that are achieved.

A focus on adequacy of inputs is aligned most closely with past research on equity of resource allocation, where fiscal neutrality, horizontal equity, and legitimate differences serve as important guideposts for policy makers who seek (or were forced) to be on the "right" equity path. Miner (1983) is an early example of this approach, where he defines adequacy essentially by identifying the required quantity of schooling inputs per pupil and determining the unit cost based on regional differences. Determining adequate investments in these inputs was seen as a means of facilitating social change.

When policy makers emphasize an input approach to adequacy, they may target the curriculum (e.g., Alexander, 2003), governance (e.g., Malen, 1994), or teaching and learning (e.g., Odden & Kelley, 1997). For instance, Alexander notes that the rigor of the curriculum has an impact on student achievement. Malen's research suggests that school governance structures can influence student performance. Odden and Kelley advocate changing teacher compensation structures in order to provide the appropriate incentives to schools and teachers to produce adequate student output. That is, individual teachers would be paid on the basis of their professional expertise and their ability to improve student performance. These findings all suggest an institutional, rather than a purely rational technical, approach to determining and achieving adequacy within an educational system.

Shifting Definitions of Adequacy from Assuring Access to Measuring Results

Researchers and practitioners have shifted their focus from inputs to processes to outputs, or what Garner (2004) describes as a shift from access to treatment to results. These shifts have led to a change in the perceived role of finance policy as a means of achieving socially desired goals. In the early stages of equity discourse, Garms (1979) recognized that "any attempt to separately analyze the effects of multiple goals must have a way of separating the allocations for those goals" (p. 416). This challenge remains as we consider what it means for a system to be "adequate." Guthrie (1983) notes, "It is difficult to define *adequate* [emphasis in original] with respect to education. Research has provided little scientific 'truth' to help in this effort, and no uniform set of societal values exists with which to measure adequacy" (p. 471).

Research on education finance is resplendent with questions regarding the most applicable approach to funding aspects of the educational enterprise. In his recent assessment of the field, Odden (2000) captures the shift in school finance discourse from a broadly appealing discussion of equity to more specific responses to adequacy,

> Long focused on fiscal equity, school finance is repositioning itself to provide for fiscal adequacy while also improving equity. This shift represents fundamental change... [and is] in the center of the education enterprise (p. 467).

Strategies for Achieving Adequacy as Measured by Results

In the quest for an adequate system, policy makers may choose to target resources (fiscal or regulatory) at any point in the education production. Odden (2000) has identified three main approaches to determining the appropriate amount of resources to use:

1. Identifying a set of inputs that educational experts presume lead to an "adequate" outcome and calculating the costs of those inputs.
2. Linking a spending amount per pupil to a desired level of student outcomes and using that amount as the basis of an adequate level of funding. Presumably the effects of differential student needs and institutional costs can be incorporated in these types of formulas.
3. Identifying the cost of comprehensive school-wide programs assumed to produce adequate outcomes and using the cost of that design as the basis for determining an adequate level of funding.

Enacted policies are important in examining the transition from equity to adequacy, but also crucial are changes in the educational practices that result. Imposed policies do not necessarily lead to implemented practices. The consequences of playing the legislative game (Firestone, 1989) may bear little resemblance to what occurs in the classroom. Thus, while it is important to view how policy makers conceptualize adequacy, it is crucial to understand how practitioners translate this concept into strategies used to educate students—including cooperative learning, block scheduling, curriculum tracking, and so on. To that end, school and system capacity must be considered more explicitly in discussions of adequacy.

Levin (1991) expresses concern that high expectations without the provision of additional resources or new strategies may be insufficient to help disadvantaged students meet increased challenges. If policy makers place standards at an "unreasonably" high level, the front-line workers (e.g., teachers, students, building administrators) needed to implement those aims may simply give up. If educators feel overwhelmed by the challenges they face, there is greater likelihood of them gaming the system (Hess, 1999). As noted by Reschovsky and Imazeki (2001), "These schools [with above-average costs] will fail, not necessarily because of their own inability to effectively educate children, but because they were provided with insufficient fiscal resources to do the job" (p. 375).

Who Gets Included in Definitions of Adequacy as an End?

Deciding who to include when we measure the adequacy of an edu-cational system is particularly important when defining adequacy as whom we include as capable of reaching a particular educational goal. Outcome standards should clearly include the performance of poor students, children of color, children with limited learning ability be included, and other students placed at risk. However, how do we build into the system a metric that identifies the different challenges faced by these groups so that while outcome standards are equal, input invest-ments are not (e.g., First and Miron, 1999)? We are faced with a problem similar to the one we faced when trying to operationalize horizontal equity: how can we shape contexts so that we are really comparing equally situated entities? When we conceptualize adequacy, to what standards should we hold children, and from there, what resources should we provide to them? Reasonable and ethical people can disagree on the appropriate response because we often face the dilemma of try-ing to "distinguish without discriminating" (Alexander, 2002) and to recognize differences without pigeonholing.

Because Guthrie and Rothstein (1999) are skeptical that states would ever fully fund education so that those students placed at risk would fully have the same opportunities as those who were more privileged, they oppose the notion that "minimally adequate outcomes should be achieved by all schools, irrespective of their students' socioeconomic characteristics" (p. 227). Later on in their discussion they raise the ques-tion that would be on the mind of many concerned with social justice:

> If we abandon Texas's [sic] one-standard-fits-all approach, do we specify, for example, that in most districts, 75 percent of students are expected to pass a proficiency test, but it is somehow acceptable for districts with mostly low-income families to have a 35 percent passage rate? (p. 228)

Once we have answered the question of who gets included, we also have to address the notion of whether democracy should promote an emphasis on liberty or equality. Should our funding system allow wide variations in the inputs that are given to children? Is that a state or a local decision? When we speak of liberty, is the freedom on the front end, in terms of the revenues raised, or in terms of what districts can do with those resources once received? Is the liberty emphasized as a direct description of what happens in the process, or is it distributed so the results of the process lead to greater freedoms among the graduates of the system?

These are all important questions that are not easily answered, but they are an essential first step in bringing into a practical realm the theory of adequacy in funding. The role of market mechanisms and rational theories in developing reasonable plans for policy makers may be limited because the key answers are assumed to be already accepted. The implication for social justice is that distribution of funds will be tied to what we think is an important path to getting priorities met in the collective.

ADEQUACY AS OVERALL STUDENT PERFORMANCE

It is not a new phenomenon for researchers and policy makers to focus on outputs (e.g., U.S. Department of Education National Commission on Excellence in Education, 1983). Guthrie (1983) writes, "Whatever the outcome of public deliberations on the context of the core curriculum, the measure of program should be students' performance—not the level of funding, the amount of time students spend in school or the classes they take" (p. 475).

Student achievement encompasses outcomes that reflect the pedagogical objectives of schools, including the educational knowledge gained by pupils, as exemplified by curriculum-based exam results or other standardized tests. Notwithstanding, Gowin (1981) has written that an "educative event" can occur only if there are at least two partners in the process, "the teacher who intervenes with the meaningful materials and the learner who chooses to grasp the meaning and *learn them*" (p. 133; emphasis added). Monk (1990) often refers to this interaction as the flow of resources. The purpose of school funding in an adequacy framework is to ensure that the flow of resources goes to those educative events that facilitate high levels of student performance or whatever the goal the community chooses. Current discussions of adequacy focus on how these outputs may be achieved by explicitly linking schooling resources, pedagogic practices, and the attainment of particular standards. While fiscal neutrality marks a focus on inputs, "results neutrality" characterizes a focus on outputs. That is, there should be no systematic associations between ascribed characteristics and desired student achievement if the appropriate funding formula for an adequate system were derived.

Tying judgments on adequacy to the performance standards set by state policy makers is consistent with recent trends in the legislative and judicial arena, including lawsuits filed in Kentucky (in the *Rose v. Council for Better Education* case of 1989); New York (Campaign for Fiscal Equity, 2000), and Ohio (Ohio Coalition for Equity and Adequacy, 2001). With the broadening of statewide assessment and accountability systems, this focus is enhanced by the increased reliance on state-established standards of proficiency and excellence. Research that develops measures of capacity that policy makers can use to assess the capability of schools to meet the established standards is an important extension of this focus.

Herrington and Weider (2001) note that "adequacy challenges have focused on whether the amount of money appropriated for public education in general is enough to meet the costs of providing the standard guaranteed in the state constitution" (p. 523). Legal approaches tend to be inductive, where the presence of high levels of illiteracy is prima facie evidence that the system is not funding its schools at an adequate level. The logic is Descartian where one can argue that high levels of illiteracy (or other standards of education) exist, therefore the system is inadequate. One difficulty in making that argument stand in state courts is the strength of the education clauses in the state constitutions. Without an explicit referral to outputs in the constitution, courts face the same difficulty that preceded the fiscal neutrality standard developed by Coons, Clune, and Sugarman (1970). In Florida, for example, the supreme court argued,

> "While the courts are competent to decide whether or not the Legislature's distribution of state funds to complement local education expenditures results in the required 'uniform system,' the courts cannot decide whether the Legislature's appropriation of funds is *adequate in the abstract*, divorced from the required uniformity. To decide such an abstract question of 'adequate' funding, the courts would necessarily be required to *subjectively evaluate* the Legislature's value judgments as to the spending priorities to be assigned to the state's many needs, education being one among them. [In this case the appellants/plaintiffs had] failed to demonstrate ... an appropriate standard for determining 'adequacy' that would not present a substantial risk of judicial intrusion into the powers and responsibilities assigned to the legislature." (Quoted in Herrington and Weider, 2001, pp. 525–526; emphasis added)

I argue that "results neutrality" should serve as the new standard by which plaintiffs can take states to court. Carnoy (1983) makes a similar claim when he refers to "schooling as equalizer" (p. 291). Consequently, plaintiffs may contend that the underperformance of students is prima facie evidence that a state has not fulfilled its responsibility to all its students. Underlying these arguments is the point made by Reschovsky and Imazeki (2001) that by not recognizing differences in schooling contexts there likely will be failure among those schools that are most in need of additional help.

Current definitions of adequacy do not necessarily address the different social contexts faced by various student groups, including students of color, English-language learners, and immigrant students. While statistical models often include variables measuring percentages of poor, percentages of minorities, and so on, they exclude more qualitative factors like institutional racism, cultural incompetence, and the like.

Input-output models and the agency framework both provide a useful backdrop for discussions on the operationalization of adequacy standards. The first conceptualization gives insights on the key inputs that go into the education of a child; the second proffers a better means of understanding the process, rather than the structure, of education. Combining an understanding of educational structures and organizational relationships can facilitate the development of a more meaningful model of the educational process, a better understanding of the impact of standards on student performance, and the role of adequacy in that context (Betts & Grogger, 2003). However, while these are necessary fixtures of an appropriate model of adequacy, they are incomplete without an explicit recognition of the cultural variants that exist in many schools and in society as a whole.

CAPACITY: AN OPERATIONALIZATION OF ADEQUACY

There is a long-established focus in the literature on the adequacy of inputs and outputs and whether they are at "high enough" or "equal enough" levels to meet standards of justice. Largely missing from the input/output discussion is a more detailed reconceptualization on the adequacy of the student learning process, which speaks to the capacity of institutions to meet the standards set (Alexander, 2003). Yet when state policy makers prescribe what level of performance students need to graduate or the results schools need to attain to be labeled as effective, they are providing a working definition of how educators in that state define the term *adequate*. That definition may be used as a benchmark to evaluate the capacity of educational programs to meet these standards and the adequacy of the system to provide a "sound basic education".

Operationalizing adequacy by measuring capacity is important. One benefit of this conceptualization of adequacy is that it ties the evaluation of an educational system to the standards used by its policy makers in their definition of an appropriate education. One disadvantage noted by First and Miron (1999) is that measure often leads policy makers to use a minimum definitional level. Notwithstanding, by using that operationalization, we are recognizing explicitly two points: (1) states have the right to determine what an appropriate secondary education is for their students; and (2) because of that right, they also have an obligation to ensure that all institutions within their jurisdictions have the capacity to provide it.

Linking Organizational Capacity to System Adequacy

Organizational capacity, system adequacy, and performance-based accountability are all important in the evolution of adequacy discourse and how it gets translated into practice. *Organizational capacity* measures the existing ability of an institution to meet the performance standards set. *System adequacy* measures the aggregate capacity of organizations within that system to meet established standards. *Performance-based accountability* is an accountability framework in which outcomes are the means by which policy makers gauge the compliance of systemic elements with policy. These are important considerations for educational policy makers and administrators as they grapple with appropriate ways to respond to the challenges of determining if they offer an adequate system of education.

Ensuring that institutions have sufficient capacity to fulfill the objectives of policy is thus important and has far-reaching implications for supporting adequate school systems once we have defined what they look like (Alexander, 2003). If Cuban's (1994) assessment regarding the need for high expectations in all schools is valid, the imposition of adequacy formulas that do not take into account fiscal and other structural differentials may exacerbate negative consequences that prevail in the most troubled schools. Ensuring that contextual differences are appropriately captured is crucial in formulating policies for funding an adequate system.

What Influences School Capacity

The capacity of schools to meet state and district requirements often depends on school size, composition, institutional setting, and cultural components. Haller, Monk, Spotted Bear, Griffith, and Moss (1990) find that larger schools offer more comprehensive programs than smaller ones, especially in the array of advanced courses provided. If policy makers consider only national or state averages in deriving adequacy, then students who are in schools that have less capacity than average will fare worse than those who are in schools with average or better capacity. Existing evidence suggests that the children who will be most disadvantaged by an "average" definition of adequacy are the ones who are also currently placed at risk. To address differential returns of schooling, Carnoy (1983) advocates establishing a variable funding system where those who receive the lowest levels of private rates of return from schooling should be the ones with the highest level of public subsidies.

Using national and state cost averages to define adequacy can obfuscate the large variation in existing capacities of schools to meet the standards set for adequacy. An examination of the ability of the organization to rise to the challenge of external actions may require taking into fuller account the descriptive "storytelling" of Delpit (1988) and Kozol (1992). Coleman (1986) addresses this need by supplementing his definition of adequacy with research that focuses on "culture as opposed to resources, the consequent emphasis on 'thick description' and the holistic concern, the belief that syndromes, configurations, patterns, are important, rather than single variables such as class size" (p. 88). The contribution of effective school research (e.g., Hallinger & Murphy, 1986) is an important basis for shaping and adding to our understanding of what it means for schools to be adequate. However, it is often difficult to balance the needs of state policy makers for generalizability, with the reality that overall averages may leave some organizations, and the individuals within them, underserved.

ADEQUACY REVISITED

The discussion in this chapter reveals that more needs to be done to focus on the contextual differences that exist among schools and among students in determining appropriate measures of adequacy. The importance of context is long noted, and the observation of Mill regarding achieving equity may be equally applied to adequacy:

> "Besides even in the same kind of work, nominal equality of labor would be so great a real inequality that the feeling of justice would revolt against its being enforced. All persons are not equally fit for all labor, and the same quantity of labor is an unequal burden on the weak and the strong, the hardy and the delicate, the quick and the slow, the dull and the intelligent." (Mill, quoted in Hartman, 1984, p. 45)

An appropriate response to achieving adequacy is to define capacity in a socially just context in which we recognize differences without pigeonholing. For that purpose, the new standard for adequacy should be results neutrality. This standard requires that there should be no systematic associations between ascribed student characteristics and desired student performance. Policies should strive to ensure that researchers cannot predict the success of a school simply by knowing its social demographics. If educational funding policies are well shaped, differences in institutional performance should not be systematically tied to demographics and institutional context. This standard is already hinted at in terms of the stated goals of No Child Left Behind, but there do not seem to be capacity-building mechanisms to ensure that the stated goals are achieved. To make capacity a more integral part of the discussion of adequacy, I propose that we:

Use the definition of *proficiency* offered by state accountability models as an anchor for the socially constructed definitions of *adequacy*.

Use existing school achievement standards as a factor for considering schooling context. Even with the possibility of inefficiency, effectiveness considerations prevail.

Calculate the adequacy of a particular system differently for subject and grade level.

Calculate the adequacy of a particular system based on the capacity of the schools within that system to meet specified goals.

Fund schools differently based on the differential capacity index that exists.

Tie in differential funding with the extra resources needed to fund either an increase in the skill of the front line workers or to develop persuasive material to increase the will of the workers in the unit.

NOTE

1. Pareto optimality refers to a context where there is an absence of waste: resources are currently being used in such a way that no one can be made better off with reallocation without making someone else worse off. By focusing on individual choice and using the price mechanism, it is assumed that equilibrium is achieved when the goods and services produced equal the goods and services demanded.

REFERENCES

Alexander, N. A. (1998). The impact of curriculum standards on student performance: The case of New York State. Unpublished empirical analysis, University at Albany, State University of New York.

Alexander, N. A. (2002). Race, poverty, and the student curriculum: Implications for standards policy. *American Education Research Journal, 39*(3), 675–693.

Alexander, N. A. (2003). Considering equity and adequacy: An examination of the distribution of student class time as an educational resource in New York State, 1975–1995. *Journal of Education Finance, 28*(3), 357–381.

Alexander, N. A. (2004). The changing face of adequacy. *Peabody Journal of Education, 79*(3), 81–103.

Allgood, W., & Rice, J. K. (2002). The adequacy of urban education: Focusing on teacher quality. In C. Roellke & J.K. Rice (Eds.), Fiscal Policy in Urban Education. A Volume in Research in Education Fiscal Policy and Practice (pp. 155–180). Greenwich, CT: Information Age Publishing.

Augenblick, J. G., Myers, J. L., & Anderson, A. B. (1997). Equity and adequacy in school funding. *Future of Children, 7*(3), 63–78.

Baldwin, G. H. (1990). The issues of equity, efficiency, and adequacy in Midwest education finance. *Planning and Changing, 21*(3), 173–180.

Barnett, W. S. (1994). Obstacles and opportunities: Some simple economics of school finance reform. *Educational Policy, 8*(4), 436–452.

Bennett, W. J., Fair, W., Finn, C. E., Jr., Flake, Rev. F., Hirsch, E. D., Marshall, W., et al. (1998). *A nation still at risk.* Washington, DC: Heritage Foundation.

Berne, R. (1994). Program equity for all children: Meaningful goal or impossible dream? *Educational Policy, 8*(4), 502–517.

Berne, R., & Stiefel, L. (1984). The measurement of equity in school finance. Baltimore: Johns Hopkins University Press.

Betts, J. R., & Grogger, J. (2003). The impact of grading standards on student achievement, educational attainment, and entry-level earnings. *Economics of Education Review, 22*(4), 343–352.

Bishop, J. (1996). Incentives to study and the organization of secondary instruction. In W. E. Becker & W. J. Baumol (Eds.), *Assessing educational practices: The contribution of economics* (pp. 99–160). New York: Russell Sage Foundation.

Brown, F. (2001). Educational adequacy: State courts remedy for school finance equity lawsuits. *School Business Affairs, 67*(11), 23–28.

Brown-Nagin, T. (1998). "Broad ownership of the public schools: An analysis of the "T-formation" process model for achieving educational adequacy and its implications for contemporary school reform efforts. *Journal of Law and Education, 27*(3), 343–400.

Campaign for Fiscal Equity. (2000). Reforming New York State's flawed school finance system. In *Evidence: Policy reports from the CFE trial* (Vol. 2). New York: Author.

Carnoy, M. (1982). *Educational adequacy: Alternative perspectives and their implications for educational finance.* In Adequate Education: Issues in Its Definition and Implementation. School Finance Project, Working Papers, p. 34–58. Washington, D.C.: Office of Educational Research and Improvement (ED).

Carnoy, M. (1983). Educational adequacy: Alternative perspectives and their implications for educational finance. *Journal of Education Finance, 8*(3), 286–299.

Chambers, J. G., Parrish, T., & Stanford University Institute for Research on Educational Finance and Governance. (1982). *The issue of adequacy in the financing of public education: How much is enough?* Stanford, CA: Institute for Research on Educational Finance and Governance, Stanford University School of Education.

Chambers, J. G., Levin, J. D., & Parrish, T. B. (2006). Examining the relationship between educational outcomes and gaps in funding: An extension of the New York adequacy study. *Peabody Journal of Education, 8*(12), 1–32.

Chubb, J. E., & Moe, T. M. (1997). Politics, markets, and the organization of schools. In E. Cohn (Ed.), *Market approaches to education: Vouchers and school choice* (pp. 275–303). New York: Elsevier Science.

Clune, W. H. (1994a). The cost and management of program adequacy: An emerging issue in educational policy and finance. *Educational Policy, 8*(4), 365–375.

Clune, W. H. (1994b). The shift from equity to adequacy in school finance. *Educational Policy, 8*(4), 376–394.

Coons, J., Clune, W., & Sugarman, S. (1970). *Private wealth and public education.* Cambridge, MA: Belknap Press of Harvard University Press.

Coons, J. E. (1978). Can education be equal and excellent? *Journal of Education Finance, 4*(2), 147–157.

Cuban, L. (1994). How can a "national" strategy miss a third of our schools? *Education Digest, 59*(5), 12–16.

Delpit, L. D. (1988). The silenced dialogue: Power and pedagogy in educating other people's children. *Harvard Education Review, 58*(3), 280–298.

DeMitchell, T. A. (1999). School finance reform: The carousel reform. *School Business Affairs, 65*(1), 42–47.

Edmonds, R. (1979). Effective schools for the urban poor. *Educational Leadership, 37*(1), 5–24.

Elmore, R. F. (1994). Thoughts on program equity: Productivity and incentives for performance in education. *Educational Policy, 8*(4), 453–459.

Engel, M. (2000). *The struggle for control of public education: Market ideology vs. democratic values.* Philadelphia, PA: Temple University Press.

Fowler, F. C. (2004). *Policy studies for educational leaders: An introduction.* 2nd edition. Upper Saddle River, N.J.: Merrill.

Firestone, W. A. (1989). Educational policy as an ecology of games. *Educational Researcher, 18*(7), 18–24.

First, P. F., & Miron, L. F. (1991). The social construction of adequacy. *Journal of Law and Education, 20*(4), 421–444.

Friedman, M. (1963). *Capitalism and freedom.* Chicago: University of Chicago Press.

Garms, W. I. (1979). Measuring the equity of school finance systems. Journal of Education Finance, 4(4), 415–435.

Garner, C. W. (2004). *Education finance for school leaders: Strategic planning and administration.* Columbus, OH: Pearson, Merrill Prentice Hall.

Goertz, M., & Edwards, M. (1999). In search of excellence for all: The courts and New Jersey school finance reform. *Journal of Education Finance,* 25(1), 5–32.

Goertz, M. E. (1994). Program equity and adequacy: Issues from the field. *Educational Policy,* 8(4), 608–615.

Gowin, D. B. (1981). *Educating.* Ithaca, NY: Cornell University Press.

Guthrie, J. W. (1983). Funding an "adequate" education. *Phi Delta Kappan,* 64(7), 471–476.

Guthrie, J. W. (2002). Who holds the purse strings? *American School Board Journal,* 189(5), 38–40.

Guthrie, J. W. and Rothstein, R. (1999). Performance standards and educational cost indexes : you can't have one without the other. In H. F. Ladd, R. Chalk, and J. S. Hansen (Eds.), Equity and adequacy in education finance (pp.). Washington, D.C.: National Academy Press.

Haller, E., Monk, D., Spotted Bear, A., Griffith, J., & Moss, P. (1990). School size and program comprehensiveness: Evidence from high school and beyond. *Educational Evaluation and Policy Analysis,* 12(2), pp. 109–120.

Hallinger, P., & Murphy, J. F. (1986). The social context of effective schools. *American Journal of Education,* 94(3), 328–355.

Hanson, R. A., & Ross, S. M. (1975). The adequacy of instructional time allocation. *Studies in Educational Evaluation,* 1(1), 23–29.

Hanushek, E. A. (1981). The impact of differential expenditures on school performance. *Educational Researcher,* 18(4), 45–62.

Hanushek, E. A. (1986) The economics of schooling: Production and efficiency in public schools. *Journal of Economic Literature,* 24(3), 1141–1177.

Hanushek, E. A. (1994). A jaundiced view of "adequacy" in school finance reform. *Educational Policy,* 8(4), 460–469.

Hanushek, E. A. (1997). Assessing the effects of school resources on student performance: An update. *Educational Evaluation and Policy Analysis,* 19(2), 141–164.

Hanushek, E. A. (2006). The alchemy of 'costing out' an adequate education. Revised version of paper prepared for the conference on *Adequacy Lawsuits: Their Growing Impact on American Education,* October 13-14, 2005, Kennedy School of Government, Harvard University. Retrieved November 9, 2006 from http://edpro.stanford.edu/hanushek/admin/pages/files/uploads/alchemy.final.pdf.

Hartman, R. H. (1984). *Poverty and economic justice: A philosophical approach.* New York: Paulist Press.

Hedges, L. V., Laine, R. D., & Greenwald, R. (1994). Does money matter? A meta-analysis of studies of the effects of differential school inputs on student outcomes. *Educational Researcher, 23*(3), 5–14.

Herrington, C. D., & Trimble, S. (1997). Educational reform in the Sunshine State: High need, low funding, and a disaffected electorate. *Educational Considerations, 25*(1), 17–20.

Herrington, C. D., & Weider, V. (2001). Equity, adequacy and vouchers: Past and present school finance litigation in Florida. *Journal of Education Finance, 21*(1), 517–534.

Hess, F. M. (1999). Spinning wheels: The politics of urban school reform. Washington, DC: Brookings Institution.

Hess, G. A., Jr. (1994). Adequacy rather than equity: A new solution or a stalking horse? *Educational Policy, 8*(4), 544–567.

Hirsch, Jr., E. D. (2002). The benefit to equity. *American Educator, 26*(2), 16–17.

Kirst, M. W. (1983). A new school finance for a new era of fiscal constraint. In A. Odden & L. D. Webb (Eds.), *School finance and school improvement linkages for the 1980s* (pp. 1–15). Cambridge, MA: Ballinger.

Kirst, M. W. (1994). Equity for children: Linking education and children's services. *Educational Policy, 8*(4), 583–590.

Kozol, J. (1992). *Savage inequalities: Children in America's schools.* New York: Harper Perennial.

Laine, R. D., Greenwald, R., and Hedges, L.V. (1996). Money does matter: A research synthesis of a new universe of education production function studies. In L. Picus and J. Wattenbarger (Eds.), *Where does the money go?* (pp. 44–70). Thousand Oaks, CA: Corwin Press.

Levin, H. M. (1991). *Accelerating the progress of all students.* Albany, NY: Nelson A. Rockefeller Institute of Government.

Linn, R. L., Koretz, D. M., Baker, E. L., & Burstein, L. (1991). The validity and credibility of the achievement levels for the 1990 National Assessment of Educational Progress in mathematics (CSE Technical Report 330). Los Angeles: University of California, National Center for Research on Evaluation Standards and Student Testing.

Lucas, S. R. (1999). *Tracking inequality: Stratification and mobility in American high schools.* New York: Teachers College Press.

Malen, B. (1994). Enacting site-based management: A political utilities analysis. Educational Evaluation and Policy Analysis, *16*(3), 249–267.

Minorini, P. (1994). Recent developments in school finance equity and educational adequacy cases. *ERS Spectrum, 12*(1), 3–11.

Monk, D. H. (1990). Educational finance: An economic approach. New York: McGraw Hill Publishing Company.

Monk, D. H. (1994). Policy challenges surrounding the shift toward outcome-oriented school finance equity standards. *Educational Policy, 8*(4), 471–488.

Monk, D. H., & Haller, E. J. (1993). Predictors of high school academic course offerings: The role of school size. *American Educational Research Journal, 30*(1), 3–21.

Murnane, R. J. (1994). Will school finance reform improve education for disadvantaged children? Research issues. *Educational Policy, 8*(4), 535–542.

Odden, A. (2000). The new school finance: Providing adequacy and improving equity. *Journal of Education Finance, 25*(4), 467–487.

Odden, A. (2003). Equity and adequacy in school finance today. *Phi Delta Kappan, 85*(2), 120–125.

Odden, A. & Kelley, C. (2002). *Paying teachers for what they know and do: New and smarter compensation strategies to improve schools.* Second Edition, Thousand Oaks, CA: Corwin Press.

Odden, A. R. & Picus, L. O. (1999). *School finance: A policy perspective.* New York: McGraw Hill Publishing Company.

Ogawa, R. T., Crowson, R.L., and Goldring, E. B. (1999). Enduring dilemmas of school organization. In J. Murphy & K. Seashore Louis (Eds.), *The handbook of research on educational administration: A project of the American Educational Research Association* (2ⁿᵈ ed. pp. 277–296). San Francisco: Jossey-Bass Inc.

Ohio Coalition for Equity and Adequacy. (2001). *Determining the cost of an adequate education: Yet another failed attempt.* Retrieved on November 9, 2006 from http://www.ohiocoalition.org/pdfs/FailedAttempt.pdf.

Okun, A. M. (1975). *Equality and efficiency: The big tradeoff.* Washington, DC: Brookings Institution Press.

Picus, L. O. (1999). Defining adequacy: Implications for school business officials. *School Business Affairs, 65*(1), 27–31.

Picus, L. O. (2001). School finance adequacy: What is it and how do we measure it? *School Business Affairs, 67*(11), 19–22.

Rawls, J. A theory of justice. Revised edition. Cambridge, Mass.: Belknap Press of Harvard University Press.

Reschovsky, A., & Imazeki, J. (2001). Achieving educational adequacy through school finance reform. *Journal of Education Finance, 26*(4), 373–396.

Rossmiller, R. A. (1994). Equity or adequacy of school funding. *Educational Policy, 8*(4), 616–625.

Sadovnik, A. R., Cookson, P. W., Jr., & Semel, S. F. (Eds.). (2001). *Exploring education: An introduction to the foundations of education* (2nd ed.). Boston: Allyn and Bacon.

Salazar, I. M. (1988, April). *The use of qualitative data as a supplement to quantitative analysis of objective survey items.* Paper presented at the annual meeting of the American Educational Research Association, New Orleans.

Slavin, R. E. (1994). Statewide finance reform: Ensuring educational adequacy for high-poverty schools. *Educational Policy, 8*(4), 425–434.

U.S. Department of Education National Commission on Excellence in Education (1983). *A Nation at Risk: The Imperative for Educational Reform.* Washington, D.C.: Author.

Verstegen, D. A. (2002). Financing the new adequacy: Towards new models of state education finance systems that support standards based reform. *Journal of Education Finance, 27*(3), 749–782.

Ward, J. G. (1987). In pursuit of equity and adequacy: Reforming school finance in Illinois. *Journal of Education Finance, 13*(1), 107–120.

Ward, J. G. (1991). Why educational adequacy remains an elusive goal. *School Administrator, 48*(8), 13–15.

Wise, A. E. (1976). Minimum educational adequacy: Beyond school finance reform. *Journal of Education Finance, 1*(4), 468–483.

Wise, A. E. (1983). Educational adequacy: A concept in search of meaning. *Journal of Education Finance, 8*(3), 300–315.

Part II

The Social Justice Implications of Contemporary School Finance Policy

5

CYCLING ON IN CULTURAL DEFICIT THINKING

California School Finance and the
Possibilities of Critical Policy Analysis

Gloria M. Rodriguez
University of California–Davis

FOR THE PAST SEVERAL YEARS, California has embraced the public reporting of academic achievement outcomes. This annual ritual (Stein, 2004) is framed as school accountability and is carried out by public officials and the media as an act of openness and service. The public reporting practices, in fact, are meant to signal transparency, and the standardized test scores are likewise presented as racially and socioeconomically neutral forms of assessment to the public (Valencia, Villarreal, & Salinas, 2002). Such accountability practices nevertheless provide, at best, an abbreviated assessment of the educational conditions that exist in California's public schools (Koski & Weiss, 2004). In addition, the annual announcement of the Academic Performance Index (API) scores serves to repeatedly highlight the persistently low rankings of school communities with the highest concentrations of low-income students and students of color. In turn, as policy makers enter their annual deliberations regarding the distribution of funding to the public school system, the evidence they must rely upon is also limited and confusing with regard to how dollars can be transformed into better outcomes for diverse students. The burning question that emerges for those of us concerned with the role of policy analysis in education finance is thus, "In whose interest do we continue a cycle of limited evaluative information, disappointing academic results, and partial explanations that belie the full challenges and potential of the California educational context?"

Indeed, given California's richness of social, linguistic, and cultural diversity, the current cycle of our educational system provides the impetus to seek out new possibilities for conducting policy analysis that can inform the investments of public resources to facilitate educational excellence. Without such efforts, California will continue to fall prey to what Valencia (1997) refers to as "cultural deficit thinking" or characterizations and explanations of schooling outcomes that render a view of low-income and ethnically or linguistically diverse students as possessing only deficiencies as learners. Moreover, as the push continues to invest educational resources in ways that maximize the opportunities and outcomes for increasingly diverse student populations, it is our responsibility as scholars in the field to leave no possibility unexplored for interrupting a cycle of disappointment in favor of better results.

With the goal in mind of improving educational investment possibilities by enriching our analyses of policy issues facing California's diverse school communities, the purpose of this chapter is to explore the use of critical policy analysis frameworks in the field of school finance. School finance policy has benefited from the theoretical frameworks offered by the fields of law, economics, sociology, and political science for many decades. Indeed, the finance systems in California and throughout the United States have shown significant improvement in inter-district funding disparities, especially those that were tied to variations in local property wealth (Odden & Picus, 2004). However, with increasing attention to the linkages between educational inputs and certain expected educational outcomes (see Alexander, this volume), it appears that the timing is right to begin expanding the possibilities once again. The persistence of outcomes disparities despite improvements in the equalization of basic funding among California's school districts creates a frustrating situation for theorists and policy makers alike. Thus, frameworks that surface the assumptions that currently prevent us from fully capturing the potential impact of our investments in diverse communities are necessary if we aim to move beyond the identification of students' deficiencies alone as a means to increase achievement.

This chapter begins by describing the "big picture" of school finance policy in California to provide the context for exploring critical policy analysis frameworks. The next discussion draws from Forester's (1993) critical public policy view and Young's (1999) "multifocal" policy studies approach that recommend a juxtaposition—and where appropriate, an integration—of conventional or standard analytical frameworks with critical frameworks to produce more comprehensive analyses. The chapter proceeds by outlining Berne & Steifel's (1984) standard school finance equity framework. This discussion is followed by the introduction of critical frameworks drawn from the theoretical work of Stein (2004), Valencia and Solórzano (1997), and Yosso (2005). The chapter explores the combined use of standard and critical policy analysis approaches to enable more systematic probing of biases emerging from cultural deficit views of low-income communities and communities of color, while pursuing the development of meaningful indicators of "cultural wealth" or "assets" (Yosso, 2005). The chapter briefly presents sample California school district data to illustrate the potential of policy analysis that incorporates critical perspectives in the effort to eradicate cultural deficit thinking and arrive at better formulations of public investments in diverse school communities. Finally, the chapter offers a reflection on the question of interests served in the current cycle of deficit thinking in California school finance policy by considering the practicalities and dilemmas inherent in combined policy analysis approaches in this field. Recommendations are made for expanding the possibilities for school finance policy that facilitates academic success among California's diverse students.

CALIFORNIA SCHOOL FINANCE: THE BIG PICTURE

In many ways, California is a good example of a "how-not-to-do-it" state. A variety of ballot initiatives and litigation over the past few decades have produced a system that is difficult to comprehend, particularly if one attempts to link the funding mechanisms to particular educational outcomes. It is a system where the minimum guarantee has become the ceiling (Picus, 2006) and where the state categorical funding does not necessarily align clearly with student needs (Timar, 2004). Moreover, as Picus (2005) points out, it is also a system sorely in need of a revamp, yet there is no clear information as to what level of funding would be sufficient to fully support all of the educational needs represented throughout California. Despite these challenges, there appears to be energy and dialogue regarding California's vision of "adequacy" in school funding, although experts in the state must still face the daunting work of defining adequacy and estimating the funding levels associated with it. And perhaps to heighten that challenge, California faces the dual conditions of declining enrollments and increasing student needs, the latter of which have become especially apparent by virtue of the school districts' attempts to comply with the requirements of the federal No Child Left Behind Act of 2001.

LITIGATION AND PUBLIC INITIATIVES
SHAPE THE SYSTEM

To preface the discussion that follows, it is useful to call attention to the uniqueness of the California policy context. The aim in doing so is to create an entry point for those who may be less familiar with school finance generally, and/or with California school finance specifically. California is a state with a public initiative process deemed by many citizens to be out of control. This political feature has produced significant shifts in direction in a wide range of policy areas, and school finance policy is a prime example. In the discussion that follows, it is helpful to keep in mind that due to the ability of individuals or groups with the resources needed to successfully place certain constitutional amendments on the ballot—and win public endorsement from voters—the school finance system reflects a variety of constituent interests and often seems to work against itself. Although the information here is presented in more or less chronological order, readers should not misconstrue that approach as signaling coherence from one policy change to the next. In fact, the incoherence and lack of responsiveness of the school finance system relative to many school communities are none better captured than in the evidence of neglect contained in the *Williams v. California* case (Decent Schools for California, 2005).

Serrano and Property Wealth Disparities

It is important to understand how schools are funded in California to appreciate the difficulties the state faces in meeting the variety of obligations it has to fully support its educational services. The constitutional challenge to the California school finance system using the state constitution's equal protection and education clauses began in 1971 with *Serrano v. Priest* (*Serrano I*), which sought to address educational expenditure disparities produced by the direct linkage between local property wealth variations and the associated variations in revenue-raising capacity among school districts throughout the state. The court challenges eventually went through three iterations before a decision in 1989 rendered the system compliant with court equalization standards set forth in *Serrano II*. The *Serrano* decisions, spanning the 1970s and 1980s, produced improved equalization of basic funding across school districts in California, though the standards set in *Serrano II* contained allowable disparities of $100 per pupil among districts in the same categories of type and size (later adjusted for inflation to result in current allowable disparities of approximately $350 per pupil). As noted by School Services of California (Goldfinger, 2006), the persistent funding disparities among districts remains an important political issue for the legislature, which has made a series of attempts to rectify the situation over the past several years.

Proposition 13

Generally speaking, California's school finance system is considered a state-funded system due to the increasing reliance on state aid by the majority of districts statewide. The shift to a state-funded system was precipitated by the passage of Proposition 13 in 1978, an initiative that was intended to curtail the increases in property taxes but which has had considerable impact on the level of services provided in the schools. The requirements of Proposition 13 placed limits on local property taxes by (1) setting a statewide rate on assessed property values, with reassessments of property values for tax purposes occurring only when property is sold; and (2) severely limiting the ability of local governments to raise or levy new special-purpose taxes, such as for local schools; hence the shift to a state-funded system. Proposition 13 removed the incentive for local districts to raise local taxes, as such revenues now simply offset the state aid that would otherwise be provided subject to revenue limits. (This change illustrates an important choice in school finance policy from serving students to protecting taxpayers). In addition, the passage of Proposition 13 also ushered in a steady decline in the state's ranking in terms of per-pupil expenditures in education (Minorini & Sugarman, 1999). According to School Services of California (SSC), the most recent available data indicates that California ranks 33rd (or 89.3% of the national average) in public education expense in the United States, with per pupil expenditures of approximately $7,860 (Goldfinger, 2006).

Proposition 4

While Proposition 13 placed limits on the state's property tax rates thus limiting the available local revenues dedicated to schools, Proposition 4, a state constitutional amendment passed in 1979, imposed limits on the growth of educational and other governmental spending. At one point in California's recent history, the Proposition 4 or "Gann Limits," named after the initiative's author, Paul Gann, carried significant implications for the allowable growth in public spending such that education would have been caught in a squeeze of limited local revenues as well as limited allowable spending growth. Given that these measures were creating a long-term trend of reductions in overall K–12 educational spending, the education community responded with yet another constitutional amendment, Proposition 98, which was intended to reverse this trend. As described below, the success of Proposition 98 in providing a response to the previous measures and limitations of equalization efforts has been extremely mixed, with the greatest difficulties faced in the most recent state budget cycles (Legislative Analyst's Office, 2005).

Proposition 98 and the Impact of the Fluctuations in State Revenues

Proposition 98 was passed by the voters in 1988 as an amendment to the state constitution. The intention was to create a minimum guarantee of funding for K–14 schools (K–12 schools and community colleges) and to tie the increases in the funding to the overall condition of the state economy as well as growth in the educational system. According to the Legislative Analyst (LAO, 2006), Proposition 98 funds totaled $49.1 billion in general funds for K–12 schools, or 49% of the $101.3 billion in general funds supporting the 2006–2007 state budget. The dollar increase in Proposition 98 funding from year to year depends heavily on the anticipated tax revenues at the state level, meaning that the increases are greater during years of revenue growth and leaner in years of decline or slower growth. Once schools receive a certain increase in funding via the Proposition 98 guarantee, that amount becomes the minimum level of funding for subsequent years unless the state legislature agrees to suspend its Proposition 98 obligation. What is not often discussed is that the legislature could actually spend more than the Proposition 98 guarantee on education; however, given the extensive competing demands for general fund support, such augmentations have not occurred—except in the mid-1990s, when California experienced considerable increases in available tax revenues.

According to the Legislative Analyst's Office, or LAO (2005), one difficulty in determining the level of funding available for public education has been the great fluctuations in state revenues. As explained in the discussion of the Proposition 98 minimum guarantee, the level of educational funding has been tied to the growth (or decline) in anticipated and actual state revenues. Although there has been growth in the level of Proposition 98 funding, the growth has not been stable over the past nearly two decades. In fact, the volatility of the state revenues requires the application of different "tests" for determining the level of Proposition 98 funding for schools, as specified in the amendment. Test 1, for example, was only used once at the initial implementation of Proposition 98, and it provided increases in the guaranteed minimum at the same level as growth in state tax revenues. However, Test 2, which has been applied most often, provides a guaranteed minimum funding equal to the prior year plus adjustments for growth in average daily attendance (ADA) and cost of living adjustments (COLA) or growth in per capita personal income. Finally, Test 3 provides yet another route for calculating the minimum guaranteed funding under Proposition 98 during times of slow growth in state tax revenues and thus is tied to the state's ability to pay versus changes in the revenues.

As a result of complex decision rules for determining the targeted minimum level of Proposition 98 funding, the inability to predict the exact increases available to public schools makes it nearly impossible for local educators to plan for the budget year in many cases. In addition, the fluctuations in state revenues also mean that other large-scale state services are affected, and even though 49% of the general fund is dedicated to K–12 education, revenues made available for innovations or initiatives to address particular student or staff needs become extremely vulnerable from one year to the next. Such unpredictability means that long-term planning is a challenge, yet given the increases in the types of student needs represented among California's public schools, lasting reforms in education become highly dependent on steady funding streams.

The Williams Settlement—Promises and Potential Shortcomings

While *Williams v. California* was not touted initially as a school finance case, the proponents of the case have certainly framed the related claims in terms of the adequacy of facilities and services for California's diverse student populations (Oakes & Saunders, 2004). The case was originally brought on behalf of the students attending the lowest-decile schools in the state using the state's API—communities whose children were attending school in dilapidated buildings, resorting to a variety of strategies to compensate for the lack of materials, textbooks, and qualified teachers. Indeed, as the case unfolded, some of the testimony documented the horrible conditions found in schools all across the state. In many regards, the focus of the case was on access to the basic materials, services, and facilities. However, advocates involved in the *Williams* case have continued to draw linkages to current debates about the adequacy of California's school finance system. Regardless of any opportunities via *Williams* to illuminate broader finance system changes needed, California governor Arnold Schwarzenegger instead reached a settlement on the case in 2004 (Goldfinger & Blattner, 2005). Basically, the settlement of *Williams* includes the following agreements, which school districts are currently involved in meeting:

- *Instructional materials:* provides funding to ensure that basic instructional materials (e.g., textbooks) are provided for every student
- *Facilities:* provides a new funding source for the repair and maintenance of school facilities; also requires notification of complaint measures to be taken at each school site to improve the cleanliness and safety of facilities
- *Teacher quality:* provides increased oversight and options for districts to obtain the services of the Fiscal Crisis and Management Assistance Team to review hiring and assignment practices to improve teacher quality, particularly in the lowest decile schools.
- *Uniform complaint form:* applies to all schools and provides notices be posted in every classroom notifying the public of how to file a complaint about certain facilities, teacher, and textbook problems, with the allowance of only 30 days to remedy the complaint

To some experts in California school finance policy, the *Williams* settlement potentially represents a "selling out" of public schools by not following through with a suit that might have resulted in greater resource investment in California's school communities. What has been produced thus far by the settlement has the risk of becoming, largely, an inventory process and grievance protocols that may not lead to actual improvements in the available stock of materials for schools or attention to the severe conditions documented by those bringing the case. In addition, the focus of the settlement also potentially diverts attention away from some of the structural and instructional aspects of the general concern for the lack of quality in the educational services being rendered in certain communities (Picus, 2006). That is, even though the basic material resources that enable schools to function may eventually be provided, it is unclear whether the lack of attention to the teaching and learning processes in those schools will be rectified. Moreover, without careful scrutiny over the types and purposes of the financial resources that schools in California do have access to (such as some categoricals), it is likely that important opportunities for greatly improving the quality of education provided could be overlooked. Indeed, the challenge of ensuring that every child has access to a school that is clean and safe and where the necessary materials and texts are provided also involves scrutiny over the actual organization of instruction, teacher-student relationships, and school-community relationships (Darling-Hammond, 2002).

Funding Structures: Revenue Limits and Categorical Funding

The California state legislature determines a "revenue limit" for each school district, which represents a district's "basic funding." Once determined, the local property tax revenues raised by each district are compared to the revenue limit figure to determine (amid a few other adjustments) the level of state aid that each district receives. The state's obligation to equalize funding among districts applies only to the revenue limit, and this amount is also adjusted annually for cost of living increases.

As with many state school finance systems, the funding a school district receives is determined by the changes in the numbers of students in ADA. One positive aspect of the determination of funding based on changes in the ADA is that the state permits districts to exercise options that enable them to most accurately represent their actual ADA from year to year. Of course, challenges exist when a school district experiences large declines in enrollment, and state policy has attempted to deal with this issue by allowing transitional funding to prevent a shock to a school district due to a significant shortage of funding from one year to the next because of declines in ADA.

While revenue limit amounts are the focus of California's equalization efforts, the categorical funding made available to schools sits outside of the equalization formula used to distribute funding to schools. On the one hand, this is helpful because it increases the possibilities for enacting categorical programs in which dollars follow needs in direct proportion to their presence among certain districts. On the other hand, because there is no attention to equalization, there is likewise no guarantee that dollars currently doled out through a variety of categorical programs address particular needs in ways that maximize teaching and learning experiences to match the great diversity of school communities across California (Timar, 2004).

California maintains a variety of categorical programs, among the largest being the Class Size Reduction Program. Several of these programs have been consolidated to ostensibly enable local educators to avail themselves of more flexibility in the use of these funds. However, the largest programs—for the most part—have been kept intact (Goldfinger & Blattner, 2005). The six areas of consolidation of categorical programs into block grants are *teacher credentialing, pupil retention, professional development, targeted instructional improvement, school and library improvement*, and *school safety*. It is interesting to note that, in their analysis of the overarching impact of this consolidation effort, SSC (Goldfinger & Blattner, 2005) indicate that the changes involving the formation of these block grants only minimally affect flexibility, do not attend to the concerns regarding equitable distribution of categorical funding across districts, and do not reflect recent efforts on the part of the educational community to increase the available funding for various purposes encompassed by these six block grant areas. Indeed, concerns over the accountability of funding uses among categorical programs—and particularly, the linkages (or lack thereof) between funding and needs—have been a perennial concern for those monitoring the proliferation of categorical programs in California over the past few decades (Timar, 2004).

Increasing Needs Tied to Accountability

A variety of student and staff needs have surfaced as a result of California's school districts' attempts to meet the multiple and often contradictory requirements of the federal No Child Left Behind (NCLB) Act. As some practitioners and scholars argue, the disaggregated data requirements produced by NCLB have led to consciousness-raising among some educators who in the past might have overlooked or purposely downplayed the lack of achievement among low-income children or children of color attending California's public schools. It is arguable that standardized test scores—particularly those that assess material that has not been taught—do not completely or reliably capture the breadth of learning that students do in their classrooms from semester to semester or year to year (Valencia, et al., 2002). However, the push for attending to the needs of all sub-groups of students does provide educators with new opportunities to improve equity conditions in the schools using data. What has become most difficult and, at times, demoralizing for schools is the tremendous energy required to meet the multitude of specific requirements set forth in the NCLB without sufficient resources to support that compliance activity. (To explore the compliance challenges of NCLB relative to teachers of English-language learners, see Gonzales & Rodriguez, this volume).

Summary of California School Finance Context

It is an understatement to refer to California's school finance system as "complex." After several years of litigation and policy intervention, we are left with a largely state-funded system, with the associated diminished local control over the decisions that guide the educational expenditures of school districts. Local control is not the only challenging aspect of California school finance for school communities, as it is also a system mired in a lack of transparency: it is commonly known that only a handful of individuals truly understand every intricate detail of the manner in which school districts obtain their funding. Most school districts fall within allowable per-pupil disparities for revenue limit (basic) funding (Picus, 2006), but there is no accountability or equalization built into the allocation and use of most categorical funding (Timar, 2004). Overall educational expenditures have decreased over time relative to other states (Goldfinger, 2006), and the system is plagued by persistent financial and non-financial resource disparities despite funding equalization efforts (Betts, Reuben, & Danenberg, 2000). The *Williams* case and settlement have illuminated the extreme neglect some school communities have endured in terms of access to basic materials, facilities, and qualified teachers (Darling-Hammond, 2004; Oakes & Saunders, 2004; Rumberger & Gándara, 2004). Together, these systemic features represent a broader cycle of policy convolution and a challenging context in which to address the presence of cultural deficit thinking in school finance.

NEW POSSIBILITIES FOR SCHOOL FINANCE POLICY ANALYSIS: COMBINING STANDARD AND CRITICAL ANALYTICAL FRAMEWORKS

Having provided a description of the California school finance policy context, the need for policy analysis approaches that serve to demystify the system becomes salient. This section seeks to explore the possibilities offered by the combined use of conventional/standard school finance equity frameworks in tandem with critical analysis frameworks. The key questions for this discussion are,

1. What is the rationale for conducting policy analysis in school finance that incorporates both conventional/standard equity frameworks and critical frameworks?
2. What are the components and processes of combined conventional/standard and critical policy analysis frameworks?
3. What can we learn about the factors that mitigate the impact of resource investments among students using combined policy analysis frameworks in school finance?

A Rationale for the Combined Use of Conventional/Standard and Critical Policy Frameworks in School Finance

The complexity of the school finance system in California certainly inspires the search for analytical approaches that enable researchers and analysts to probe the system and reveal its inner workings. However, the introduction of critical analysis frameworks—that is, analytical approaches that are informed by one or more critical perspective (e.g. critical theory, critical race theory, feminist theory, etc.)—suggests that the problem to be analyzed may have dimensions that are not easily revealed if one relies on more traditional or conventional approaches alone. In the case of school finance policy, the key issue that would benefit from the introduction of critical analysis is the persistence of disappointing or frustrating results from the educational system despite years of reform in the distribution of financial and non-financial resources to public schools. Moreover, the repetitive cycle involves the stigmatized characterizations of large (and growing) numbers of students—those who are from low-income backgrounds and/or of color—such that their potential as learners and contributors to our society is obscured and remains untapped.

Drawing upon the work of Forester (1993) and Young (1999), it is clear that there are also broader considerations in the rationale for applying critical perspectives to policy analysis. Both Forester and Young provide cogent arguments for the use of "critical public policy" and "multifocal policy research" approaches, respectively, which are distinct yet complementary. Forester (1993) argues that policy analysis should allow us to understand not only the most straightforward aspects of our practice in the public arena, but also the ways in which policies help to produce and reproduce certain conditions and relationships among the populations who are affected by them. The conditions and relationships that are produced and reproduced by various policy actions may, in turn, influence or mitigate the policy outcomes that were being sought.

In the case of school finance, Forester's view would encourage us to use available theoretical/analytical approaches to understand not only whether the distribution of funding proceeds as the regulations dictate or how school funding is used to accomplish certain organizational objectives. We would also use analyses to understand what patterns of participation or exclusion emerge among all affected constituents from the current formulations of school finance policy. Typically, we are exposed through the media to the high-level political interests that are negotiated in educational policy contexts, especially relative to the distribution of funding. However, Forester's rationale for applying critical theory in policy analysis is to advance a deeper understanding of the issues for which policy intervention is sought and to facilitate more inclusiveness among communities most directly affected by the policies in question. According to Forester, critical theory enables us to accomplish these purposes by encouraging analysis that shifts the focus to those aspects of policy development and formulation that go unquestioned: the subtle, taken-for-granted power relations, modes of engaging with the process, and the modes of excluding certain parties from full, democratic participation.

Young's (1999) work in developing "multifocal policy research," or what she also refers to as "multiple-framed" analysis, is introduced as a means for expanding the possibilities for policy studies in education. Although it is arguable that not everyone involved in school finance undertakes policy analysis that is designed as formal research, there is great relevance for scholars and analysts who seek opportunities to contribute to the policy debates in ways that expand or deepen our understanding of the issues at hand. In Young's illustrative case, she examines the notion of parental involvement in education using a multiple-frame approach that incorporates both traditional and critical research designs using qualitative methods that align with each of these paradigmatic perspectives.[1] She situates herself as a researcher and explains that she

> employed ... a critical theory that is concerned with policy rhetoric and reality; the unequal distribution of power, resources, and knowledge; social stratification; institutionalization; and resistance. In this form, critical theory ... seeks to provide an empirical account of the contextual and contingent reproduction—through policy and practice—of social inequality. (1999, p. 689)

Given the shared concerns that many school finance researchers and analysts have for the seeming permanence of certain disparities among school communities and the salience of race and class in those analyses, Young's reasoning for engaging critical theory in educational policy studies is especially pertinent to school finance. Perhaps the dimensions of exploration that she describes may seem daunting to researchers who seek to better understand the relationship between inputs and outcomes in schools (e.g. for determinations of adequacy in school finance). I would argue that Young's use of critical theory actually introduces a way to stop chipping away at symptoms (e.g., low test scores) and instead to get at the root problems (e.g., institutionalized biases that mitigate full educational participation) that prevent us from realizing our shared goals for educational success among diverse communities.

Of course, Young recognizes the analytical force of research and policy work that relies upon multiple frames and methods to construct deeper meanings from the experiences involved in different educational settings. In very practical terms, Young goes on to explain that the value of the combined use of conventional/standard and critical frameworks is also realized in the ways in which the associated methods can be compatible or can surface contradictory findings that help to raise new questions for still deeper understanding—an important form of triangulation. Such analytical power holds great promise in addressing the many puzzles of school finance policy, which may represent a complexity of as-yet-uninterrogated assumptions about the means and ends of educational investments on behalf of communities variously situated in our society. The promise and potential of this approach is that we can begin to locate the problems of disparate inputs and outcomes in sites other than the cultural backgrounds of the students and their communities, thereby increasing the usefulness of policy analysis as a lever to interrupt repetitive and disappointing cycles in education.

Both Forester and Young provide rationales for the use of combined analytical frameworks in public and educational policy, which are compelling and applicable to school finance. The discussion proceeds from here by outlining the components and processes that characterize two frameworks to explore conceptually the power of the combined analytical approaches in school finance. The first is the *standard school finance equity framework*, introduced originally by Berne and Stiefel (1984) and elaborated further by Odden and Picus (2004). The second, which I am calling the *critical community strength framework*, draws from the theoretical and empirical work of Stein (2004), Valencia & Solórzano (1997), and Yosso (2005).

The Standard School Finance Equity Framework—Components and Process

In 1984, Berne and Stiefel introduced a framework that has become the touchstone of school finance equity analysis for over two decades. Their book, *The Measurement of Equity in School Finance: Conceptual, Methodological, and Empirical Dimensions*, provided an analytical approach that draws upon their prior work examining wealth distribution, public finance, and school finance. To date, the majority of school finance equity analyses incorporate at least partial recognition of this four-question framework, which asks, "Equity for whom? Of what object? Determined by what principles? And assessed by what measures?" (Berne & Stiefel, 1984).

One of the most compelling statements made by the authors in explaining the purposes of their analytical framework is how they were motivated, in part, by the need they saw to make the value judgments in equity analyses more explicit:

Equity concerns emanate from many sources, but all have one thing in common. All incorporate specific values, either implicitly or explicitly, where values are preferences for what should be and for what should not be. In many cases equity analyses are unnecessarily confusing, in part because the values embedded in the assessment are hidden or surpressed [sic]. To clarify and improve equity analyses, we have developed a four-dimensional framework in which each dimension helps bring certain kinds of value judgments to the forefront. (p. 272)

Notably, while most school finance researchers have embraced Berne & Stiefel's framework and extensive methodological contributions, seldom, if ever, do scholars reference the purpose of using the framework to make the values and value judgments embedded in their analyses more explicit. In this regard, Odden and Picus (2004) have elaborated further upon the use and potential of Berne and Stiefel's original framework to broaden the analyst's perspectives about elements of schooling that matter most in equity analyses. For example, the authors point out that while Berne & Stiefel focused on educational inputs and outcomes captured, respectively, by dollars per pupil and standardized test scores, researchers may deem other educational inputs and outcomes as better indicators of the equity status of different student populations served by the systems they are evaluating (Odden & Picus, 2004). Embedded in this elaboration is the encouragement to consider what is of value in the educational system in question and to shape one's analysis according to the particular value judgments that produce an articulation of "what should be and what should not be" the schooling conditions for various groups served by the system being evaluated.

The process embodied in four questions enables school finance researchers and analysts to specify the focal group, equity standards, and key indicators that will be used to assess the equity conditions in a given school finance system. The first question—"Equity for whom?"—is helpful to distinguish between analyses that focus on students and those that focus on taxpayers, as these are typically the two major constituents of concern for school finance researchers. The second question—"Of what object?"—identifies the distribution of a specific resource (or, as Odden and Picus suggest, the specific outcome) that is to be assessed for equity purposes. The third question—"Determined by what principles?"—directs the researcher's attention to the equity standards that may be most relevant in light of the particular concerns to be addressed by the analysis. (I will return to this question shortly). The fourth question—"Assessed by what (statistical) measures?"—sets forth an operationalization, in more concrete terms, of an assessment of the distribution patterns of certain resources. Most often, the responses to the fourth question are stated in terms of statistical measures of resource distributions across various student or taxpayer populations. Related to the indicators is the consideration of level of analysis, since the measures can be developed for districts within states or schools within districts (Odden & Picus, 2004).

The four questions contained in the standard school finance framework provide a process to establish the parameters of school finance analysis. In addition, another set of critical components—used to respond to the third question—"Determined by what principles?"—are the three principles of (a) horizontal equity; (b) vertical equity; and (c) fiscal neutrality (also referred to as "equal opportunity"). Briefly, these principles are defined as follows:

a. *Horizontal equity*—equal treatment of equals—requires the establishment of an identified group of "equal" to which the school finance system should provide equal distributions of specified resources. Example: equal dollars per pupil across school districts.

b. *Vertical equity*—differential distribution of resources according to variations in need (or for taxpayers, revenue-raising capacity)—requires the establishment of an identified group of individuals to which the school finance system should provide varying levels of resource distribution in direct proportion to an identified need; it also reflects the notion that "equal treatment is not always fair treatment." Examples: Special purpose revenues targeted as compensatory educational funding or targeted toward the accomplishment of an articulated educational goal; pupil weights that represent the additional educational expenditure required to reflect the cost of educating students with special educational needs.

c. *Fiscal neutrality* eliminates the systematic relationship between local property wealth and educational expenditures, typically, through the distribution of state equalization aid; also referred to as "equal opportunity" to reflect the notion that students served by the same state school system are secured an equal opportunity in education regardless of the neighborhood in which they happen to reside. Example: state aid that is distributed to school districts in inverse proportion to the local property wealth revenues raised for educational expenditure purposes.

Taken together, the key components and process of the standard school finance equity framework provide a starting point for understanding the equity status of different populations served (or not served) by the California school finance system.

The Critical Community Strength Framework— Components and Process

The critical policy analysis approach that is presented here draws from the theoretical and empirical work of Stein (2004), Valencia & Solórzano (1997), and Yosso (2005), each of whom has examined the over-reliance of educational policy and practice on cultural deficit explanations for poverty, "failing" schools, low academic achievement, and limited educational attainment. The development of this proposed framework is undertaken out of concern about the repeated cycle in school finance and accountability practices that rely upon stigmatized characterizations of low-income students and students of color in their explanations for their lack of academic achievement and success. By specifying the key components and processes of this critical framework, the potential also exists for engaging in more comprehensive analyses of the subtle, unquestioned power relations and underlying assumptions that serve to perpetuate social inequality within and beyond schools (Forester, 1993; Young, 1999).

The critical community strength framework that I propose in this exploratory work consists of five key components that emerge from the educational research undertaken by scholars employing both cultural and critical race theory (CRT) analyses of educational policy and practice, as well as the schooling experiences of low-income communities and children of color (Stein, 2004; Valencia & Solórzano, 1997; Yosso, 2005). This first attempt to articulate a critical policy analysis framework applicable to school finance is aimed at identifying an approach that can first build upon conventional treatments of school finance equity, and then shed light on taken-for-granted assumptions and new areas of inquiry to enhance our ability to address persistent disparities in both resources and outcomes in education. Of particular concern is the impact that current school finance policy formulations have (and do not have) upon the educational prospects of the diverse student populations who currently attend California's public schools. The five components of the framework are as follows:

1. Raising awareness of institutional bias within educational (finance) policy (Stein, 2004)
2. Raising awareness of the manifestations of cultural deficit thinking as it pertains to low-income children and children of color (Valencia & Solórzano, 1997)

3. Positioning communities of color and low-income communities at the center of school finance policy analysis to consider how policy impact might differ or shift (Yosso, 2005; Young, 1999)
4. Reframing cultural deficits by resisting the use of white, middle-class communities as the universal norm and recognizing the power of diverse histories, perspectives, worldviews, and experiences (Valencia, 1997; Yosso, 2005)
5. Questioning and dialogue to surface potential sources of cultural wealth or assets in service of facilitating high academic achievement and success among low-income students and students of color (Forester, 1993; Stein, 2004; Yosso, 2005)

Acknowledge Institutional Bias in Educational Policy The salience of institutional bias and cultural deficit thinking in educational policy is well documented in Stein's (2004) *The Culture of Education Policy*. Stein undertakes an analysis of congressional hearings and school community implementation activities related to the federal Elementary and Secondary Education Act (ESEA), which has undergone several reauthorizations between its inception in 1965 and the most recent No Child Left Behind Act of 2001. Stein's analysis is framed by her "Culture of Policy Conceptual Model" (p. 13) which asserts that the culture of educational policy positions government as a corrective agent for the variety of deficiencies that the beneficiaries of policy—in this case, low-income children and children of color—are thought to possess. Stein's model also posits that given the relationship that exists between the government and beneficiaries of policy, incentives are produced in the educational system to identify potential beneficiaries by their deficiencies and to perpetuate this status to secure access to the resources that flow in proportion to the deficiencies. Although Stein notes a difference in the language of "failing schools" that is embedded in NCLB, her analysis reveals that children affiliated with schools not meeting the (increasingly lower and narrower) educational expectations are nevertheless stigmatized. The fact remains that "failing schools" are typically those serving low-income children and children of color. Within the field of school finance, the level of awareness of institutional bias against low-income students or students of color is relatively minimal. In fact, quite similar to Stein's analysis of the proceedings to reauthorize the ESEA (focusing on Title I), the discourse typically reflects a well-intended, charitable response to the educational challenges of low-income students. Often subtle, the "helping" approach in policy obscures institutional bias that privileges the experiences and educational participation practices of white, middle-class children and their families (Pincus, 2000). As Wildman and Davis (2000) explain, "The normalization of privilege means that members of society are judged, and succeed or fail, measured against the characteristics that are held by those privileged. The privileged characteristic comes to define the norm" (p. 53). Thus, the first part of the process of applying a critical framework to school finance policy is to acknowledge and make explicit for others the institutional biases and norms upon which policy in this field is based.

Acknowledge Cultural Deficit Thinking in Educational Policy In the edited volume *The Evolution of Deficit Thinking: Educational Thought and Practice* (Valencia, 1997), the contributors painstakingly chronicle the history, development, manifestations, and impact of cultural deficit explanatory models and theories that are well established in the field of education. Over time, Valencia explains, the models have ranged in their disciplinary grounding, including genetics, cultural anthropology, psychology, and sociology, and have incorporated what he considers a "pseudoscience" meant to establish the intellectual and cultural superiority of white, middle-class individuals. What the models bear in common is their use as explanatory theories for the educational failure, underperformance, disengagement, and other negative outcomes ascribed to low-income students and students of color (Valencia 1997). In their examination of contemporary manifestations of cultural deficit thinking, Valencia and Solórzano (1997) also highlight the enduring influence of the myth of low-income parents of color as being non-participants in the education of their children—parents who neither value nor inculcate in their children an appreciation for learning and education. Similarly, they take up the popularized construct of "at risk" (pp. 195-198) and contend that this label is yet another term that represents cultural deficit thinking by emphasizing the individual student as the source of educational failure and neglecting to give attention to "how schools are institutionally implicated in ways that exclude students from learning.... The deficit model turns students into burdens and trades potential for risk" (p. 196).

Position Affected Communities at the Center of Policy Analysis Building on the preceding two components, the act of positioning communities of color at the center of policy analysis is a logical step in raising our awareness of biases and confronting limiting explanatory theories. To be clearer, such positioning is not merely determining the impact of policy as it is intended—or as it proceeds from institutional objectives.

Rather, as Forester (1993), Yosso (2005), and Young (1999) explain, this positioning (or re-positioning) involves analyzing the impact of policy from the perspective of the affected parties. In school finance policy analysis, this would require us to re-formulate questions about how to raise achievement *in spite* of high concentrations of students of color or low-income students in a school to instead focus on how learning and achievement are construed by communities of color—and how they view the investment of certain resources as either facilitating or hindering their progress in school and beyond. As Young (1999) explains, such a stance in policy analysis encourages researchers to generate new research questions by examining not only why and how the intended policy impact does not occur, but also how similar objectives embodied in the policy (in her case, the promotion of parental involvement) *are* being accomplished, but in ways that reflect the worldviews, problem solving, and sense making of the affected communities. In school finance, such an approach might enable us to see beyond the disappointing cycle of persistent outcomes disparities despite increases in funding to raise new questions about how the input/outcomes relationship is construed and acted upon by communities of color or low-income communities, thus leading to more responsive school finance policies and structures.

Reframe Cultural Deficit: Resist Universalized Norms and Recognize Diverse Perspectives and Experiences   In her article, "Whose culture has capital? A critical race theory discussion of community cultural wealth," Yosso (2005) provides an important reframing of the enduring "cultural deficit" explanations offered by many researchers and educators for the lack of academic success among children of color (and low-income communities; as indicated by Valencia, 1997). Yosso's reframing draws upon the extensive CRT literature—which embodies not only a recognition of institutional and structural racism,[2] but also the intersection of this form of subordination with the many forms of subordination that are enacted or that are embedded in American social institutions (for a more extensive examination of CRT perspectives, see Alemán, this volume) to instead consider the cultural "wealth" or "assets" that children of color do bring to the school setting. Drawing from CRT and incorporating the findings of Oliver and Shapiro's (1995) examination of the concept of "wealth" in the black community, Yosso identifies at least six forms of what she terms *community cultural wealth* that reflect many of the perspectives and experiences that combine to shape the lives of students of color. These forms of cultural wealth are seldom recognized as the strengths or skills available to overcome some of the challenges and obstacles these students encounter in their academic careers. Briefly listed, Yosso (1995) defines these assets as:

1. *Aspirational capital:* "the ability to maintain hopes and dreams for the future, even in the face of real and perceived barriers" (p. 77)
2. *Linguistic capital:* "the intellectual and social skills attained through communication experiences in more than one language and/or style" (p. 78)
3. *Familial capital:* "the cultural knowledges nurtured among [families] that carry a sense of community history, memory, and cultural intuition" (p. 79)
4. *Social capital*[3]: "networks of people and community resources ... [that] can provide both instrumental and emotional support to navigate through society's institutions" (p. 79)
5. *Navigational capital:* "the skills of maneuvering through social institutions [inferred historically as] maneuvering through social institutions not created with People of Color [*sic*] in mind" (p. 80)
6. *Resistance capital:* "knowledges and skills fostered through oppositional behavior that challenges inequality ... [including] maintaining and passing on the multiple dimensions of community cultural wealth" (p. 80)

Yosso's community cultural wealth model (2005) provides a means to begin pushing for new indicators reflecting the untapped potential of students of color and low-income students, thus enabling the analyses—including the discourse of our research and policy analysis questions—to surface prohibitive operating assumptions and counteracts cultural deficit thinking to envision improvements that are relevant and effective.

Question and Create Dialogue to Inform Policy Analysis In order to arrive at better formulations of a school finance policy that facilitates academic success among diverse communities, a crucial component of the critical community strength framework is to maintain a stance of inquiry to promote equity. Forester (1993) describes this activity as "questioning" (see pp. 48–53) to create interactions that serve our broader democratic purposes in policy analysis and development by ensuring that multiple perspectives are included and that critical analysis leads to positive social change. In the same spirit, Stein (2005) concludes her analysis by inviting educators, researchers, and analysts to consider the importance of critical dialogue to deconstruct the "culture of policy" while also situating one's experiences and biases to surface the ways in which those biases influence policy formulations. Finally, as Young (1999) argues, the incorporation of multiple frames confronts institutional biases and raises the rigor of our investigations as policy researchers in pursuit of such questions as how school finance policy can facilitate better results among diverse communities.

An Illustration of Possibilities Using Sample California School District Data

To explore the possibilities offered by the combined standard school finance equity and critical community strength frameworks,[4] this discussion considers a dataset consisting of 20 California unified school districts, which were selected to generally represent several major regions of the state covering nine counties. These data were obtained online from various sources linked to the California Department of Education (CDE).[5] The 20 districts (see Table 5.1) were specifically selected to reflect the large presence of Latina/o students in California's public school system, and they are distinguishable as school districts with high (30% or more) concentrations of Latina/o and low-income students. The idea is to use these data to push our creative thinking in the combined conventional/standard and critical policy analysis approaches to explore how we might (1) envision the full impact of school finance policy on diverse communities; and, (2) expand our ability to refrain from an over-reliance on stereotypes of cultural deficiency that influence decisions on resource distribution. Indeed, part of what both standard and critical frameworks rely upon is transparency in the values, value judgments, and perspectives that inform our choices for the distribution of resources to schools. Thus, one objective in this illustrative process is to begin to surface flawed or unquestioned assumptions about school communities with large concentrations of Latina/o students. As noted in the preceding discussion, the over-reliance on unquestioned deficit-centered explanations has led to obstructed views of the full scope of policy options available to us to invest resources in ways that transform dollars into positive outcomes.

Table 5.1 provides a listing of the 20 unified districts by county, including the state capital, Sacramento County; Alameda, Contra Costa, and Santa Clara Counties in the greater San Francisco Bay Area; Fresno and Tulare Counties in the state's Central/San Joaquin Valley; Los Angeles and Orange Counties to the south; and, farther south, San Diego County, near the California/Mexico border. The concentrations of Latina/o students for 2005–2006 range from 30.3% (Santa Clara;

Table 5.1 Twenty California Unified School Districts with High Concentrations of Latina/o Students by County, Academic Performance Index (API), and Revenues per Student in Average Daily Attendance (ADA), 2004–2005

County	Unified School District	% Latina/o Students	API Score for District	Revenue Limit per Student (ADA)	Total Revenues per Student (ADA)
Alameda	Hayward	51.0	675	$5,070	$7,612
	Oakland	35.0	634	$5,319	$9,871
	San Lorenzo	44.1	674	$5,022	$7,166
Contra Costa	West Contra Costa	40.3	655	$5,150	$8,584
Fresno	Central	44.6	707	$4,901	$6,745
	Fresno	56.5	644	$4,926	$8,147
	Kings Canyon Joint	81.7	663	$4,895	$7,524
Los Angeles	Compton	72.3	592	$5,002	$8,152
	Long Beach	50.1	713	$4,825	$7,503
	Los Angeles	73.2	649	$4,862	$8,790
Orange	Santa Ana	91.9	656	$5,070	$8,019
Sacramento	Sacramento City	31.2	700	$4,997	$7,569
San Diego	Oceanside	52.3	728	$5,049	$7,638
	San Diego	43.5	728	$5,257	$8,899
	Vista	49.4	712	$5,130	$7,630
Santa Clara	Gilroy	67.0	710	$5,027	$7,196
	San José	50.6	737	$5,110	$8,271
	Santa Clara	30.3	741	$5,250	$7,308
Tulare	Porterville	63.6	657	$5,464	$7,955
	Visalia	54.3	683	$4,876	$7,062
State Figures		47.6	709	$4,927	$7,569

Sources: California Department of Education, 2006

Notes: Unified school districts are comprised of elementary, middle, and high schools. "High concentration" for purposes of this table is defined as districts with 30% or greater proportion of Latina/o students enrolled. The term *Latina/o* is use in place of the CDE's term *Hispanic or Latino*. API scores range from 200 to 1000. District revenue limit amounts represent "basic funding" as established by legislative action and are funded primarily by local property taxes and state aid; Total revenues are comprised of each district's revenue limit, combined with state categorical (special purpose) funding, federal funding, and other local revenues. ADA is defined by the CDE as the "total days of student attendance divided by the total days of instruction" with restrictions specified in statute. Information for percentage of Latina/o students is reported for 2005–2006, the most recently available demographic data. All other information is reported for 2004–2005, the most recently available API and financial data.

Santa Clara County) to 91.9% (Santa Ana; Orange County). For the same year, the three districts with the lowest enrollments (see Table 5.2) include Kings Canyon Joint (9,235), Gilroy (9,961), and San Lorenzo (11,613). Among the highest enrollments are Los Angeles (727,319), San Diego (132,482), Long Beach (93,589), and Fresno (79,046). It is striking to see that the Los Angeles Unified School District—second in size only to New York City's public school system—is both the largest district in California and has a concentration of Latina/o students of 73.2% (see Table 5.2).

To facilitate a more systematic exploration of the use of the standard and critical frameworks, Table 5.3 encapsulates the key questions to be considered in our illustrative analysis. These include the four questions that make up the standard school finance equity framework, as well as the three equity principles embedded in it (Berne & Stiefel, 1984; Odden & Picus, 2004). Sample indicators are reiterated in accordance with each question and principle. Likewise, key questions emerging from the five elements of the critical community strength framework are presented, along with some proposed sample indicators that would align with the framework's elements.

Discussion of Illustrative Analysis Using Standard and Critical Frameworks

Using the standard school finance equity framework questions, concepts, and indicators provides an important starting point for considering the extent to which California's school finance policy reflect equitable distributions of resources to support student academic success. As noted in the contextual discussion regarding the equity standards established in *Serrano II*, the data in Table 5.1 reflect a distribution of the revenue limit (basic aid) per ADA that falls within the allowable disparity (adjusted for inflation) of $350 among the sample districts. According to Picus (2006), all of the unified districts in this sample are considered to be "large" districts and thus comparable to each other for *Serrano II*–mandated equity purposes. Conceptually speaking, this "allowable" disparity satisfies both the horizontal equity consideration and the fiscal neutrality principle by distributing revenues in ways that reduce variations otherwise produced by reliance on local property wealth alone.

A brief examination of the total revenues per ADA, which includes the revenue limit plus the additional allocations of federal and state special/categorical funds, reveals a much less clear picture of whether the vertical equity principle is satisfied. In fact, given the concentrations of

Table 5.2 Twenty California Unified School Districts with High Concentrations of Latina/o Students by County and Selected Characteristics, 2005–2006

County	Unified School District	Enrollment	% Latina/o	% English Learners	% Fluent English Proficient	% Graduates with UC/CSU Courses Completed	% Fully Credentialed Teachers	% Eligible Free/ Reduced Price Meals
Alameda	Hayward	22,236	51.0	34.5	25.9	36.2	98.0	56.5*
	Oakland	48,135	35.0	28.4	17.3	28.5	86.9	66.9
	San Lorenzo	11,613	44.1	26.8	19.7	34.0	96.1	39.0
Contra Costa	West Contra Costa	32,197	40.3	30.8	17.0	14.0	90.6	58.5
Fresno	Central	12,713	44.6	17.2	13.6	30.6	95.7	46.8
	Fresno	79,046	56.5	28.3	14.9	34.9	97.6	82.1
	Kings Canyon Joint	9,235	81.7	48.3	10.2	19.3	93.2	65.8
Los Angeles	Compton	30,233	72.3	54.0	12.6	22.5	74.6	95.2
	Long Beach	93,589	50.1	23.6	24.3	35.3	94.0	68.5
	Los Angeles	727,319	73.2	40.4	27.0	47.5	91.0	79.8
Orange	Santa Ana	59,310	91.9	55.8	29.0	22.6	97.1	74.1
Sacramento	Sacramento City	50,408	31.2	28.8	9.8	35.4	92.7	65.5

continued on next page

Table 5.2 (continued) Twenty California Unified School Districts with High Concentrations of Latina/o Students by County and Selected Characteristics, 2005–2006

County	Unified School District	Enrollment	% Latina/o	% English Learners	% Fluent English Proficient	% Graduates with UC/CSU Courses Completed	% Fully Credentialed Teachers	% Eligible Free/ Reduced Price Meals
San Diego	Oceanside	21,367	52.3	26.2	17.0	29.6	93.1	50.0
	San Diego	132,482	43.5	28.0	24.9	39.5	90.9	61.3
	Vista	26,207	49.4	25.7	13.5	19.0	97.3	40.1
Santa Clara	Gilroy	9,961	67.0	28.6	12.8	26.7	92.6	51.2
	San José	31,646	50.6	25.3	21.9	65.7	94.4	42.3
	Santa Clara	14,129	30.3	26.0	19.0	35.5	97.5	46.5
Tulare	Porterville	13,373	63.6	19.0	28.6	14.8	97.7	77.1
	Visalia	26,105	54.3	19.9	14.1	28.3	98.4	52.4
State Totals		6,312,103	47.6	24.9	17.6	35.2	94.2	50.8

Source: California Department of Education, 2006.

Notes: Unified school districts are comprised of elementary, middle, and high schools. "High concentration" for purposes of this table is defined as districts with 30% or greater proportion of Latina/o students enrolled. The term Latina/o is used in place of the CDE's term Hispanic or Latino. Percentage of graduates with complete UC/CSU–required courses was calculated by the author using number of graduates with completed UC/CSU courses divided by number of graduates, multiplied by 100. Graduate figures are reported by the CDE for the prior year in this report. Free/reduced-price meals figure unavailable for 2005–2006; a comparable figure for 2004–2005 was used.

Latina/o students and indicators of particular educational needs, such as the percentages of English-language learners presented in Table 5.2, the levels of total revenues per ADA do not follow a discernible pattern. These data begin to confirm the assertions that Timar (2004) has made regarding the lack of transparency, accountability, and relationship with student need that is pervasive among California's categorical (special funds) programs.

The starting point for exploring the use of the critical community strength framework is to consider momentarily that the 20 districts presented in Tables 5.1 and 5.2 match the typical depiction of high concentrations of students of color and low-income students, as well as relatively low standardized achievement levels, reflected in API scores of less than 750 out of 1000. These data certainly make it easy for the analyst to rely upon the readily available explanations of low achievement despite relatively equalized basic funding; indeed, it does require a significant shift in practice to engage in locating evidence of community/student strengths upon which to build to overcome academic challenges. (For another model of this approach in teacher practice, see González, Moll, & Amanti, 2005).

If we apply the components encompassed in this critical community strength framework, we can begin to speculate about the strengths or assets that exist among the students and communities that are represented in the sample districts. This exploration is not meant to be a quixotic exercise that serves only to gloss over the challenges that truly exist for districts, such as these, that do encounter real (not just perceived) shortages of financial and human resources to meet their students' needs. (Indeed, one need only refer to the data presented for the Compton Unified School District, which appears to be sorely underresourced in terms of access to credentialed teachers and extremely high percentages of low-income students, as indicated by 95% eligibility for free/reduced-price meals). Rather, the framework helps to surface areas of real (not just perceived) strengths that communities of color or low-income communities can utilize to further maximize the available resources and thus garner additional resources and opportunities for advancing more equitable educational outcomes.

To continue this exploration, the critical framework enables us to appreciate the consideration of level of analysis: institutional bias and reliance on cultural deficit explanatory models may take on different forms at the state level than at the district or school levels. Likewise, in the spirit of promoting dialogue, questioning (Forester, 1993), and participatory inquiry, the proposed sample indicators of the six types

Table 5.3 Summary of Key Questions, Guiding Principles, and Sample Indicators for Standard School Finance Equity and Critical Community Strength Frameworks

Framework	Key Questions	Conceptual Focus and Definitions	Operational Focus and Definitions (Sample Indicators)
Standard School Finance Equity	1. Equity for whom?	Students, taxpayers	Individual students, school enrollments, district ADA
	2. What equity object?	Resources/inputs [or outcomes] distributed among focal constituents	Inputs: total revenues, special purpose revenues, teachers Outputs: graduation rates, college-preparatory course completion (used less often)
	3. Determined by what guiding principles?		
	a. Horizontal Equity	Equal treatment of equals	Equal revenues per pupil; flat grants
	b. Vertical Equity	Differential treatment according to need or additional investment required to obtain comparable benefit from the same school system	Special purpose funding distributed proportionately to eligible/targeted populations; categorical grants
	c. Fiscal Neutrality ("Equal Opportunity")	No systematic relationship between local property wealth and educational expenditures	State aid distributed to districts in inverse proportion to local property tax revenues
	4. Assessed by what measures?	Statistical measures of the distributional patterns revealed by applying the guiding principles and reflecting normative standards for equitable distributions	Depending upon guiding principle employed, can include: correlation coefficient, indexes measuring distributions above or below the median resource level (see also Odden & Picus, 2004)

Critical Community Strength	1. What institutional biases exist in the school finance policy?	Terminology, location of power or authority, organizational structures that reflect unconscious or unquestioned assumptions undergirding or otherwise embedded in the policy	Examination of school finance policy substance and processes to determine: patterns of public and professional participation/exclusion; transparency of content or structures; patterns of prioritization/ marginalization of constituents by need, region, district type, property wealth or other class status, voting patterns, race
	2. Are there manifestations of cultural deficit thinking in the school finance policy?	Terminology, explanatory statements, rationales in the school finance policy that emphasize only or primarily the perceived deficiencies represented among affected students/ communities; distribution of resources linked primarily to perceived deficiencies embodied in various educational outcome patterns	Examination of government and media reports, district and school documents, and records of public proceedings to identify patterns of language and/or treatment that reflect primarily the perceived deficiencies of students Examination of special funding or program eligibility criteria and participation patterns to determine level of emphasis on perceived deficiencies
	3. How does perceived impact/assessment of the school finance policy shift when constituents' perspectives on the policy are placed at the center?	Assessment of policy impact is conducted in partnership with communities of color and/or low-income communities utilizing a variety of methods (case studies, ethnography, participatory action research, focus groups, participant observation) to surface community perspectives, expectations, and goals relative to school finance policy	Evidence (news reports, newsletters, records of organized community action, etc.) of actions taken by community members or groups to access resources perceived to be facilitative of community educational goals Evidence (as above) of actions taken by community members or groups to counteract/resist policy impact perceived to hinder community educational goals

continued on next page

Table 5.3 (continued) Summary of Key Questions, Guiding Principles, and Sample Indicators for Standard School Finance Equity and Critical Community Strength Frameworks

Framework	Key Questions	Conceptual Focus and Definitions	Operational Focus and Definitions (Sample Indicators)
	4. What is the cultural wealth represented among the students/communities affected by the school finance policy?		
	a. Aspirational capital	Ability to maintain hopes and dreams in the face of real or perceived barriers	Participation in college-preparatory programs or coursework; evidence of academic goal-setting; participation in extra-curricular programs reflecting academic and nonacademic interests and talents
	b. Linguistic capital	Intellectual and social skills attained through community experiences in more than one language and/or style	Percentages of English learners; percentages of bilingual or multilingual students; participation in extracurricular activities focused on language use, e.g. debate, spoken word, rap, etc.
	c. Familial capital	Cultural knowledge nurtured among families that carry sense of community history, memory, cultural intuition	Evidence of sibling participation in similar academic/nonacademic activities Evidence of student/family participation in neighborhood social institutions (e.g. churches, community centers); Presence of cultural heritage centers in school district or communities and evidence of participation

d. Social capital	Networks of people/community resources that provide both instrumental and emotional support to navigate society's institutions	In addition to the above indicators of familial capital, evidence of mentoring relationships among teachers/school leaders and students Patterns of participation in college-preparatory programs/services; Record of school/district alumni currently attending colleges that serve as formal and informal conduits of information and support for siblings, younger students, e.g. peer tutoring, peer counseling.
e. Navigational capital	Skills of maneuvering through social institutions, historically inferred as those not created with people of color in mind	In addition to the indicators of linguistic capital, evidence of students taking responsibility at home for assisting parents with English translations in meetings with school officials or other social service providers; In addition to the indicators of aspirational capital, evidence of participation in "mainstream" organizations or learning environments with relatively low representations of students of color or low-income students, e.g. (in some schools) student government

continued on next page

Table 5.3 (continued) Summary of Key Questions, Guiding Principles, and Sample Indicators for Standard School Finance Equity and Critical Community Strength Frameworks

Framework	Key Questions	Conceptual Focus and Definitions	Operational Focus and Definitions (Sample Indicators)
	f. Resistance capital	Knowledge/skills fostered through oppositional behavior that challenges inequality, including maintaining/passing on community cultural wealth	Assessment of community access to data regarding patterns of schooling outcomes among students by race, gender, class, physical limitations, sexual orientation, and other characteristicsIn addition to nearly all other forms of cultural capital listed, evidence of participation in community organizing activities; student leadership activities; parental and community leadership focused on educational (e.g., representatives on school bilingual education advisory committees) or broader community needs/demands; patterns of representation of community interests during regular, daily school activities; evidence of community accountability mechanisms beyond standard state- or school district–centered accountability

of community cultural wealth are likely to be better determined at the school level than at the state level. Examining these sample districts briefly, one can identify possible evidence of linguistic capital (percentages of English-language learners and fluent English proficient students indicate the potential for bilingualism); aspirational capital (some of the districts have both high concentrations of Latina/o students and are at or above state average rates of University of California/California State University required course completion), which could be a foundation upon which to build a college-going culture within these districts. This exploration of potential cultural capital indicators also begins to surface new (and hopefully more productive) questions that can help shape better policy guiding the investment of financial and non-financial resources. Certainly, the high percentage of credentialed teachers among most of these districts is both a strength and an important area of inquiry regarding how well matched the teachers are for the types of diverse communities in which they teach. Readers are encouraged to continue their own speculation and questioning, as these data are meant to inspire new possibilities and resistance to the "easy answer" of cultural deficits and community deficiencies for why educational results across California schools do not reflect our professed commitment to equity and excellence.

CONCLUSION: A REFLECTION ON THE INTERESTS SERVED, PRACTICALITIES, AND DILEMMAS OF COMBINED STANDARD AND CRITICAL POLICY ANALYSIS IN SCHOOL FINANCE

On the Practicality of Multifocal Policy Analysis in School Finance

A guiding premise of the standard equity framework in school finance is to make explicit the values by which we as a society determine the focus of our distribution of funding to schools (Berne & Stiefel, 1984). Within critical frameworks, a guiding premise is to use systematic analysis to illuminate and eradicate the oppressive elements of our social institutions, which includes making a conscious effort to rid ourselves of the elements of institutionalized racism and other biases that continue to weaken our educational systems in their ability to be responsive to students of all backgrounds. Knowing what we know about the impact of cultural deficit thinking in education, how can we, in school finance, not engage in more complex analyses that enable us to see the flaws in even our most well-intentioned attempts to support and encourage certain educational activities and achievements?

An Emerging Dilemma: When Dollars are Linked to Perceived Cultural Deficits

In truth, we may find a less-than-eager audience of school finance colleagues ready to engage in multifocal policy analysis (Young, 1999) to expand our understanding of the impact and limitations of educational policy that is otherwise portrayed as racially and class neutral. We nevertheless seem to share with many scholars a frustration about the continually unsatisfactory educational outcomes experienced by many of our public school students. However, as Stein (2004) and Valencia and Solórzano (1997) illustrate, the interests served by perpetuating a cycle of resources tied to deficit-centered analyses do not reflect our espoused interests in using education as a means to counteract social inequality. Nevertheless, the challenge to conventional systems that rely upon the dollars/deficits relationships implies the need for reasonable approaches that prevent a sense of powerlessness among school communities in the face of such dilemmas. To the degree that, in this case, California's future hinges on both the strengths and challenges of our diverse student populations, it behooves us minimally to seek out analytical methods that inform us about the policy levers that appropriately facilitate the recognition, development, and utilization of community assets (i.e. cultural wealth, as described by Yosso, 2005 or funds of knowledge, as theorized by González, et al., 2003) to get us closer to our shared democratic goals of self-determination, full participation, and positive contributions to California and society at large.

NOTES

The author wishes to thank Daniel Solórzano (University of California–Los Angeles) for his guidance and suggestions throughout the inception of this chapter, and Tara J. Yosso (University of California–Santa Barbara), and Julie López Figueroa (California State University–Sacramento) for their invaluable input during the completion of this chapter.

1. It is striking to consider qualitative research as "traditional," given that qualitative research is minimally represented in the field of school finance. Yet it is becoming increasingly featured as part of the recent adequacy studies involving "professional judgment panels" and case study methods used by scholars such as Chambers, Parrish, Picus, and Odden, among others.

2. Pincus (2000) distinguishes among three forms of discrimination—individual, institutional, and structural—to explicate the functioning of these phenomena in society. According to Pincus, institutional discrimination (racism, in this use) would involve institutional practices that reinforce the exclusion and subordination of groups or individuals based on race, e.g. through unwritten but still enacted hiring practices. Structural discrimination/racism is more subtle, in that one must turn to patterns of systematic impact that grow out of practices and policies that are presented as neutral but which reflect a legacy of institutional discrimination and differential patterns of historical participation (e.g. banks' lending practices, segregated neighborhoods, etc.). These definitions help us to understand that when we hear the term racism we often first (or only) think of overt, individual acts of racial discrimination versus the institutional and structural forms of racism that permeate our social institutions in the United States.
3. Yosso (2005) acknowledges the extensive literature on this single concept, but she emphasizes the definitions and interpretations utilized by scholars such as Stanton-Salazar and Valenzuela.
4. Unified school districts operate elementary, middle, and high schools.
5. Indeed, several scholars have noted the challenge of conducting school finance research in California because the pertinent data are scattered across a number of databases; however, efforts have been underway for some time to begin to integrate these sources and also make them more widely and readily available to researchers and the public.

REFERENCES

Berne, R., & Stiefel, L. (1984). *The measurement of equity in school finance: Conceptual, methodological, and empirical dimensions.* Baltimore: Johns Hopkins University Press.

Betts, J. R., Reuben, K. S., & Danenberg, A. (2000). *Equal resources, equal outcomes? The distribution of school resources and student achievement in California.* San Francisco: Public Policy Institute of California.

Darling-Hammond, L. (2002). *Redesigning schools: What matters and what works.* Stanford, CA: Stanford University School Redesign Network.

Darling-Hammond, L. (2004). Inequality and the right to learn: Access to qualified teachers in California's public schools. *Teachers College Record, 106*(10), 1936–1966.

California Department of Education. (2005). *Selected county level data—Alameda, Contra Costa, Fresno, Los Angeles, Orange, Sacramento, San Diego, Santa Clara, Tulare—for the year 2004–05. Educational Demographics Unit.* Retrieved August 30, 2006, from http://data1.cde.ca.gov/dataquest.

California Department of Education. (2006). *Selected county level data—Alameda, Contra Costa, Fresno, Los Angeles, Orange, Sacramento, San Diego, Santa Clara, Tulare—for the year 2005–06. Educational Demographics Unit.* Retrieved July 6, 2006, from http://data1.cde.ca.gov/dataquest.

Decent Schools of California. (2005). *Papers filed with the court.* Retrieved May 1, 2006, from http://www.decentschools.org/.

Ed-Data. (2006). State-level and school district financial reports for 2004–2006. Educational Data Partnerships. Retrieved August 30, 2006, from http://ed-data.k12.ca.us.

EdSource. (2004). *Resource cards on California schools.* Retrieved August 5, 2006 from http://www.edsource.org.

Forester, J. (1993). *Critical theory, public policy, and planning practice: Toward a critical pragmatism.* Albany: State University of New York Press.

Goldfinger, P. M. (2006). *Revenues and revenue limits: A guide to school finance in California* (2006 ed.). Sacramento: School Services of California.

Goldfinger, P. M., & Blattner, B. (2005). *Revenues and revenue limits: A guide to school finance in California* (2005 ed.). Sacramento, CA: School Services of California.

González, N., Moll, L. C., & Amanti, C. (2005). *Funds of knowledge: Theorizing practices in households, communities, and classrooms.* Mahwah, NJ: Lawrence Erlbaum Associates.

Koski, W. S., & Weis, H. A. (October 2004). What educational resources do students need to meet California's educational content standards? A textual analysis of California's educational context standards and their implications for basic educational conditions and resources. *Teachers College Record, 106*(10), 1907–1935.

Legislative Analyst's Office (LAO). (2005). *Analysis of the 2005–06 budget: Education.* Sacramento: Author.

Minorini, P. A., & Sugarman, S. D. (1999). School finance litigation in the name of educational equity: Its evolution, impact, and future. In H. F. Ladd, R. Chalk, & J. S. Hansen (Eds.), *Equity and adequacy in education finance: Issues and perspectives* (pp. 34–71). Washington, DC: National Academy Press.

Oakes, J., & Saunders, M. (2004). Education's most basic tools: Access to textbooks and instructional materials in California's public schools. *Teachers College Record, 106*(10), 1967–1988.

Odden, A. R., & Picus, L. O. (2004). *School finance: A policy perspective* (3rd ed.). New York: McGraw-Hill.

Picus, L. O. (2005, October. *Funding California's schools: How do we assure an adequate education for all?* Paper prepared for the Policy Analysis for California Education legislative briefing, Sacramento, CA.

Picus, L. O. (2006, March). *Funding California's schools: Past, present, and future?* Paper prepared for the annual meeting of the American Education Finance Association, Denver, CO.

Pincus, F. L. (2000). Discrimination comes in many forms: Individual, institutional, and structural. In M. A. Adams, W. J. Blumenfeld, R. Castañeda, H. W. Hackman, M. L. Peters, & X. Zuñiga (Eds.), *Readings for diversity and social justice: An anthology on racism, antisemitism, sexism, heterosexism, ableism, and classism* (pp. 31–35). New York: Routledge.

Rumberger, R. W., & Gándara, P. (2004). Seeking equity in the education of California's English learners. *Teachers College Record, 106*(10), 2032–2056.

Serrano v. Priest, 5 Cal.3d 584 (1971). (*Serrano I*)

Serrano v. Priest, 18 Cal.3d 728 (1976). (*Serrano II*)

Serrano v. Priest, 20 Cal.3d 25 (1977). (*Serrano III*)

Stein, S. J. (2004). *The culture of education policy.* New York: Teachers College Press.

Timar, T. B. (2004). *Categorical school finance: Who gains, who loses?* Working Paper Series 04-2. Berkeley, CA: Policy Analysis for California Education.

Valencia, R. R. (Ed). (1997). *The evolution of deficit thinking: Educational thought and practice.* Stanford Series on Education and Public Policy. London: Falmer Press.

Valencia, R. R., & Solórzano, D. G. (1997). Contemporary deficit thinking. In R. R. Valencia (Ed.), *The evolution of deficit thinking: Educational thought and practice* (pp. 160–210). Stanford Series on Education and Public Policy. London: Falmer Press.

Valencia, R. R., Villarreal, B. J., & Salinas, M. F. (2002). Educational testing and Chicano students: Issues, consequences, and prospects for reform. In R. R. Valencia (Ed.), *Chicano school failure and success: Past, present, and future* (2nd ed., pp. 253–309). London: Routledge-Falmer.

Wildman, S. M. & Davis, A. D. (2000). Language and silence: Making systems of privilege visible. In M. A. Adams, W. J. Blumenfeld, R. Castañeda, H. W. Hackman, M. L. Peters, & X. Zuñiga (Eds.), *Readings for diversity and social justice: An anthology on racism, antisemitism, sexism, heterosexism, ableism, and classism* (pp. 50–60). New York: Routledge.

Yosso, T. J. (2005). Whose culture has capital? A critical race theory discussion of community cultural wealth. *Race, Ethnicity and Education, 8*(2), 69–91.

Young, M. (1999). Multifocal educational policy research: Toward a method of enhancing traditional educational policy studies. *American Educational Research Journal, 36*(4), 677–714.

6

THE RESOURCE IMPLICATIONS OF NCLB FOR THE RECRUITMENT, PREPARATION, AND RETENTION OF HIGHLY QUALIFIED TEACHERS FOR ENGLISH LEARNERS IN CALIFORNIA

Sarah A. Gonzales

California State University–East Bay

James L. Rodriguez

San Diego State University

EDUCATIONAL ACCOUNTABILITY HAS BEEN, and continues to be, the focus of political and educational reform efforts across the nation; and, this effort is reflected in federal and state policies that influence improvement efforts in public schools. The most recent and prominent national accountability reform effort is the No Child Left Behind (NCLB) Act of 2001. NCLB embodies four principles of President George W. Bush's educational reform plan: (1) stronger accountability as determined by data-driven results; (2) expanded flexibility and increased local control of resources; (3) additional options for parents; and (4) an emphasis on empirically tested teaching methods (No Child Left Behind, 2002). This last principle led to the attempt of placing highly qualified teachers in every classroom by 2005 through greater flexibility in federal spending on hiring new teachers, increasing teacher pay, and improving teacher development. In addition, the call for empirically tested teaching methods in NCLB was supposed to address the quality of programs for

English learners (referred to in the law as limited English proficient, or LEP students). NCLB did not define specific methodology for teaching English to immigrant students other than to stipulate that LEP students must be taught using "effective methods" as defined by scientifically based methods. The law also requires that teachers who work with English learners be fluent in English and any other language used in the English learning (EL) program.[1] However, NCLB does not provide resources to conduct specific research on effective methodologies for EL students and does not specify criteria to determine what constitutes a "highly qualified" teacher for EL students.

Furthermore, the concerns with NCLB for EL students in the California educational context are significant given the student demographics in the state. According to the California Department of Education (CDE), one of every four students in the state is an EL student, and in grades K–1, one-third of all children are EL students. While Spanish is by far the most common native language spoken by California's EL students, over 65 languages are represented in public schools statewide (California Department of Education, 2006).

An analysis of ethnic and linguistic diversity in California schools shows that between the years 1985 and 1995, the number of English learners grew 141%, with Spanish speakers representing over 78% of all EL students (California Department of Education Superintendent's Hispanic Advisory Task Force, 1997). A decade later, state statistics for 2004–2005 indicate that Spanish speakers now comprise 85% of the total EL population in California (CDE, 2006). Much to the dismay of both educators and Latino/a community advocates, California's Spanish-speaking EL students consistently post low academic achievement scores and high dropout rates (García & Wiese, 2002; Olsen & Jaramillo, 1999; Rumberger & Rodriguez, 2002; SHATF, 1997). As the number of EL students has increased steadily, the percentage of students in classrooms with a bilingual teacher has decreased, and EL students increasingly are placed in English-dominant classroom settings. According to the CDE, of the 1.6 million EL students in California, 47% are enrolled in "structured English immersion" settings,[2] and 39% are enrolled in an "English language mainstream class" for students meeting district-specified criteria for a "good working knowledge" of English (CDE, 2006).[3]

In some cases, extremely high levels of linguistic diversity exist within individual school districts if not within individual schools. As this demographic picture of California takes shape, current educational policy discussions in the state continue to focus on ensuring high student achievement, supporting quality teacher preparation, and allocating school funds to promote positive outcomes, driven primarily by the requirements of NCLB. Curiously, amid all these discussions, EL students and the implications of their growing presence are conspicuously missing.

With this magnitude of growth comes the demand for teachers who are well prepared to meet the academic and linguistic needs of EL students. Clearly, the research indicates that the quality of teaching, especially with EL students, is critical (Rumberger & Gándara, 2004). The literature also reveals that there exists a great shortage of teachers with the special skills to teach this ever-growing population—as indicated by the percentage of EL students exceeding the percentage of teachers with specialized training for teaching linguistically diverse student populations threefold. Flores and Clark (1997) assert that specialized training is essential for the academic success of EL students, noting, "The limitations of existing pedagogical training for bilingual populations, along with the increasing failure of language minority children, further support the need for the recruiting and retaining of prospective minority/bilingual teachers" (p. 337).

When viewed through a social justice frame that centers on educational equity, it becomes impossible to ignore the unique needs of EL students in California. Through this lens, the issues related to the resource implications of recruiting, preparing, and retaining highly qualified teachers for EL students that are examined in this chapter are:

1. The resources that are necessary to prepare and retain high-quality teachers in research-based programs for EL students
2. The common description of highly qualified teachers under NCLB and beyond
3. The social justice benefits of targeting human resources efforts on recruiting and retaining high-quality teachers for EL students
4. The implications of this policy with regard to the attainment of social justice and educational equity in the instruction of EL students and their teachers

This chapter attempts to capture, define, and discuss the resources required to provide high-quality instruction for EL students. In order to further advance our effort, the chapter will focus on the dynamics in California related to resource issues for the recruitment, preparation, and retention of highly qualified teachers for EL students. In addition, we will address the significant gap between the resources needed and available to ensure effective, high-quality education for all students and, more specifically, for EL students.

A BROADER DEFINITION OF RESOURCES
TO SUPPORT ENGLISH LEARNERS

A broader definition of educational resources is used in this chapter to take into account the nonfinancial resources, including time and decision making power, that are critical in supporting the teaching and learning activities that are best suited to promote equitable outcomes for EL students. For example, a common concern among educators is the availability of time to co-construct new curricula, instructional approaches, and staffing arrangements (Gándara, 2000). Similarly, school communities with a vision for supporting EL students in a more culturally responsive and relevant manner might seek to integrate the richness of their neighborhood resources into the schools' activities.

Even within the confines of the school itself, the reality that the majority of public funds must be spent on personnel means that personnel decisions become some of the highest leverage activities for enacting high-quality EL teaching and learning. Who the teachers are, how they and other staff work together, and the relationships built through shared professional learning experiences all require a careful allocation of the school resources available—both financial and (perhaps more important) nonfinancial. Of course, this view does not preclude attention toward the reallocation of additional funding to support innovative and visionary EL services. On the contrary, our use of a broader definition of the term *resources* suggests that we not overlook the opportunities to change the nature of the schooling arrangements to serve linguistically diverse students, and in this process, discover innovations that position our schools to maximize the possibilities afforded by any additional funding (Odden, Archibald, Ferminich, & Gross, 2003; Parrish, 1994).

A THEORETICAL FRAMEWORK OF EDUCATIONAL
RESPONSIVENESS TO EL STUDENT NEEDS:
LINKING SCHOOL RESOURCES TO BEST PRACTICES

The theoretical framework guiding this chapter draws on the scholarship that conceptualizes "responsiveness" in education. Within the field of school finance, Berne and Stiefel (1984) have introduced the concept of *vertical equity*, which we view as a useful way to see responsiveness in terms of resource allocation. Specifically, *vertical equity* refers to the differential investment of resources to address (or respond to) the differential needs that exist among student populations to enable them to benefit comparably from the same school system. In practice, such allocations may involve extra resources allocated for particular instructional purposes—in our case, to support high quality EL instruction. Or, such allocations may involve targeted investments to accomplish a particular educational goal, such as ensuring that all EL students acquire proficiency in English while maintaining their native language skills.

This chapter is further framed by the view that educational responsiveness is enacted in the professional practices of teachers who are attuned to and engaged with the cultural, social, and linguistic diversity of their students to promote learning and high achievement (García, 2001; Ladson-Billings, 1994). That is, in the examples we have available where low-income children and children of color are able to perform well academically in public schools, considerable investments in meaningful professional development and collegial relationships have been undertaken to ensure such improvements (Darling-Hammond & Snyder, 2003; Delpit, 1995; Miles & Darling-Hammond, 1998). For schools populated by large or growing numbers of EL students, one is likely to encounter a variety of staff needs (e.g., adjustments in pedagogy, capacity building for collaborative work, improved skills in identifying and addressing varying learning styles, training in EL instructional methods, and so forth) that require both financial and nonfinancial resource investment for schools to be truly educationally responsive. Thus, an application of this framework implies that we view the schools' attempts to meet the needs of EL students and the preparation of their teachers through the lens of educational responsiveness, which might be manifested by resource allocation aligned with student needs; resource allocation aligned with staff needs; and/or resource implications revealed by the use of particular "best practices" in classrooms demonstrating high levels of success in meeting their EL students' and staff needs.

SCHOOL FINANCE AND ENGLISH LEARNER SUPPORT: THE CALIFORNIA CONTEXT

The school finance context in California presents several important dynamics for exploring teacher quality and programs to meet the needs of linguistically diverse students. First, California continues to rank among the top in terms of student diversity and near the bottom in terms of basic per-pupil expenditures in education (EdSource, 2004; Goldfinger & Blattner, 2005; Rodriguez, this volume). A wide variety of special or "categorical" funds are made available beyond basic expenditures to address multiple, often equity-related concerns. Nevertheless, California does not have a mechanism in place to ensure that the additional special dollars will flow to the associated needs represented among its districts to ensure equitable educational opportunities and outcomes (Picus & Wattenbarger, 1995; Timar, 1994).

A second and related dynamic discussed by the California Legislative Analyst's Office (2005) is that nearly 40% of California's school districts are experiencing enrollment declines of a magnitude that will continue to result in school closures and discontinuation of certain special programs. However, even in districts with declining enrollments, the proportion of EL students continues to increase. Declining enrollments lead directly to reductions in basic educational funding for the affected districts, many of which are in larger, urban communities with the most linguistically diverse student populations. Many of the remaining school districts experiencing large increases in enrollments, largely rural and suburban, are also located in areas that have high or increasing concentrations of Latino/a and Spanish-speaking populations. However, despite the additional basic funding flowing to districts with increases in student enrollments, the current funding mechanisms in California are not likely to render sufficient special funds to support the increased language needs represented by higher concentrations of EL students in those districts.

A third contextual dynamic is reflected in the persistent mismatch between the articulation of best practices via the research on bilingual education and language acquisition, among other areas, and the anti-immigrant climate that has resurfaced repeatedly in recent years. Many of California's higher education institutions have made significant contributions to the scholarship and policy approaches used in contemporary bilingual education circles. Yet, changes in the state's policy environment over the last two decades alone have thwarted the efforts to ensure that immigrant children are able to access high quality learning opportunities and support for English language acquisition. Moreover, unlike other states with large immigrant populations, California specifically earmarks limited categorical funds for EL support through its basic funding formula with few categorical programs designated for districts with high concentrations of *either* EL students *or* low-income students (CDE, 2006; EdSource, 2004; Goldfinger & Blattner, 2005).[4]

A fourth important dynamic emerges from the greater attention in the policy arena to educational accountability and the national movement via the NCLB Act of 2002 toward narrower indicators of learning and achievement. Due to the mandates associated with NCLB, California faces the dual pressures of meeting increased accountability requirements and the diverse needs of EL students. This results in the assessment of EL students on material that they have not been taught or in a language in which they are not yet proficient (Rumberger & Gándara, 2004). For example, EL students are held to the same standards for passing on the California Standards Test (CST) as native English speakers are, without regard to the EL students' limited exposure to the English language. The CST, one of the most rigorous such tests in the nation, is used to determine whether a school is designated as a program improvement school for not meeting achievement goals and therefore subject to sanctions under NCLB (CDE, 2005). In many cases, school districts that continually fail to meet the achievement growth mandated by NCLB find in their EL populations a ready explanation for poor performance that only adds to the perception that this important population represents a burden to public school systems. Together, these contextual dynamics provide a complex backdrop and bring to light the challenges involved in describing what it takes to ensure that EL students and their teachers receive the attention and support they need to be successful.

HIGHLY QUALIFIED TEACHERS
AND STUDENT ACHIEVEMENT

One of the most significant resources in public school systems across the nation are their human resources (Elmore & Rothman, 1999). Public school systems expend 80–90% of their revenues on overall personnel salaries and benefits. Districts expend in the range of approximately 55–65% specifically on certificated teachers' salary and benefits. The allocation of fiscal resources toward teacher salaries and benefits could be viewed from different perspectives. The first perspective is that the resources committed to recruiting, hiring, and retaining teachers signal the importance of identifying and keeping highly qualified teachers. Another perspective is the importance of ensuring that highly qualified teachers are distributed across school districts, schools, and classrooms in an equitable manner. A disturbing pattern exists in which schools and classrooms with higher concentrations of EL students tend to have less experienced, lesser qualified, and often unprepared teachers (Education Trust, 2005). In other recent literature, there is strong indication that quality teachers clearly impact in positive ways the academic achievement of students, especially if teachers are prepared to work with linguistically and culturally diverse students. There is growing evidence that fully prepared, trained teachers do impact the achievement outcomes of students, and more specifically in urban areas and with student populations with special language-learning needs (Gándara & Maxwell-Jolly, 2000; Haberman, 1996; Haycock, 1998).

An important aspect of preparing quality teachers for urban and special language-learning needs populations is the continuous support for ongoing development of teachers. Teachers are prepared by teacher education programs to enter the profession and quality teaching requires a propensity for continuous learning. According to Darling-Hammond (1999),

> There is no silver bullet, no single simple reform that will change chalkboard lecturers into inspirational educators. But a critical first step is establishing a context for teaching as a learning profession that is widely recognized and supported by schools, policy makers and the public.... it is fair to say that a great deal of evidence points to the importance of a well-integrated, carefully planned approach to educating teachers. This approach begins with pre-service education, is bolstered by a supportive induction process for beginning teachers, and is made robust by continuing professional development. (p. 3)

Language in the NCLB Act clearly supports the notion that teacher quality needs to be a major goal for school districts. Financial resources are provided for in the NCLB Act that support the initial training of teachers along with the continuous efforts to support teacher professional development in order to ensure that all schools have "highly qualified teachers" by 2005. While the intent of the policy seems to be a "silver bullet" to improve student achievement, the implementation is focused on compliance rather than on quality teaching. In reality, compliance assures that teachers possess a certificate rather than possessing the unique skills to teach students with English-language needs. For example, a teacher may be possess a certificate to teach mathematics and is therefore compliant with NCLB's "highly qualified" teacher definition, but the same teacher may not possess the skills, experience, or sensibilities to teach students whose native language is not English.

Unfortunately, in California, as in many states, the definition of "highly qualified teacher" has been reduced to bureaucratic paperwork that deals mostly with compliance rather than to assure actual higher quality of instruction resulting in improved student achievement. In the official publication of the California Teachers Association, a teacher trainer states,

> "the most important thing teachers should realize is that the term 'highly qualified teacher' has nothing to do with whether teachers are, in fact, highly qualified. The legislation does not measure effectiveness in the classroom or how good a teacher is at his or her craft." (Quoted in Posnick-Goodwin, 2004, p. 6)

The CTA makes the argument that this requirement of NCLB is more about being "NCLB compliant" rather than "highly qualified" (Posnick-Goodwin, 2004). The controversy surrounding the requirements for identifying a teacher as highly qualified has obscured the argument about what resources are necessary to ensure quality instruction for students with English-language learning needs.

The origin of the disagreement about the meaning of "highly qualified teacher" comes from the U.S. Department of Education and its secretary's report on teacher quality. In the report, the secretary presents "scientific evidence" that teacher quality depends more on content knowledge and experience with that knowledge rather than teacher certification processes and methodology courses (U.S. Department of Education, Office of Postsecondary Education, 2002). In essence, the secretary opines that if a teacher knows a subject, a teacher can teach it without necessarily needing training on how to teach or how to teach special needs students. In this report, the secretary asserts that there is substantial "scientific evidence" to support his notion of the impact of teacher quality on student achievement being based primarily on content knowledge.

This assertion is contradicted by teacher educators who claim that the report "cites almost no research that would meet scientific standards, misrepresents findings from a large number of sources, and includes unsupported statements of teacher education and teacher certification" (Darling-Hammond & Youngs, 2002). In a review of the research on alternative certification programs (ACPs), Darling-Hammond and Youngs found no evidence that ACPs showed any positive impact on student achievement. In fact, they found that traditional university-based teacher certification programs actually increase student achievement. They also found that teacher education programs that supported teacher performance outcomes and retention and more carefully designed programs for teacher preparation actually produced more positive changes in student achievement (Darling-Hammond & Youngs, 2002).

TEACHER PREPARATION TO SERVE EL STUDENTS

California is sorely in need of a teacher workforce that is prepared to work with ever-increasing numbers of EL students, the largest group being Spanish-speaking Latinos/as. The challenges that teachers face in supporting EL students toward proficiency in English are daunting when one considers the circumstances under which they work and the lack of professional support needed to ensure success. Until recently,

California's teacher education institutions attempted to address the needs of its linguistically and ethnically diverse students by preparing teachers through two comprehensive credential programs that, to varying degrees, focused on the development of linguistically and culturally sensitive teaching competencies. Individuals were able to pursue the cross-cultural language academic development (CLAD) credential, which infused first- and second-language development, English language development methodologies, and cultural awareness in course requirements. In addition to the CLAD requirements, the bilingual cross-cultural language academic development (BCLAD) credential included coursework in primary language instructional methodology and a deeper background in linguistics (Walton & Carlson, 1994). Beyond these coursework requirements, BCLAD candidates were required to demonstrate a depth of knowledge in the culture and proficiency in the language of emphasis prior to gaining the certificate.

With the passage of California Senate Bill 2042 in 1998, the CLAD and BCLAD programs were phased out and a new credential program was initiated in which content and pedagogical approaches that address cultural and linguistic diversity are embedded within the program, as opposed to being explicitly addressed by specific courses. There are at least two major concerns to be raised. The first is that the preparation of new teachers to engage with EL students has diminished with the conversion of content-specific courses geared toward their needs to "embedded" content throughout credential coursework. The second concern is that the uncertainty surrounding the bilingual credential might result in decreasing numbers of bilingual candidates whose specialized training is sorely needed as the number of EL students in the state increases. In addition, there is still no provision in 2006 for bilingual credentials under SB 2042, although bilingual training and certification continues by way of special contract. The impact of SB 2042 teacher certification programs on English learners has yet to be determined.

CURRICULUM AND INSTRUCTIONAL SUPPORT FOR EL STUDENTS

The preparation of teachers in adequate numbers to meet the needs of EL students through quality programs is situated within the context of a series of structural and systemic issues. These issues affect the availability of highly prepared teachers, access to the curriculum for EL students, and the instructional approaches used with EL students.

The most prevalent of these issues is the de facto segregation of EL students, especially at the high school level, in large urban or remote rural schools. These same schools tend to have higher percentages of low-income students, higher rates of teacher turnover, higher numbers of novice educators, higher numbers of teachers providing instruction outside of their expertise, and lesser financial resources. As a result, EL students are more likely to be taught by less-experienced and under-qualified teachers who may or may not have the appropriate training to work with students who are learning English as a second language (Education Trust, 2005; García, 2001).

The preparation and availability of qualified teachers has an impact on classroom culture and the instructional approaches utilized with EL students. Central to the implementation of any curriculum is a teacher's beliefs in regard to the role of culture and language in a student's intellectual development and learning. Learning and development are not dependent on the curriculum alone, but the manner in which curriculum is implemented. Teaching practices employed by teachers who highly value a student's cultural and linguistic competencies are consistent with practices considered to be culturally responsive or culturally relevant to the needs and strengths that students bring to the classroom (Hollins, 1996; Jones, Pang, & Rodriguez, 2001; Ladson-Billings, 1994).

Researchers have noted the significance of allowing EL students to express their language, values, and norms while also taking into account the strengths they bring with them (García, 2005, Valdés, 2001, Valenzuela, 1999). Teachers who gain an understanding of their students' cultural backgrounds are more likely to utilize teaching practices that are culturally responsive. Such practices integrate students' everyday experiences into classroom instruction and allow for conceptual bridges between prior knowledge and new information (Au, 1990; Tharp & Gallimore, 1988). In addition to classroom conditions, the use of effective instructional approaches and the implementation of curriculum there are issues of access to curriculum for EL students (August & Hakuta, 1997; Valdés, 2001; Valenzuela, 1999). If EL students are to have full access and educational opportunity, then materials responsive to their needs must be available across content areas, as opposed to any single curricular area such as English Language Development. In sum, there is a dynamic interrelationship between the resources available to EL students in the form of well-prepared and -qualified teachers, the instructional practices utilized, and access to the whole curriculum.

As this chapter is being written, most states including California are falling short of meeting the NCLB requirement for a highly qualified teacher in every classroom. We contend that this is a most critical issue in providing a quality education to all students, including EL students. Conversation and debate among academics, educators, and policy makers is also sharpening as the reauthorization of NCLB approaches. In California, this conversation is especially salient given the increasing number of EL students in public schools and concerns over their achievement. It is imperative that these conversations and debates focus on the need for additional resources for the instruction of EL students and, perhaps more importantly, the need to strategically target resources toward the recruitment, preparation, and retention of highly qualified teachers, counselors, and administrators to serve the ever-growing population of EL students in California. In turn, these highly qualified individuals can contribute toward the development of a school culture that is responsive to student needs that lead to effective educational practices and experiences that promote higher levels of student achievement for all. When this concept finally comes to fruition, California schools will promote a more socially just educational system.

NOTES

The authors wish to acknowledge the invaluable feedback and advice on this chapter provided by Barbara A. Storms, professor of educational leadership at California State University–East Bay.

1. For purposes of this chapter, we are using the Language Census (R30-LC) criteria established by the California Department of Education to define English-learning students.
2. "Structured English immersion" is a program in which instruction is provided to EL students overwhelmingly in English with some support in the students' native language.
3. An "English language mainstream class" is a program in which instruction is provided to EL students completely in English, with no support in the students' home language. Students must perform at proficient levels as determined by state and district assessments to show that they have a "good working knowledge" of English.
4. Under AB 825, set to go into effect in 2006, six state block grants were established to enable school districts to exercise greater flexibility among a wide range of categorical programs, thus releasing them from having to spend these designated funds for the originally intended purposes (Goldfinger & Blattner, 2005).

REFERENCES

Au, K. (1990). Changes in a teacher's view of interactive comprehension instruction. In Moll, L. (Ed.), *Vygotsky and education* (pp. 271–286). New York: Cambridge University Press.

August, D., & Hakuta, K. (Eds.). (1997). *Improving schooling for language-minority children.* Report of the National Research Council Committee on Developing a Research Agenda on the Education of Limited-English-Proficient and Bilingual Students. Washington, DC: National Academy Press.

Berne, R., & Stiefel, L. (1984). *The measurement of equity in school finance: Conceptual, methodological, and empirical dimensions.* Baltimore: Johns Hopkins University Press.

California Department of Education (CDE). (2005). "State schools Chief Jack O'Connell's statement regarding Rand, Fordham reports on California schools." Retrieved August 29, 2006, from http://www.cde.ca.gov/nr/ne/yr05/yr05rel1.asp.

California Department of Education (CDE). (2006). "English learners, instructional settings and services." Educational Demographics Unit. Retrieved July 25, 2006 from http://data1.cde.ca.gov/dataquest.

California Department of Education Superintendent's Hispanic Advisory Task Force. (1997). *Mandate for excellence: A call for standards, assessment, and accountability in the education of California's Hispanic students.* Sacramento, CA:. Author.

California Legislative Analyst's Office. (2005). *Analysis of the 2005-06 budget: Education.* Sacramento: Author.

Carlson, R., & Walton, P. H. (1994). CLAD/BCLAD: California reforms in the preparation and credentialing of teachers for a linguistically and culturally diverse student population. Paper presented at the Annual Meeting of NABE's International Bilingual/Multicultural Education Conference. Los Angeles, CA.

Darling-Hammond, L. (1999). *Professional development for teachers: Setting the stage for learning from teaching.* Santa Cruz, CA: Center for the Future of Teaching and Learning.

Darling-Hammond, L., & Snyder, J. (2003). Organizing schools for student and teacher learning: An examination of resource allocation choices in reforming schools. In M. L. Plecki & D. H. Monk (Eds.), *School finance and teacher quality: Exploring the connections* (pp. 179–205). Larchmont, NY: Eye on Education.

Darling-Hammond, L., & Youngs, P. (2002) Defining "highly-qualified teachers": What does "scientifically-based research" actually tell us? Retrieved May 26, 2005, from http://www.aera.net/pubs/er/vol21_09/AERA310903.pdf.

Delpit, L. (1995). *Other people's children: Cultural conflict in the classroom.* New York: New Press.

EdSource. (2004). *Resource cards on California schools.* Retrieved September 18, 2005 from http://www.edsource.org.

Education Trust (2005). *The funding gap 2005: Low-income and minority students are shortchanged by most states.* Washington, DC: Author.

Education Trust–West (2005). *California's hidden teacher spending gap: How state and district budgeting practices shortchange poor and minority students and their schools.* Oakland, CA: Author.

Elmore, R., & Rothman, R. (Eds) (1999). *Testing, teaching and learning: A guide for states and school districts.* Washington, DC: National Academy Press.

Flores, B., & Clark, E. (1997). High-stakes testing: Barriers for prospective bilingual education teachers. *Bilingual Research Journal, 21*(4), 334–356.

Gándara, P. (2000). *The dimensions of time and the challenge of school reform.* Albany: State University of New York Press.

Gándara, P., & Maxwell-Jolly, J. (2000). *Preparing teachers for diversity: A dilemma of quality and quantity.* Santa Cruz, CA: Center for the Future of Teaching and Learning.

García, E. E. (2001). *Hispanic education in the United States: Raíces y alas.* Lanham, MD: Rowman and Littlefield.

García, E. E. (2005). *Teaching and learning in two languages: Bilingualism and schooling in the United States.* New York: Teachers College Press.

García, E. E., & Wiese, A. (2002). Language, public policy, and schooling: A focus on Chicano English language learners. In R. R. Valencia (Ed.), *Chicano school failure and success: Past, present, and future* (2nd ed., pp. 149–169). London: Routledge-Falmer.

Goldfinger, P., & Blattner, B. (2005). *Revenues and revenue limits.* Sacramento, CA: School Services of California.

Haberman, M. (1996). "Selecting and preparing culturally competent teachers for urban schools," In J. Sikula (Ed.), *Handbook of Research on Teacher Education* (pp. 747–760). New York, NY: Macmillan.

Haycock, K. (1998). *Good teaching matters a lot.* Washington, DC: Educational Trust.

Hollins, E. R. (1996). *Culture in school learning.* Mahwah, NJ: Lawrence Erlbaum Associates.

Jones, E. B., Pang, V. O., & Rodríguez, J. L. (2001). Culture matters: Teaching social studies in the elementary classroom. *Theory into Practice, 40*(1), 35–41.

Ladson-Billings, G. (1994). *The dreamkeepers: Successful teachers of African American children.* San Francisco: Jossey-Bass.

Miles, K. H., & Darling-Hammond, L. (1998). Rethinking the allocation of teaching resources: Some lessons from high-performing schools. *Educational Evaluation and Policy Analysis, 20*(1), 9–29.

No Child Left Behind (2002). Retrieved October 17, 2006, from http://www.ed.gov/nclb/index/az/index.html

Odden, A., Archibald, S., Ferminick, M., & Gross, B. (2003). Defining school-level expenditure structures that reflect educational strategies. *Journal of Education Finance, 28*(3), 323–356.

Olsen, L., & Jaramillo, A. (1999). *Turning the tides of exclusion: A guide for educators and advocates for immigrant students.* L. Woodlief & C. Dowell (Series Eds.), *California Tomorrow Equity-Centered School Reform Series.* Oakland, CA: California Tomorrow.

Parrish, T. B. (1994). A cost analysis of alternative instructional models for limited English proficient students in California. *Journal of Education Finance, 19*(3), 256–278.

Picus, L. O., & Wattenbarger, J. (Eds.). (1995). *Where does the money go? Resource allocation in elementary and secondary schools.* Thousand Oaks, CA: Corwin Press.

Posnick-Goodwin, S. (2004). "Are you highly qualified?" *California Educator, 8*(5), 6.

Reynolds, A., Ross, S. M., & Rakow, J. H. (2002). "Teacher retention, teaching effectiveness, and professional preparation: A comparison of professional development school and non-professional development school graduates." *Teaching and Teacher Education, 18*(3): 289–303.

Rumberger, R. W., & Gándara, P. (2004). Seeking equity in the education of California's English learners. *Teachers College Record, 106*(10), 2032–2056.

Rumberger, R. W., & Rodriguez, G. M. (2002). Chicano dropouts: An update of research and policy issues. In R. R. Valencia (Ed.), *Chicano school failure and success: Past, present, and future* (2nd ed., pp. 114–146). London: Routledge-Falmer.

Tharp, R., & Gallimore, R. (1988*). Rousing minds to life: Teaching, learning, and schooling in social context.* New York: Cambridge University Press.

Timar, T. B. (1994). Politics, policy, and categorical aid: New inequities in California school finance. *Educational Evaluation and Policy Analysis, 16*(2), 143–160.

U.S. Department of Education, Office of Postsecondary Education. (2002). *Meeting the highly qualified teacher challenge: The secretary's annual report on teacher quality.* Washington, DC: Author.

Valdés, G. (2001). *Learning and not learning English: Latino students in American schools.* New York: Teachers College Press.

Valenzuela, A. (1999). *Subtractive schooling: U.S.-Mexican youth and the politics of caring.* Albany: State University of New York Press.

7

INVESTING IN STUDENT LIVES OUTSIDE OF SCHOOL TO INCREASE ACHIEVEMENT INSIDE SCHOOLS

David C. Berliner

Arizona State University

IN THE UNITED STATES, SCHOOLS FOR THE POOR are only occasionally successful and rarely stay successful over long periods of time. Even many schools identified on the basis of achievement test scores as successful for poor children often have high dropout rates between 8th and 12th grade, and lower than desired rates of college attendance. There are surely many reasons why poor children have less access to successful schools than do wealthier children, but among the most likely is that we treat the poor as if they are not deserving. Integral to America is its belief in individualism, so help for poor people has often been given grudgingly. Furthermore, the most visible poor often are minorities living in urban areas, and the majority, a politically powerful middle-class white population, has had little interest in the people whom they helped to segregate by class and race.

The major mechanism chosen for the reduction of poverty among all Americans has been heralded in our myths and in our legislation: public schooling. But this represents a misunderstanding of what schooling can ordinarily accomplish. We sometimes forget that schooling is a relatively weak treatment, often limited in its accomplishments by the poverty that exists outside the classroom. These limiting outside-of-school factors are the focus of this chapter. Although there are schools that occasionally beat the odds, it is recognized that the vast majority of schools for the poor will be helped by working on outside-of-school issues as much, or more, as by continued work on improving conditions inside of schools.

THE LIMITED POWER OF SCHOOLING
ON THE LIVES OF THE POOR

It is a fact of contemporary American life that many of the poorest of the children who come to our schools have spent no time at all in school-like settings during the first five years of their life. And then, when of school age, children only spend about 30 hours a week in our schools, and they do that for only about two-thirds of a year. The arithmetic is simple. In the course of a full year, students might spend just over 1000 of their waking hours in school, and almost five times that amount of time in their neighborhood and with their families. For poor children, what is learned in those 5000 hours in nonschool settings can be unhelpful. It was Anyon, among others, who some time ago alerted us to the fact that many of the families in those impoverished neighborhoods are so poorly equipped to raise healthy children that the schools those children attend would have a hard time educating them, even if they weren't also so poorly organized and run. I agree with Anyon (1995), who posits,

> It is has become increasingly clear that several decades of educational reform have failed to bring substantial improvements to schools in America's inner cities. Most recent analyses of unsuccessful school reform (and prescriptions for change) have isolated educational, regulatory, or financial aspects of reform from the social context of poverty and race in which inner city schools are located. (p. 69)

> .... the structural basis for failure in inner-city schools is political, economic, and cultural, and must be changed before meaningful school improvement projects can be successfully implemented. Educational reforms cannot compensate for the ravages of society. (p. 88)

As educators and scholars we continually talk about school reform as if it must take place inside the schools. Most of us advocate for adequacy in funding so that we can attract higher-quality teachers for the poor; encourage professional development of the staff in schools for the poor, thus increasing their pedagogical and subject matter knowledge; provide more technologically enhanced instruction; increase the time students spend in schooling, perhaps through after-school programs, Saturday programs, and summer school; and so forth. Some of the most lauded of our school reform programs in our most distressed schools do show some success, but success often means bringing the students who are at the 20th percentile in reading and mathematics up to the 30th percentile in those skills. Statistical significance and a respectable effect size for a school reform effort is certainly worthy of our admiration, but it does not accomplish as much as our nation needs to accomplish. School reform efforts for poor children almost always will be unsuccessful if they do not consider the outside-of-school conditions that affect the ability to teach and learn successfully inside of school.

The economist Richard Rothstein understands this. In his recent book *Class and schools* (2004), he states,

> Policy makers almost universally conclude that existing and persistent achievement gaps must be the result of wrongly designed school policies—either expectations that are too low, teachers who are insufficiently qualified, curricula that are badly designed, classes that are too large, school climates that are too undisciplined, leadership that is too unfocussed, or a combination of these.

> Americans have come to the conclusion that the achievement gap is the fault of "failing schools" because it makes no common sense that it could be otherwise....This common sense perspective, however, is misleading and dangerous. It ignores how social class characteristics in a stratified society like ours may actually influence learning in schools. (pp. 9–10)

Like Anyon, Rothstein goes on to note,

> For nearly half a century, the association of social and economic disadvantage with a student achievement gap has been well known to economists, sociologists and educators. Most, however, have avoided the obvious implication of this understanding—raising the achievement of lower-class children requires the amelioration of the social and economic conditions of their lives, not just school reform. (p. 11)

Anyon, Rothstein, and others provide the framework for the issues I raise in this chapter.

AMERICA'S POVERTY PROBLEM

The Innocenti Foundation (UNICEF Innocenti Research Centre, 2005), is among the most recent to reliably document our nations' poverty problem. Their entire report is summarized quite simply in one graph,

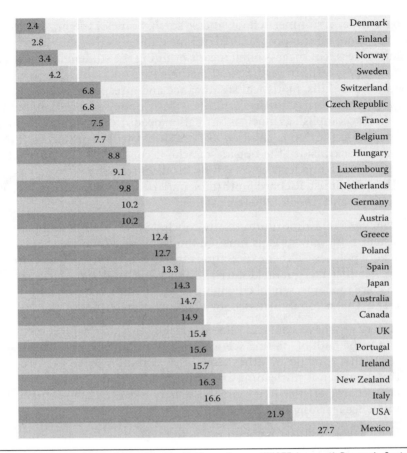

Figure 7.1 Poverty Rates Among Wealthy Nations. *Source:* UNICEF Innocenti Research Centre, 2005.

as presented in Figure 7.1. In this set of wealthy nations, through the 1990s, the United States is among the leaders in childhood poverty. The only nation with a record worse than ours is Mexico, and, contrary to UNICEF, I would not consider Mexico a rich nation. Using 2003 data to compute gross national income per capita (using purchasing power parity, or PPP, as the method of comparison), the United States ranked fourth, at $37,750 per capita, while Mexico ranked 80th, with $8,900 per capita (World Bank, 2005). As a nation we should not be in the same league as Mexico, but, alas, we are closer to them in children's poverty rate than to others whom we might, more commonly, think of as our peers. Our leadership in rate of childhood poverty has been remarkably steady for over a decade (Berliner & Biddle, 1995). What is abundantly

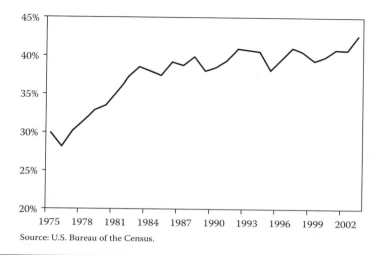

Source: U.S. Bureau of the Census.

Figure 7.2 Percentage of the Poor Living at Half the Official Poverty Line. *Source:* Mishel, Bernstein, & Allegretto, 2005, p. 323.

clear is that if we cared to do something about it we could emulate the economic policies of other industrialized nations and not have the high rate of poverty that we do.

Using internal U.S. data, which probably underestimates the percentage of youth in poverty, we note a current rate of about 18%. But we see also that fully one-third of U.S. children live in households where no parent has full-time, year-round employment (Anne E. Casey Foundation, 2006), indicating considerable job insecurity for American families. Still another measure of the magnitude of the poverty problem in the United States is the percentage of people who are living at *half* the rate of those classified as merely being poor. These data are given in Figure 7.2. These are the poorest of the poor in our nation, constituting over 40% of the tens of millions of people that are officially classified as "poor" by our government. As bad as this trend appears, the situation is probably worse. Most economists believe that the level of income at which the government declares a person to be poor misleads us into thinking there are fewer poor than there really are. So it is likely that there are many more very poor people than this graph suggests.

Something else needs to be noted about the poverty we see among children: it is not random. Poverty is unequally distributed across the many racial and ethnic groups that make up the American nation. Figure 7.3 makes clear that poverty is strongly correlated with race and ethnicity. New immigrants, African-Americans, and Hispanics, particularly those who live in urban areas, are heavily overrepresented in the groups that

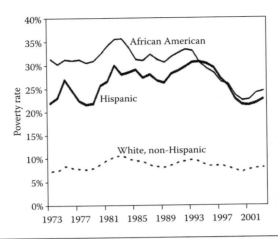

Figure 7.3 Poverty Rates by Race and Ethnicity. *Source:* Mishel, Bernstein, & Allegretto, 2005, p. 323.

suffer severe poverty. Class and race are strongly correlated in American society, making this chapter about the school achievement of the poor a problem of school achievement for children of color, as well.

Because our nation's poverty problems are clear, we actually have developed many programs to help parents and children in poverty. But these programs are too often fragmented, do not cover everyone eligible, and are subject to year-to-year variability in funding. Thus, such programs end up not nearly as good, nor as consistent, as those in many other countries. Table 7.1 illustrates the problem. We are identified as a leader among the rich nations of the world in failing to help people exit from poverty once they have fallen into poverty. One column in this table shows the percentage of individuals who became impoverished once in a three-year time period—through, say, illness, divorce, childbirth, or job loss—the big four poverty producers among those who had not previously been poor. Here we see that the U.S. rate is quite high, but not much different than that of many other nations. Poverty befalls many people, in many countries, once in a while.

Our national problem shows in the next column, displaying the percentage of people who stayed poor for the entire three years after they had fallen into poverty. At a rate roughly twice that of other wealthy nations, we lead the industrialized world. Unlike other wealthy countries, we have few mechanisms to move people out of poverty once they fall into it.

In the last column of the table we can see how awful it can be to stumble into poverty in the United States when compared to other

Table 7.1 Poverty in OECD Countries Over a Three-Year Period During the 1990s

Country	Percent Poor Once in Three Years	Percent Poor for All Three Years	Percent in Nation Permanently Poor
United States	23.5	9.5	14.5
Denmark	9.1	0.8	1.8
Ireland	15.3	1.3	5.3
Netherlands	12.9	1.6	4.5
France	16.6	3.0	6.6
Italy	21.5	5.6	10.4
United Kingdom	19.5	2.4	6.5
Canada	18.1	5.1	8.9
Belgium	16.0	2.8	5.2
Germany	19.2	4.3	8.1
Finland	25.1	6.5	12.2
Portugal	24.2	7.8	13.4
Spain	21.3	3.7	8.7

Source: Mishel, Berstein, & Allegretto, p. 409.

nations. In that column we see the percentage of people who stayed below the poverty level on a relatively permanent basis. On the basis of these data we can claim the title for the highest rate of the permanently poor in all the other industrialized nations. If the data from Denmark, Ireland, or the Netherlands are compared to that of the United States, it is easy to see the difference between societies that abhor poverty, and one such as ours, that accepts poverty as a given.

POVERTY AND STUDENT ACHIEVEMENT

Credible evidence suggests that the rates of childhood poverty in the United States are high, poverty in the United States is racialized, and those who once get trapped in poverty have a hard time getting out of it. So what does this mean for our nation in terms of student achievement and the international competitiveness of our students? The international tests of achievement provide some clues. The results of the recent Trends in International Mathematics and Science Study, known as TIMSS 2003, are representative (Gonzales et al., 2004). Table 7.2 presents data on mathematics and science scores for American fourth- and eighth-grade youth disaggregated by the degree of poverty in the schools they attend.

In this table, three aspects of our performance with regard to other nations are instructive. First, our scores in both subject areas and at both grade levels were correlated perfectly with the percentage of poor students who attend a school. In the five categories presented, schools with the wealthier students had the highest average score; the next wealthier set of schools had students who had the next highest average score; and so forth, until we see that the schools with the poorest students had the students who scored the lowest. This pattern is common.

The second thing to note is that the average scores for the schools with *less* than 50% of their students in poverty exceeded the U.S. average score, while the average scores for the schools with *greater* than 50% of their students in poverty fell below the U.S. average score. This tells us who is and who is not succeeding in the United States.

The third thing to notice pertains to the schools that serve the most impoverished students, where 75% or more of the students are eligible for free or reduced lunch. That is, almost all the students in these schools live in extreme poverty. These are the students that fall well below the international average achieved in this study. In general, Table 7.2 informs us that our poor students are not competitive internationally while our middle classes and wealthy public school children are doing extremely well in comparison to the pool of countries that made up TIMSS 2003.

There are more international data to support this finding. The Organization for Economic Cooperation and Development (OECD) has instituted a three-year cycle for looking at reading, mathematics, and science for 15-year-olds, called the PISA studies, for the Program for International Student Assessment (Lemke, et al., 2001). Unfortunately, the PISA doesn't do a very good job of breaking down the data by social

Table 7.2 Fourth Grade and Eighth Grade Mathematics and Science Scores from TIMSS 2003

Poverty level of school (percent free or reduced lunch)	Fourth Grade Math Scores	Fourth Grade Science Scores	Eighth Grade Math Scores	Eighth Grade Science Scores
Less than 10% in poverty (schools with wealthy students)	567	579	547	571
10%–24.9% in poverty	543	567	531	554
25%–49.9% in poverty	533	551	505	529
50%–74.9% in poverty	500	519	480	504
75% or more in poverty (schools with poor students)	471	480	444	461
U.S. average score	518	536	504	527
International average score	495	489	466	473

class. So I report on ethnicity and race to discuss the effects of poverty on achievement. Given the high correlations among poverty, ethnicity, and school achievement in our country, it is (sadly) not inappropriate to use ethnicity as a proxy for poverty in reporting student achievement.

Tables 7.3, 7.4, and 7.5 display the performance in 2000 of U.S. 15-year-olds in mathematics, literacy, and science in relation to other nations. What stands out first is a commonly found pattern in international

Table 7.3 Mathematics Scores (Mean 500) from PISA 2000

Country	Score
Japan	557
Korea, Republic of	547
New Zealand	537
Finland	536
Australia	533
Canada	533
United States Average Score for White Students	**530**
Switzerland	529
United Kingdom	529
Belgium	520
France	517
Austria	515
Denmark	514
Iceland	514
Sweden	510
Ireland	503
Norway	499
Czech Republic	498
United States Average Score	**493**
Germany	490
Hungary	488
Spain	476
Poland	470
Italy	457
Portugal	454
Greece	447
Luxembourg	446
United States Average Score for Hispanic Students	**437**
United States Average Score for African-American Students	**423**
Mexico	387

Table 7.4 Literacy Scores (Mean 500) from PISA 2000

Country	Score
Korea, Republic of	552
Japan	550
United States Average Score for White Students	**538**
Finland	538
United Kingdom	532
Canada	529
New Zealand	528
Australia	528
Austria	519
Ireland	513
Sweden	512
Czech Republic	511
France	500
Norway	500
United States Average Score	**499**
Hungary	496
Iceland	496
Belgium	496
Switzerland	496
Spain	491
Germany	487
Poland	483
Denmark	481
Italy	478
Greece	461
Portugal	459
United States Average Score for Hispanic Students	**449**
United States Average Score for African-American Students	**445**
Luxembourg	443
Mexico	422

studies of achievement—namely, that U.S. average scores are very close to the international average. But in a country as heterogeneous and as socially and ethnically segregated as ours, mean scores of achievement are not useful for understanding how we are really doing in international comparisons. Such data must be disaggregated. I have done that in each of the three tables presenting the PISA data. From those tables we see clearly that our white students (without regard for social class) were among the highest performing students in the world. But

Table 7.5 Science Scores (Mean 500) from PISA 2000

Country	Score
Korea, Republic of	552
Japan	550
Finland	538
United States Average Score for White Students	**535**
United Kingdom	532
Canada	529
New Zealand	528
Australia	528
Austria	519
Ireland	513
Sweden	512
Czech Republic	511
France	500
Norway	500
United States Average Score	**499**
Hungary	496
Iceland	496
Belgium	496
Switzerland	496
Spain	491
Germany	487
Poland	483
Denmark	481
Italy	478
Greece	461
Portugal	459
Luxembourg	443
United States Average Score for Hispanic Students	**438**
United States Average Score for African-American Students	**435**
Mexico	422

our African American and Hispanic students, also undifferentiated by social class, were among the poorest performing students in this international sample.

Looking at all three tables reveals something very important about inequality in the United States. If the educational opportunities available to white students in our public schools were made available to all our students, in 2000, the United States would have been the seventh-highest-scoring nation in mathematics, the third-highest-scoring nation in reading, and the fourth-highest-scoring nation in science. Public schooling for tens of millions of U.S. white children is clearly working quite well. On the other hand, were our minority students themselves nations, they would score almost last among the industrialized countries in the world.

Given these findings, we should ask what plausible hypotheses might differentiate the education of white, African-American, and Hispanic students from one another. Segregated schooling seems to be one obvious answer. Orfield and Lee (2005), in their report on school segregation, make clear how race and schooling are bound together. Only 12% of white children go to schools in which the majority of the students are not white. And only 1% of white students go to schools that comprise over 90% minority students. Eighty-eight percent of white children are attending schools that are predominantly white. In contrast, almost all African-American and Latino students, usually poorer than their white age-mates, are in schools where there are students very much like them racially and socioeconomically. Latinos and African-Americans are as segregated by poverty as they are by race and ethnicity, which may be the more important issue with which our schools have to deal.

Other international and national data repeatedly make the same point. White Americans of all classes, and relatively wealthy Americans of all races and ethnicities, do well in school. Poor children and most children of color do not. Poverty is strongly associated with low school achievement. It is worth thinking about the fact that after hundreds of studies showed that cigarettes were related to serious illnesses, the world eventually came to believe that the relationship between smoking and cancer was causal. This conclusion was reached despite the fact that none of the studies done with humans were experimental. In contrast, we now have thousands of studies showing correlations between poverty and academic achievement (Sirin, 2005), and no such causal relationship is recognized. The connections between poverty and educational attainment are stronger than we ever found for the link between cigarettes and smoking. But to explain the relationship between students in poverty and low school achievement we constantly look for other mechanisms of causality, such as the low expectations of teachers, or the quality of teachers' subject matter knowledge, or the rigor of the curriculum. Of course, the low expectations of teachers, their subject-matter competency, and the rigor of the curricula for poor students are important. But so, too, are the exercise patterns, the diets, and the alcohol consumption of smokers, yet it never prevented the nation from determining that smoking is causally related to cancer, emphysema, heart disease and other illnesses, independent of other factors and without a single experimental study. It is quite clear that the relationship between social class and test scores is positive, high, and well embedded in theories that can explain the relationship. What makes the poverty–achievement relationship different from the cigarette smoking–cancer relationship? What interests are served by refusing to regard poverty as causally related to school performance? Perhaps there is a hypothesis that is frightening to hear uttered in a capitalist society—namely, that if the incomes of our poorest citizens were to go up, so might the achievement test scores of their children. Sometimes a correlation exists precisely *because* causation exists.

HOW POVERTY AFFECTS ACHIEVEMENT

Poverty affects school achievement through all sorts of stresses on families: illness and accident, abandonment and divorce, heavy workloads necessitating long hours away from home by parents, and so forth. But two of the primary mechanisms through which poverty affects schooling are (1) children's health and (2) the social conditions of the neighborhood in which poor youth are raised. As will be made clear, a bit more money for the poor—increases in minimum wages, earning a livable wage, the provision of health insurance, subsidized housing in middle-class neighborhoods, and so forth, all could moderate these effects. And the effects of poor health and inadequate neighborhoods do need to be attenuated, since their effects on achievement are quite strong.

Health Issues Affecting the Poor

The many medical problems that are related to social class provide obvious and powerful examples of problems affecting school achievement that are remediable with a little extra money. For example, at the simplest level are such medical problems as otitis media and those associated with vision. Otitis media is a simple and common childhood ear infection, frequently contracted by rich and poor children alike between birth and three years of age. In a number of studies, recurring otitis media in the first three years of life has been related to hearing impairments, and thus to language development, and thus to reading problems in school, and therefore to deficits on tests such as the Stanford-Binet Intelligence Test. Otitis media is also implicated in the development of attention deficit hyperactivity disorder (ADHD; see, for example, Agency for Healthcare Research and Quality, 2005; Hagerman & Falkenstein, 1987; Knishkowy, Palti, Adler & Tepper, 1991; Luotonen et al., 1996). This literature makes clear that poor children have more untreated cases of otitis media than do those that are financially better off—especially those with medical insurance. The cause of otitis media may not be directly linked to poverty, but its prevalence and lack of treatment in children is quite clearly affected by poverty.

Recurrent otitis media, as well as other childhood diseases before age three, are found to be strongly and negatively related to breast-feeding—the less breast-feeding the greater the rate of a number of childhood diseases. But breast-feeding of infants in America is done significantly less frequently by women who are poor. It is also done significantly less often by those who only have high school degrees or have not finished high school, and by those mothers who are under 19 and who are not married (Centers for Disease Control and Prevention, 2005).

In other words, poverty affects otitis media and other childhood diseases indirectly through home practices that are more common among the poor and less common in the middle class. Another example makes this point as well. The relationship to recurring otitis media is also strongly positive for pacifier use (Niemela, Pihakari, Pokka, Uhari, & Uhari, 2000). But pacifiers are used more commonly, and for longer periods of time, among the lower social classes. In the final analysis, while otitis media isn't a disease of the poor, the characteristics of child rearing and of home environment among the poor of all races and ethnicities leads to more medical problems for the children of the poor. And then, since the poor often lack proper medical insurance, they have a much greater chance of having hearing handicaps at the stage in their lives where language is being developed; in just a few years those handicaps will emerge as reading problems in the classroom.

Vision is another simple case of poverty's effects on student behavior outside the teachers' control. For example, two different vision screening tests, one among the urban poor in Boston and one among the urban poor in New York, each found that over 50% of the children tested had some easily correctable vision deficiency, but most such cases were not followed up on or corrected (Gillespie, 2001). An optometrist working with poor children notes that the mass screening vision tests that schools typically use rarely assess the ability of children to do close-up work—the work needed to do reading, writing, arithmetic, and engage in computer-mediated learning (Gould & Gould, 2003). What optometrists point out is that a better set of mathematics standards seems less likely to help these students improve in school than does direct intervention in their health and welfare, perhaps most easily accomplished by ensuring that the families of these children earn adequate incomes and are provided medical insurance.

The complexity of medical problems increases when we discuss asthma, which has now reached epidemic proportions among poor children. One survey in a South Bronx neighborhood of New York City found a fourth grade teacher of whose 30 students 12 have asthma and 8 of those have to bring their breathing pumps to school every day (Books, 2002). Almost a decade ago, according to the National Institutes of Health, asthma alone resulted in 10 million missed school days a year, with many individual children missing 20 to 40 school days a year (National Institutes for Health, 1998, cited in Books, 2002. More recently, however, a survey puts missed school days due to asthma at 21 million (Schulman, Ronca & Bucuvalas, Inc., 2005). Asthma is simply preventing millions of children of all social classes from attending school and studying diligently. But asthma's effects on children from middle-income families are not nearly as severe as they are on the children of low-income families. Time on task, as we all know, is one of the strongest predictors of learning in schools. So it is no great leap of logic to point out that poor children, compared to their middle-class counterparts, will be missing a lot more school because of asthma, and thus will be learning a lot less.

Another level up in the seriousness of the medical problems that afflict the poor has to do with the effects of lead on mental functioning. Martin (2004), of the Arizona School Boards Association, has convinced me that this is much more of a problem than I had thought. No one I could find in the medical profession disputes the fact that very small amounts of lead can reduce intellectual functioning and diminish the capacity of a child to learn. The damage that lead does is almost always permanent. The good news is that lead poisoning is in decline; the bad news is that the Centers for Disease Control and Prevention still estimate that some 450,000 children in the United States between 1 and 5 years of age show levels of lead in their blood that are high enough to cause cognitive damage (Centers for Disease Control and Prevention, 2004). A simple extrapolation gives us a K–6 schooling population of another half million students with levels of lead in the blood high enough to cause neurological damage, and another half million permanently brain damaged students are apparently enrolled in our middle and high schools. Whether the effects of lead poisoning are small or large, whatever damage is done is usually permanent.

Do the millions of children affected in small and big ways by lead poisoning have anything in common? They sure do: they are mostly poor and mostly children of color. The poor live in older inner-city buildings where lead contamination from paint, and lead dust from many other sources, is prevalent. The poor also attend the oldest schools, and these have also been found to contain dangerous levels of lead. But the poor cannot move and neither landlords nor school districts will spend the money to make these buildings safe.

The literature on the symptoms of lead poisoning reminds me of the problems new teachers tell me about when they teach in schools that serve the poor. A lead-damaged nervous system is associated with a variety of problems including learning disabilities, ADHD, increased aggression, and lower intelligence, and those symptoms among older children are also linked with drug use and a greater likelihood of criminal behavior (see Books, 2002; Rothstein, 2004). Though a reduction of, say, four or five IQ points is not disastrous in a single poisoned child, that IQ reduction in a population will increase by 50% the number of children who qualify for special education, just about what we see in the schools serving the poor. Bailus Walker, a member of both the National Academy of Sciences and the Institute of Medicine, notes,

> The education community has not really understood the dimensions of this because we don't see kids falling over and dying of lead poisoning in the classroom. But there's a very large number of kids who find it difficult to do analytical work or [even] line up in the cafeteria because their brains are laden with lead. (Cited in Martin, 2004)

What is important to note is that the symptoms presented by lead exposure, like ADHD, irritability, problems of concentration, and the like are problems that schools must cope with and are not fixable by having better teachers or a more rigorous curriculum. There is absolutely no safe level for lead, and it almost always causes negative cognitive and behavioral effects (Lanphear, Dietrich, Auinger, & Cox, 2000). So it is to be expected that more poor children will have negative school experiences. They are bound to receive more negative evaluations and punishment than might their healthier middle-class peers.

There is another medical problem that is directly related to poverty. Premature births and low-birth-weight children are much more common problems among the poor. Neural imaging studies show that premature and low-birth-weight children are several times more likely to have anatomic brain abnormalities than do full-term, full-birth-weight controls (Peterson et al., 2003). Quantitative comparisons of brain volumes in eight-year-old children born prematurely and age-matched full-term control children also found that brain volume was less in the prematurely born. The degree of these morphologic abnormalities was strongly and inversely associated with measures of intelligence (Peterson et al., 2000). Unfortunately, social class and birth defects have been found to be significantly correlated in hundreds of studies. Some of the relationships seem associated with lifestyle problems (drug and alcohol use, vitamin deficiencies), while some seem neighborhood related (waste sites, lead, pesticides). But in either case, the children will still go to public schools five years later and become a problem for teachers and budgets alike.

How Neighborhood Poverty Affects Achievement

Neighborhood socioeconomic factors have an impact on achievement even beyond the impact of various health practices. For example, Garner and Raudenbush (1991) looked at student achievement in literacy in 16 secondary schools and in 437 neighborhoods in a set of school districts. The neighborhoods were scaled to reflect sociodemographic characteristics. These included overall unemployment rate, youth unemployment rate, number of single-parent families, percentage of low-income wage earners, overcrowding, and permanently sick individuals. When hierarchical linear modeling was used to analyze these data, significant school-to-school variance was found even when controlling for family background and neighborhood. Happily, this tells us that we should continue working on making schools better. This study and many others demonstrate that school effects are real and powerful: schools do exert positive influences on the lives of the poor.

But the analysis did not stop there. The neighborhood socioeconomic conditions variable showed a negative effect on educational attainment even after variation in the individual students and the schools they attend were stringently controlled. This was not a trivial statistical finding. For two students with identical prior backgrounds in achievement, with identical family backgrounds, and even with identical school membership, the differences in their educational attainment as a function of their neighborhood socioeconomic conditions was estimated to be a difference of between the 10th and the 90th percentile on achievement tests. More recently, sociologists Catsambis and Beveridge verified these finding using 1988 National Educational Longitudinal Survey (NELS 88) data with mathematics achievement as the outcome (2001). They found that neighborhood had significant direct and indirect effects on achievement, often by depressing parental practices that were usually associated with better student achievement. Because neighborhood effects are strong, good parents too frequently lose their children to the streets. Poverty traps people in neighborhoods that affect their children separately from the effects of home and school.

In sum, zip codes matter; they determine who is around to exert an influence during a child's formative years. In this way, zip codes can determine school achievement as much or more than can the influence of a person's family. Thus, several empirical studies have found that attending a middle-class school exposes minority students to higher expectations and more educational and career options. One team of researchers studied voluntary transfer policies in metropolitan St. Louis (Wells & Crain, 1997). They observed that minority students who attend middle- and upper-class schools had higher educational achievement and college attendance rates than their peers in schools where poverty was concentrated. Studies of Boston students who attended suburban public schools revealed that they had access to knowledge and networks of knowledge that their peers in inner-city Boston lacked (Eaton, 2001). These experiences increased their educational and professional opportunities. The famous Gautreaux study of Chicago made this plain years ago (Rubinowitz & Rosenbaum, 2000). In that natural experiment a random set of families received vouchers to move from their urban neighborhoods to the suburbs. Their children succeeded much better than did an equivalent control group. The Gautreaux study provides convincing evidence of the power of neighborhood, and the schools available to those neighborhoods, to influence our nation's youth.

Other Factors Contributing to the Low Achievement of the Poor

There are many other factors that contribute to poor students' low achievement levels. For example, the rates of hunger among the U.S. poor continue to be high for an industrialized nation (Nord, Andrews & Carlson, 2004). In 2003, about 12.5 million households—around 36 million people—suffered food insecurity. About 4 million of those households, or around 9.5 million people, actually went hungry at some time in that year. And sadly, one-third of this group experienced *chronic* hunger. Seventeen percent of the households with food insecurity have children, and these children do not ordinarily learn well. Perhaps equally unfortunate is the fact that the neighborhood norms for people who are poor promote non-nutritional foods and diets that lead to medical problems. Anemia, vitamin deficiencies, obesity, diabetes, and many other conditions that affect school learning help to keep the academic achievement of poor children lower than it might otherwise be.

The lack of high-quality affordable day care and quality early childhood learning environments is a problem of poverty that has enormous effects on later schooling. The early childhood educational gap between middle-class and poor children is well documented by Lee and Burkham (2002). More recent studies of the economic returns to society of providing better early childhood education for the poor have looked at the most famous of the early childhood programs with longitudinal data. From projects such as the Perry Preschool, the Abecedarian Project, the Chicago Child-Parent Centers, and the Elmira Prenatal/Early

Infancy Project, scholars find that the returns to society range from $3 to almost $9 for every dollar invested. Grunewald and Rolnick, of the Minneapolis Federal Reserve, have noted that when expressed as a rate of return, "the real (adjusted for inflation) internal rates of return on these programs range from about seven percent to above 16 percent annually" (2004, p. 6; see also Lynch, 2004, for a similar argument). Thus, since the return on investment to society for making high-quality early childhood programs available to all of our nation's children is remarkably large, why are we *not* making those investments?

The effects of smoking, alcohol and other drugs, lack of adequate dental and medical care, increased residential transiency, fewer positive after-school groups in which to participate, and many other factors all take their toll on the families and children of the poor. While these factors all interact with the quality of the teachers and the schools that poor children attend, these social, educational, medical, and neighborhood problems are also independent of the schools, and thus beyond their control. That is the crux of the argument: poverty severely limits what our schools can be expected to accomplish.

Let me take stock, here, so my argument is clear. I have provided reliable information that (1) we have the largest percentage of poor children in the industrialized world, (2) people stay poor longer in the United States than elsewhere in the industrialized world, (3) poverty is negatively related to school achievement and poverty's effects on our international competitiveness appear to be serious, and (4) poverty has powerful effects on individuals' educational achievement and attainment. This leads to the major point of this chapter: *improvement in the school achievement of students from low income families will have to come as much from improvements in their outside-of-school lives as from their inside-of-school lives.* And, because the outside-of-school environment is so important an influence on the academic attainment of poor people, there is every reason to suspect that changes in the income of poor families will lead to changes in the school-related behavior and achievement of their children.

HOW INCREASED FAMILY INCOME AFFECTS STUDENT BEHAVIOR AND SCHOOL ACHIEVEMENT

Two studies from a growing number about the effects of income growth on families and children have impressed me. First is the study by Dearing, McCartney, and Taylor (2001), who used as a measure of poverty the ratio of income available to the needs faced by a family. A ratio of 1.00 means that the family is just making it, that their family income and their needs such as housing, food, transportation, and so forth, are matched. A ratio of 3.00 would be more like that of a middle-class family, and a ratio of .8 would indicate poverty of some magnitude. A large and reasonably representative sample of poor and nonpoor families was followed for three years and their income-to-needs ratios computed regularly, as were their children's scores on various social and academic measures. What was found was that as poor families went from poor to a lot less poor, for whatever reasons, their children's performance began to resemble that of the "never poor" children with whom they were matched. The research literature suggests that bigger changes are expected to occur for the poor than the nonpoor as positive changes in their environments occur. That occurred in this study. When the never poor increased in income, their children's performance did not improve. But when poor families increased in income, the performance of their children did show gains. Also worth noting is that Duncan and Brooks-Gunn (2001) have found that the greatest impact of family income on children's academic outcomes is when they are the youngest—and this was a study of children from birth to three years of age.

In an interesting follow-up to the original study, these researchers went on to estimate the effect size of making the income changes that had occurred permanent in the sample of poor families, and comparing that effect size to those that the U.S. Department of Health and Human Services estimates for the early Head Start program (Taylor, Dearing, & McCartney, 2004). Both in the Head Start study and this one, the same mental development index was used to look at intellectual functioning and both studies measured students' negative behavior, as well. The interesting findings are presented here in Table 7.6.

In the first row of Table 7.6 we see that Head Start researchers estimate that children enrolled in that program increased between 12% and 15% of a standard deviation on the mental development index. These children also showed a decline of 10–11% of a standard deviation in their negative behavior. Those outcomes are socially significant and large enough to claim effectiveness for the gigantic Head Start apparatus. The second row of this table are Taylor, Dearing, and McCartney's (2004)

Table 7.6 Comparison of Head Start Program Effects with Those from Family Growth in Income

	Mental Development Index (percent of a standard deviation)	Negative Behavior Index (percent of a standard deviation)
Head Start Program	Up 12–15%	Down 10–11%
Income Growth Study	Up 15%	Down 20%

estimates of what would happen were the income of the poor families in their study increased one standard deviation, or about $13,000 per year. This estimate shows that the children form low-income families would have had gains in IQ of about 15% of a standard deviation, and that the children would decline in negative behavior about 20% of a standard deviation.

The success brought about by an increase in the incomes of poor families apparently matches or exceeds the success our nation obtains from running a giant program like Head Start, which enrolls only about 60% of those that are eligible. Equally intriguing in this study is that raising the income of families to improve the lives of poor children is actually a bit less expensive than the annual cost per child of attending Head Start. It is impossible not to speculate about what the results might be for our society if we combined both approaches to school improvement, providing both high-quality early childhood programs and better incomes for the poor.

The second study of income change and school success is from North Carolina, and is almost a natural experiment in income redistribution (Costello, Compton, Keeler, & Angold, 2003). A Duke University team noticed that their study of psychiatric disorders and drug abuse within a rural community included a group of people who had risen out of poverty because of the income derived from a recently opened gaming casino. During these changes the researchers had been giving annual psychiatric assessments to about 1,400 children, 350 of them American Indians, and they did so over an eight-year period. The children ranged in age from 9 to 13 and were in three distinct groups: those who had never been poor, those who had been persistently poor, and a group that had been poor until the casino came to the reservation.

The researchers discovered that moving out of poverty was associated with a decrease in frequency of psychiatric symptoms over the ensuing four years. In fact, by the fourth year, the psychiatric symptom level was the same among children whose families moved out of poverty as it was among children whose families were never in poverty. A small replication of the findings was available for a group of non-Indians who also moved out of poverty over this same time period. Once again, as in the Dearing, McCartney and Taylor (2001) study, and in the main part of this study, negative psychiatric symptoms disappeared as income rose. The researchers offered an explanation for these findings—namely, that relieving poverty appeared to increase the level of parental supervision of children. One last finding of interest from this study is that additional income for the families of the never poor had no effect on frequency of behavioral or emotional symptoms. As is common in this area of research, and noted earlier, improving the income of the very poor has large effects, while improving the income of the less poor has negligible effects.

Although the literature is not voluminous, these are not the only studies to show that a lessening of poverty helps young children succeed better at school and in life. The negative income tax was studied over 20 years ago and it revealed that increases in family income resulted in increased school attendance and better school achievement for the families that gained in income (Salkind & Haskins, 1982). The work-assistance programs of the 1990s have also been examined, and again there is some evidence that as family income went up the achievement and behavior of children in those families improved (Huston et al., 2001). The evidence of the positive influence on student achievement when families are able to leave poverty is consistent and replicable, suggesting that inside-of-school reform needs to begin with outside-of school reform.

WHAT WE NEED TO DO

It is not easy for most educators to overcome the effects that poverty has on the lives of their students. Poverty in a community almost ensures that many of the children who enter their neighborhood schools cannot maximally profit from the instruction provided. Helping to eliminate some of that poverty is not just morally appropriate—though it is that, first of all. But, to a convincing degree, finding ways to reduce poverty to improve schooling is evidence based: it takes no great wisdom to realize that families with increasing fortunes have more hope, and are thus able to take better care of their children, than do families in more dire straits, where anxiety and despair are the more common emotional reactions. So when we push for higher qualifications for the teachers of the poor, as we should, we should also push ourselves and others to stop buying from companies that do not provide decent wages and health insurance to their workers.

The logic of this is simple: if we want to primarily hold our teachers responsible for increasing their students' educational attainment, then we need to provide those teachers with children who enter their classrooms healthy and ready to learn. Wal-Mart, now the nation's largest employer, and companies like it, do not provide the great majority of their employees the income, medical insurance, or retirement plans needed to promote healthy families or raise healthy children. Wal-Mart and companies like it have a terrible record in their treatment of women employees with children, a group who make up a big share of the poor households in this country (Shulman, 2003). Thus, Wal-Mart and companies like it are an impediment to school reform. When we push for more rigorous standards in our schools we need to also push for a raise in the minimum wage—or better yet, for livable wages. If we do not do this, then we will ensure that the vast majority of those meeting the increasingly rigorous requirements for high school graduation will be those students fortunate enough to be born into better-resourced families. If we really want a more egalitarian set of educational outcomes, our nation needs a more equalitarian wage structure.

While it is appropriate that we push for more professional development for teachers and mentoring programs for new teachers, such activities might still not be helpful to poor students if women workers in America continue to make poverty wages. So we need also to demand that women's wages be set equal to those of men doing comparable work, since it is working women and their children who make up a large percentage of America's poor. When we push for advanced placement courses or college preparatory curricula for all our nation's students, we must simultaneously demand universal medical coverage for all our children. Only then will all our children have the health that allows them to attend school regularly and learn effectively, instead of missing opportunities to learn due to a lack of medical treatment.

When we push for all-day kindergarten, or quality early childhood care, or detracked schools, we need also to argue for affordable housing throughout our communities, so that neighborhoods have the possibility of exerting more positive influences on children and people can move from lead- and mercury-polluted areas to those that are less toxic, and thus less likely to cause birth defects. This goal requires educators, parents, and other concerned citizens to be in the forefront of the environmental fight. To fight for clean air and water, and for fewer untested chemicals in all our food products, is not just a rational response to modern living; it is also a fight to have more healthy children for our schools to educate. The financial and psychological costs to families because of students needing special education can be markedly reduced by our demands for a healthier environment.

In my estimation, we will get better public schools by requiring concern for the out-of-school factors as much as by concern for the inside-of-school factors. It is silly to worry about whether teachers have enough phonics knowledge or whether school standards are rigorous enough when we send to the schools children who are not able, due to out-of-school circumstances, to fully benefit from that best that our schools have to offer.

CONCLUSION

Schools alone cannot do what is needed to help more people achieve higher levels of academic performance in our society. As Anyon has put it, "Attempting to fix inner city schools without fixing the city in which they are embedded is like trying to clean the air on one side of a screen door" (1997, p. 168). To clean the air on both sides of the screen door we need to begin thinking about building a two-way system of accountability for contemporary America. The obligation that we educators have accepted to be accountable to our communities must become reciprocal. Our communities must also be accountable to those of us who work in the schools, and they can do this by creating social conditions for our nation that allow us to do our jobs well. Our whole society must be held as accountable for providing healthy children, who are ready to learn, as our schools are for delivering quality instruction. One-way accountability, where we are always blaming the schools for the faults that we find, is neither just nor likely to solve the problems we want to address.

REFERENCES

Agency for Healthcare Research and Quality (2005). *Otitis media with effusion in young children.* Archived Clinical Practices Guidelines, National Library of Medicine, No. 12. Retrieved May 17, 2005, from http://www.ncbi. nlm.nih.gov/entrez/query.fcgi?cmd=Search&db=books&doptcmdl= GenBookHL&term=otitis+media+AND+hstat%5Bbook%5D+AND+ 342118%5Buid%5D&rid=hstat6.section.23571#top.

Anne E. Casey Foundation (2006). *Kids count data book.* Baltimore: Author. Retrieved June 20, 2006, from http://www.aecf.org/kidscount/sld/ databook.jsp.

Anyon, J. (1995). Race, social class, and educational reform in an inner city school. *Teachers College Record, 97*(1), 69–94.

Anyon, J. (1997). *Ghetto schooling: A political economy of urban school reform.* New York: Teachers College Press.

Berliner, D. C., & Biddle, B. J. (1995). *The manufactured crisis: Myth, fraud, and the attack on America's public schools.* Reading, MA: Addison-Wesley.

Books, S. (2002). Poverty and environmentally induced damage to children. In V. Polakow (Ed.), *The public assault on America's children: Poverty, violence, and juvenile injustice* (pp. 42-58). New York: Teachers College Press.

Catsambis, S., & Beveridge, A. W. (2001). *Sociological Focus, 34*(4), 435–457.

Centers for Disease Control and Prevention (2004). *Children's blood lead levels in the United States.* Retrieved May 15, 2005, from http://www.cdc.gov/ nceh/lead/research/kidsBLL.htm.

Centers for Disease Control and Prevention (2005). *Breastfeeding Practices: Results from the 2003 National Immunization Survey.* Retrieved May 17, 2005, from http://www.cdc.gov/breastfeeding/NIS_data/.

Cooper, H., Nye, B., Charlton, K., Lindsay, J., & Greathouse, S. (1996). The effects of summer vacation on achievement test scores: A narrative and meta-analytic review. *Review of Educational Research, 66*(3), 227–268.

Costello, E. J., Compton, S. N., Keeler, G., & Angold, A. (2003). Relationships between poverty and psychopathology: A natural experiment. *Journal of the American Medical Association, 290*(15), 2023–2029.

Dearing, E., McCartney, K., & Taylor, B. A. (2001). Change in family income-to-needs matters more for children with less. *Child Development, 72*(6), 1779–1793.

Duncan, G. J., & Brooks-Gunn, J. (2001). Poverty, welfare reform, and children's achievement. In B. J. Biddle (Ed.), *Social class, poverty, and achievement* (pp. 49–75). New York: Routledge-Falmer.

Eaton, S. (2001). *The other Boston busing story: What's won and lost across the boundary line.* New Haven, CT: Yale University Press.

Garner, C. L., & Raudenbush, S. W. (1991). Neighborhood effects on educational attainment: A multilevel analysis. *Sociology of Education, 64*(4), 251–262.

Gillespie, K. (2001, 17 April). How vision impacts literacy: An educational problem that can be solved. Harvard Graduate School of Education News. Retrieved May 15, 2005, from http://www.gse.harvard.edu/news/features/vision04172001.html.

Gonzales, P., Guzmán, J. C., Partelow, L., Pahlke, E., Jocelyn, L., Kastberg, D., et al. (2004). *Highlights from the Trends in International Mathematics and Science Study (TIMSS) 2003.* U.S. Department of Education, National Center for Education Statistics, NCES 2005–005. Washington, DC: U.S. Government Printing Office. Retrieved May 15, 2005, from http://nces.ed.gov/pubs2005/2005005.pdf.

Gould, M., & Gould, H. (2003). A clear vision for equity and opportunity. *Phi Delta Kappan, 85*(4), 324–328.

Grunewald, R., & Rolnick, A. (2004). *A proposal for achieving high returns on early childhood development.* Minneapolis, MN: Federal Reserve Bank of Minneapolis. Retrieved May 16, 2005, from http://minneapolisfed.org/research/studies/earlychild/draft_ecd_proposal.pdf.

Hagerman, R. J., & Falkenstein, A. R. (1987). An association between recurrent otitis media in infancy and later hyperactivity. *Clinical Pediatrics, 26*(5), 253–257.

Huston, A. C., Duncan, G. J., Granger, R., Bos, J., McLoyd, V., Mistry, R., et al. (2001). Work-based antipoverty programs for parents can enhance the school performance and social behavior of children. *Child Development, 72*(1), 318–336.

Knishkowy, B., Palti, H., Adler, B., & Tepper, D. (1991). Effect of otitis media on development: A community-based study. *Early Human Development, 26*(2), 101–111.

Kozol, J. (1995). *Amazing grace: The lives of children and the conscience of a nation.* New York: Crown.

Lanphear, B. P., Dietrich, K., Auinger, P., & Cox, C. (2000). Subclinical lead toxicity in U.S. children and adolescents. *Public Health Reports, 115,* 521–529. Retrieved May 15, 2005, from http://www.nmic.org/nyccelp/ medical-studies/Lanphear-Cognitive-Deficits-under-10ugdl.pdf.

Lee, V. E., & Burkam, D. T. (2002). *Inequality at the starting gate.* Washington, DC: Economic Policy Institute.

Lemke, M., Calsyn, C., Lippman, L., Jocelyn, L., Kastberg, D., Liu, Y. Y., et al. (2001). *Outcomes of Learning: Results from the 2000 Program for International Student Assessment of 15-year-olds in reading, mathematics, and science literacy.* National Center for Education Statistics, NCES 2002–115. Washington, DC: U.S. Department of Education, National Center for Education Statistics.

Luotonen, M., Uhari, M., Aitola, L., Lukkaroinen, A., Luotonen, J., Uhari, M., et al. (1996). Recurrent otitis media during infancy and linguistic skills at the age of nine years. *Pediatric Infectious Disease Journal, 15*(10), 854–858.

Lynch, R. G. (2004). Exceptional returns: Economic, fiscal, and social benefits of investment in early childhood development. Washington, DC: Economic Policy Institute.

Martin, M. (2004). *A strange ignorance: The role of lead poisoning in "failing schools."* Retrieved May 15, 2005, from http://www.azsba.org/lead.htm.

Mishel, L., Bernstein, J., & Allegretto, S., (2005). *The state of working America 2004/2005.* Washington, DC: Economic Policy Institute/Ithaca, NY: Cornell University Press.

Niemela, M., Pihakari, O., Pokka, T., Uhari, M., & Uhari, M. (2000). Pacifier as a risk factor for acute otitis media: A randomized, controlled trial of parental counseling. *Pediatrics, 106*(3), 483–488.

Nord, M., Andrews, M., & Carlson, S. (2004). *Household food security in the United States, 2003.* Food Assistance and Nutrition Research Report No. FANRR42. Washington, DC: United States Department of Agriculture, Economic Research Service. Retrieved May 16, 2005, from http://www.ers.usda.gov/publications/fanrr42/.

Orfield, G., & Lee, C. (2005). *Why segregation matters: Poverty and educational inequality.* Cambridge, MA: Harvard University Civil Rights Project. Retrieved May 15, 2005, from http://www.civilrightsproject.harvard. edu/research/deseg/Why_Segreg_Matters.pdf.

Peterson, B. S., Anderson, A. W., Ehrenkranz, R., Staib, L. H., Tageldin, M., Colson, E., et al. (2003). Regional brain volumes and their later neuro-developmental correlates in term and preterm infants. *Pediatrics, 111*(5), 939–948.

Peterson, B. S., Vohr, B., Staib, L. H., Cannistraci, C. J., Dolberg, A., Schneider, K. C., et al. (2000). Regional brain volume abnormalities and long-term cognitive outcome in preterm infants. *Journal of the American Medical Association, 284*(15), 1939–1947.

Rector, R. E., & Johnson, K. A. (2004). *Understanding poverty in America.* Washington, DC: Heritage Foundation. Retrieved May 15, 2005, from http://www.heritage.org/Research/Welfare/bg1713.cfm.

Rothstein, R. (2004). *Class and schools: Using social, economic, and educational reform to close the black-white achievement gap.* Washington, DC: Economic Policy Institute.

Rubinowitz, L. S., & Rosenbaum, J. E. (2000). *Crossing the class and color lines: from public housing to white suburbia.* Chicago: University of Chicago Press.

Salkind, N. J., & Haskins, R. (1982). Negative income tax: The impact on children from low-income families. *Journal of Family Issues, 3*(2), 165–180.

Shulman, B. (2003). *The betrayal of work: How low-wage jobs fail 30 million Americans.* New York: New Press.

Schulman, Ronca & Bucuvalas, Inc. (2005). *Children and asthma in America.* New York: Author, for GlaxoSmithKline. Retrieved May 15, 2005, from http://www.asthmainamerica.com.

Sirin, S. R. (2005). Socioeconomic status and academic achievement: A meta-analytic review of research 1990–2000. *Review of Educational Research, 75*(3), 417–453.

Taylor, B. A., Dearing, E., & McCartney, K. (2004). Incomes and outcomes in early childhood. *Journal of Human Resources 39*(4), 980–1007.

UNICEF Innocenti Research Centre (2005). *Child poverty in rich countries, 2005.* Innocenti Report Card No. 6. Florence, Italy: Author. Retrieved May 16, 2005, from www.unicef.org/irc.

Wells, A., & Crain, R. (1997). *Stepping over the color line: African-American students in white suburban schools.* New Haven, CT: Yale University Press.

World Bank (2005). *World development indicators database.* Retrieved May 15, 2005, from http://www.worldbank.org/data/databytopic/GNIPC.pdf.

8

ON THE INTERNATIONAL DIMENSION OF EDUCATION AND SOCIAL JUSTICE

Stephen P. Heyneman
Vanderbilt University

THROUGHOUT HISTORY, PEOPLE HAVE FOUND ONLY FIVE WAYS to choose leaders: by inheritance, force, chance, political loyalty, or achievement. Only with the last—achievement—has there been an attempt to question how opportunity for participation might be equitably distributed. Broad access to schooling has been society's way to ensure that future leaders might be drawn from the population at large, with a universal opportunity to participate. Plato might have been the first to propose that occupational preparation be renewed with each generation and based upon what each individual was able to achieve for himself. Thus, the social justice rationales (i.e., the equitable distribution of opportunity) for education are both radical and ancient.

Implementation of this "footrace" remained relatively dormant until the Industrial Revolution. Before then, families were the primary economic unit and the appropriate function of education was to maintain the productivity of the family. Skills were passed from parent to child. Until the time when children were not expected to remain within the family economic unit, educational opportunity, much less equality of opportunity, was hardly relevant. Today, in spite of the concerns of many social liberals, occupational choice is less determined by family of birth than at any time in human history. Only in the most isolated geographical areas (e.g., among desert nomads and forest tribes) is parent-to-child occupational transfer automatically conducted without intervening influence from the economy or the state. This worldwide change in the nature of occupational selection makes the quality of educational opportunity a universal issue.

DEFINITIONAL REQUIREMENTS
OF EQUAL OPPORTUNITY

An equal-opportunity strategy is justified by the premise that human beings differ, and therefore some will utilize resources more efficiently and more quickly than others. The purpose of all equal-opportunity strategies is to assure that, as nearly as is feasible, all will have equal chances to utilize resources. Key to the concept is the notion of equal exposure to the resources necessary to participate. Whether those resources are equally utilized does not determine whether equal opportunity has been achieved. Equal opportunity acknowledges that inequalities in utilization will not disappear.

Whether some inequality is morally acceptable in a just society is the subject of a dialogue between some fields of sociology and moral philosophy (Bane, 1975; Coleman, 1973, 1974; Nozick, 1975; Rawls, 1958, 1971). The pro-and-con arguments hinge on the following: if one accepts an equal-opportunity strategy, it implies that one must accept the existence of appropriate or proper differences among people. Society must agree that these differences are just and have been achieved fairly—as in, for example, differences in achievement in sports, chess, and physics.

When faced with a demand for equalizing geographical opportunity within a country, several definitional criteria might be utilized. As a practical matter, the four checks proposed by Bell and Robinson (1978), Berne and Stiefel (1984), and Rice (2004) seem pertinent: (1) that the criteria be based on something that can in fact be distributed; (2) that a unit of analysis such as neighborhood, region, or individual be specified; (3) that the degree of distribution be measurable; and (4) that the consumers agree that the item is a good measure of what should be fairly distributed.

EQUAL OPPORTUNITY OF EDUCATION
AMONG NATIONS

A new international definition of basic human rights emerged from the United Nations agreements signed at the end of World War II. There were guarantees of freedom of many kinds—from hunger, persecution, and prejudice based on race, gender, religion, and national origin—as well as a guarantee of education. In the English and American legal context, the rights of individuals were thought of as being constituted prior to the state itself. In Europe, the rights of individuals were thought of as being guaranteed by the states (Bendix, 1964). Because there is no single authority that can operate above the nation-state, individual rights have been thought of as being part of a natural law applicable to all human beings. This is the natural law cited as the source of authority by the United Nations in its declaration of human rights (Lauren, 2000).

Now, a half century later, it might be worthwhile to ask what has been accomplished. One could hardly argue that the world is free of prejudice or persecution. Hunger, malnutrition, and disease continue to be serious problems. One arena in which the world can demonstrate advancement is the field of education. This advancement has been made in spite of the obvious handicaps frequently cited in the development economics literature: population growth, civil war, disease, political and economic inexperience of local leaders, poverty, and competing economic and social priorities.

The explanation for this advancement is not difficult to discern. The world's first experience with public education was in the late 18th century in Prussia. It arose from a need to achieve social cohesion across a community suddenly divided by Catholic and Protestant citizens (Heyneman, 2000). Thus precedent was established for some citizens in order to help finance the education of other citizens to whom they were not directly related. In the United States, equal opportunity has recently been defined as equality of opportunity across school districts within the same state. Recent state supreme court rulings have now made interschool district financial redistribution the norm in most places (Baicker & Gordon, 2004; Berne & Stiefel, 1999; Corcoran, Evans, Godwin, Murray, & Schwab, 2003).

This equality of opportunity strategy has generated both support and protest. In the United States and other places, since educational finance is often dependent on local property taxes and since local property taxes require a public vote, it has been argued that a reallocation toward lower income school districts will lower the incentive for the public to tax itself for education. In fact, some high-income school districts have established educational foundations as a partial response to reallocation of educational resources. Some see this as a means by which wealthy parents provide educational quality for their children while avoiding providing resources for others' children (Carr & Furman, 1999). However resisted, in some respects reallocation of educational resources across school districts is parallel to financing a public good by taxing citizens in a graduated fashion according to differences in property or income.

It is assumed that the poor would benefit from a source of revenue that they did not directly generate. But why would wealthy citizens agree to tax themselves for the benefit of the less wealthy? What helps determine the willingness to be taxed for the benefit of someone else's children? As a human right, education is unique in that it is as much in the interest of the geographic periphery as the geographic center. Education investments made in rural Mississippi may have important and positive externalities in New York. Although New York has many priorities and demands on public expenditure, when New Yorkers pay federal taxes, in essence they are taxing themselves to support Head Start education in Mississippi. They do this because there is a general consensus across the states that one legitimate function of the central government is to assist in the provision of educational opportunity for citizens whose resources are too modest to provide it for themselves. And they have agreed to use these tax resources for citizens who may live in communities far away from their own. This is roughly analogous to the current discussion over international tax-supported assistance to provide basic education in low-income countries.

Education investments are of value to both geographic donors and geographic consumers because the economic benefits accrue to both producers and consumers of a public good. Parents may think of schools as instruments to affect individual occupational life chances. In many low-income countries the evidence of upward mobility through education has been dramatic (Heyneman, 1982, 2004). Parental demand for educational opportunity, coupled with the economic and political obligation of state authorities to provide it, accounts for the recent expansion of formal schooling at levels unprecedented in human history. Since the end of World War II, universal primary enrollment has been achieved in 85 countries, including most of Central Asia, Europe, and Latin America; much of Eastern Asia; Iraq, Jordan, and Tunisia; and Algeria, Botswana, Gabon, Lesotho, South Africa, Swaziland, Togo, and Uganda (UNESCO, 2002, p. 46). About nine nations remain with gross enrollment rates at or below 70%, although there are many additional countries where recent data are not sufficient to determine enrollment rates.

An international standard has been established of having equal access to a basic education opportunity consisting of about nine grades. Approximately 20% of the age cohort between 18 and 22 today have an opportunity to attend some form of postsecondary education (World Bank, 2004). The unprecedented growth in access to schooling would suggest that we are living in a period of the largest educational oppor-tunity in recorded history. In spite of this universal growth in access, most countries fall short of the standard of universal completion of grade 9. But the reason these countries fall short has changed. In West and Central Africa and in South Asia, about one-third of the deficit from universal completion of grade 9 can be attributed to "dropouts." In Central America and in Eastern and Southern Africa, about 70% of the deficit can be attributed to dropouts. In Europe and Central Asia, dropouts constitute about 80% of the deficit, and in South America dropouts account for 92% of the deficit (Pritchett, 2004, p. 181). The main problem in basic education today is not lack of access, but the lack of progress through primary school once entry has been attained.

While there are some school systems that have been found to operate efficiently despite low levels of resources (Heyneman, 1997, 2004), it is also the case that differences in resources constitute the largest source of low achievement (Heyneman & Loxley, 1983). Because low achieve-ment is associated with leaving schools early, and because inequality of resources is a principal contributor of the achievement problem, it is rea-sonable to conclude that inequality in the distribution of resources is the principal cause of the inequality in educational results across countries.

Yet how unequal is the distribution of educational resources? Within the United States, financial disparities among districts and states range from a ratio of 1:2 to perhaps as high as 1:3. For instance, in New York in 2001–2002, per-pupil expenditures ranged from $10,214 in the bot-tom 10% of its districts to a high of $16,355 in those at the top 90%, a difference of 1:1.6 (New York State Education Department, Fiscal Analysis and Services Unit, 2004). It might also be relevant to look at the extreme difference between the poorest and the wealthiest districts. The New York district of Broadalbin-Perth in Fulton County was able to spend only $8,701 per student in 2001–2002, yet Kiryas Joel Village in Orange County was able to spend $69,140 per student, a difference of 1:7.9 (NYSED, 2004). In 2003–2004, interstate differences ranged from a low of $5,091 in Utah to a high of $13,317 in the District of Columbia, a difference of 1:2.6 (National Education Association, 2005).

It is difficult to calculate the same measures across countries. Purchasing-power value differs between currencies; salaries and wages are often not well recorded; figures on government expenditures range in quality and in coverage. And international statistical agencies are only beginning to hold low-income countries to the same standards of transparency and statistical professionalism in education that they expect in other fields such as health, trade, and public accounts (Heyneman, 1999). Nevertheless, recent efforts have made it possible to estimate expenditures using purchasing-power parity in a sufficient variety of countries to give us a picture of the order of magnitude of the differences in educational opportunity. There is more variation between wealthy and impoverished areas of the world than there is between wealthy and impoverished regions within the United States.

For each country for which we have reliable information, we have taken (1) the level of public expenditure on education as a percentage of gross domestic product (GDP); and (2) the level of GDP expressed in terms of purchasing-power parity (PPP). From these two figures we have calculated (3) the money spent on education in U.S. dollars. We have then taken the total expenditures and divided by the number of school-age children in the population and divided that by educational

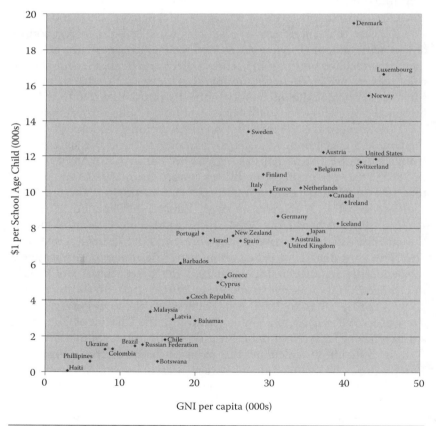

Figure 8.1 Equity of international educational resources. *Sources:* United Nations Development Programme, 2004; UNESCO, 2002.

expenditures to achieve (4) the expenditure for each school age child in each nation.

As one might expect, the very-low-income nations are able to allocate only a small fraction of what a high-income country is able to allocate. Bangladesh spends about $157 per school-age person. This compares unfavorably with Angola, which allocates $209; Azerbaijan, with $486; Brazil, with $1,450; South Africa, with $2,287; Bahrain, with $3,600; Spain, with $7,300; Germany, with $8,673; Canada, with $9,791, the Netherlands, with $10,233; Switzerland, with $11,658; Norway, with $15,409; and Denmark, with $19,468. These differences are illustrated in Figure 8.1 on the opposite page.

THE INTERNATIONAL SEARCH FOR SOCIAL JUSTICE IN EDUCATION

International legal structures to propose, negotiate, and ratify binding treaties are in place and already operating in diverse fields of human rights causes such as ethnic cleansing, war crimes, narcotics trafficking, and involuntary servitude, as well as in more technical areas such as nuclear disarmament and nonproliferation, transport safety, and telecommunications standards. The procedures of international law are implemented on a daily basis. The United Nations Convention on the Rights of the Child, adopted in 1989, is the most widely ratified treaty in the world. Virtually all of the industrial democracies have signed this convention and their legislatures and parliaments have ratified it. All of them are required to submit reports, every five years, on what they are doing to make those rights effective (Melchiorre, 2002, p. 3). Article 28 of the Convention on the Rights of the Child includes the obligation of the state to:

Make primary education compulsory and available to all;

Encourage the development of different forms of secondary education, including general and vocational education, make them available and accessible to every child, and take appropriate measures, such as the introduction of free education and offering financial assistance in case of need;

Make higher education accessible to all on the basis of capacity by every appropriate means;

Make educational and vocational information and guidance available and accessible to all children;

Take measures to encourage regular attendance at schools and the reduction of dropout rates;

Take all appropriate measures to ensure that school discipline is administered in a manner consistent with the child's human dignity;

Promote and encourage international cooperation in matters relating to education, in particular with a view to contributing to the elimination of ignorance and illiteracy throughout the world and facilitating access to scientific and technical knowledge and modern teaching methods. *In this regard, particular account shall be taken of the needs of developing countries.* (Reproduced in Melchiorre 2002, p. 6; emphasis added)

What are the "needs" of developing countries, and what does "take into account" imply? Normally, the latter implies that the ability of a poor nation to adhere to rules and regulations is attenuated because of its poverty. It does not mean that poor countries have a right to abrogate their agreements. No country is excused from the prohibition on slavery on the grounds that it is poor. In essence, this phrase acknowledges that low-income countries cannot be expected to enforce universal schooling agreements without assistance for education.

Since World War II, industrial democracies have allocated a proportion of their public finance as assistance to less wealthy nations, including their efforts to educate their citizens. This aid flows through private voluntary organizations such as CARE; through bilateral organizations such as USAID; and through multilateral organizations such as the World Bank and the regional development banks. Industrial democracies have not legally obligated themselves to allocate a particular proportion of their wealth to foreign aid, but it is generally acknowledged that approximately one percent of GDP is a reasonable target. In the first years following World War II, the United States was extraordinarily generous with its assistance, which in 1950 amounted to just under 3% of GDP. U.S. foreign aid dropped over the next 20 years. In 1997 it reached its lowest level ever, at 0.16% of GDP, with the number of employees working for USAID dropping from 8,200 in 1962 to about 2,000 today (Tarnoff & Nowels, 2002, p. 15). In 2002, the United States ranked 22nd in its allocation of foreign aid (see Figure 8.2).

The U.S. economy is the world's largest, and though foreign aid in 2004 accounted for only 0.9% of federal government expenditures (see Figure 8.3), the amount of aid in terms of dollars is still the world's largest among the industrial democracies (see Figure 8.4).

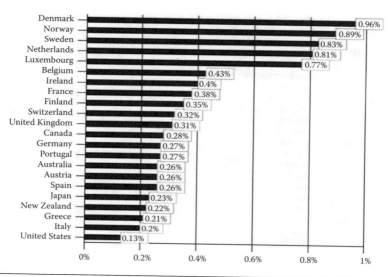

Figure 8.2 Economic aid as a percentage of GNI from major donors, 2002. *Source:* Tarnoff & Nowels, 2002.

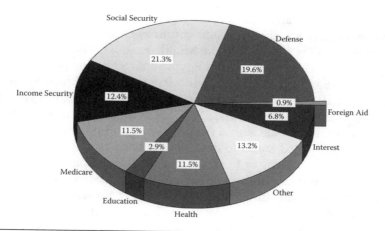

Figure 8.3 U.S. budget outlays, FY2004. *Source:* Tarnoff & Nowels, 2004.

The problem is not only that foreign aid is too small, but also that it is allocated to many priorities other than education. Only about half of the U.S. foreign aid budget is allocated for purposes of economic development or humanitarian-based relief. The other half is allocated either to military purposes or to economic and political purposes. Military purposes accounted for 23% in 2004; economic and political and security purposes accounted for 26%.

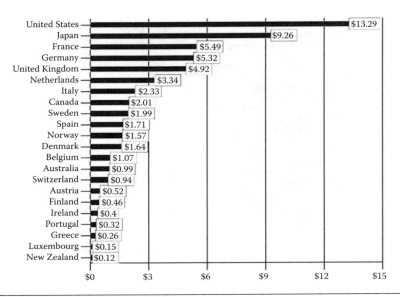

Figure 8.4 Economic aid in dollars from major donors, 2002. *Source:* Tarnoff & Nowels, 2004.

Another handicap is the tendency to allocate foreign aid to a small number of strategically important countries. A significant portion of U.S. foreign aid is allocated to the Middle East, with Israel accounting for almost $3 billion per year and Egypt about $2 billion per year. Four recipients—Egypt, Israel, Jordan, and Palestine—accounted for about one half of all U.S. foreign assistance until recently. This has changed since the events of September 11, 2001, with the growth in assistance to Afghanistan, Iraq, and Central Asia, but the point is constant. Foreign aid from the United States to date has not been targeted primarily to humanitarian concerns or to education. Education accounts for about 6% of U.S. economic and social assistance, with assistance for basic education accounting for about 3.9% (Tarnoff & Nowels, 2002, p. 10).

Is the United States less concerned with education than other industrial democracies that have lower military and security concerns? Not exactly. Of all official development assistance (ODA) in 2002, the total education assistance of U.S. $3.8 billion accounted for only a small portion of overall aid. Education assistance was only 8% of the total level of assistance to Eastern Europe, and in the region which arguably needs it most, Sub-Saharan Africa, aid to education amounted to only 10% of the total aid allocation (Organization for Economic Cooperation and Development, 2002). But foreign assistance is in fact only a small percentage of the total flow of capital to and from developing countries. In 2000, capital flows amounted to U.S. $463 billion (with U.S. $161

Table 8.1 Capital Flows to Developing Countries in 2000 (in U.S. $ Billions)[1]

	E. Asia	ECA[2]	LAC[3]	MENA[4]	S. Asia	SSA[5]	Total	(% of Total)
Foreign Direct Investment	58	29	76	5	3	7	178	38.4%
Portfolio Equity Flows	29	6	10	1	2	1	49	10.6%
Aid	3	8	3	3	3	10	30	6.5%
Remittances	2	6	15	12	18	2	55	11.9%
Debt Repayment	−33	−5	−47	−11	1	−6	−101	−21.8%
Profits on Foreign Investment	−17	−3	−22	−2	−1	−5	−50	−10.8%
Total (Net)							161	Positive
							463	Total Flow

Notes:
1. Developing countries are those that are allowed to borrow from the Multilateral Development Banks.
2. ECA = Europe and Central Asia region.
3. LAC = Latin America and the Caribbean region.
4. MENA = Middle East and North Africa region.
5. SSA = Sub-Saharan Africa.

Source: World Bank, 2001.

billion net inflow). Aid amounted to only 6.5% of this, and was dwarfed by the amount of capital flowing via foreign direct investment at 38.4% (Table 8.1).

There is no enforceable mandate for wealthy nations to share their resources to achieve a principle that they take as sacrosanct within their own countries. But there is a moral and an economic case for achieving a rough equality of educational access around the world. If this was accepted as an international responsibility, what would it cost? The World Bank, UNICEF, and UNESCO have each done cost estimates. Because their assumptions differ, their estimates differ. UNESCO believes it would require additional resources of about U.S. $4.3 billion per year; UNICEF believes it would require about U.S. $4.9 billion; and the World Bank suggests that it would require about U.S. $8.4 billion (see Table 8.2). The most important differences in these estimates derive from differences in unit expenditures (UNESCO assumes $188 per student per year; UNICEF assumes $42 per student) and whether the target outcome is enrollment or completion. The World Bank's estimate,

Table 8.2 Average Annual Cost to Achieve Universal Primary Education by 2015 (by Source of Estimate)

Source	Cost (U.S. $ Millions)
UNESCO[a]	4,294
UNICEF[b]	4,939
World Bank[c]	8,357

[a] 100% Net Enrollment Rate projected unit cost $198; current cost $188.
[b] 100% Net Enrollment Rate projected unit cost $140; current cost $42.
[c] 100% completion; projected unit cost $79; current cost $79.
Source: UNESCO, 2002, p. 136.

for instance, is based on the proportion of children in the relevant age cohort able to complete primary education within the allotted time.

Estimates also differ in regard to potential additional funding sources. But all estimates assume that the resources would need to be derived from a mixture of external aid and internal savings and tax receipts, with the majority of the new resources coming from internal sources even for the 47 poorest countries of the world (see Table 8.3).

Whatever the outcome, it must be acknowledged that the highest of the three estimates of the additional external funds needed to achieve basic international equality of educational opportunity, U.S. $2.4 billion, is less than 1% of the flow of capital between low- and high-income countries and only 8% of the current flow of aid. If the cost is so low in comparison to the resources available, what are the prospects of establishing a new dimension of social justice in the field of education? In fact, the prospects are quite good.

Table 8.3 Annual Funding Requirements to Achieve Universal Primary Education by 2015 (in U.S. $ Billions)

	Source		
	Domestic	External	Total
47 poorest countries	4.1	2.1	6.1*
All developing countries	2.3	0.3	2.6
Total	6.4	2.4	8.8

* Includes 0.6 billion to support AIDS orphans.
Source: World Bank, 2002, table 4.13.

THE NEW INTERNATIONAL DIMENSION
OF SOCIAL JUSTICE IN EDUCATION

There has been a great deal of discussion about the effectiveness of foreign aid. Some have argued that it has been ineffective because the aid has been targeted to comparatively wealthy countries with low need. Others have argued that aid was directed at countries whose economic policies were hopelessly mired in distortions (Dollar & Pritchett, 1998). Some have suggested that foreign aid has simply supplanted normal expenditures, allowing local governments to use aid to pay for expenditures they would have made anyway while shifting other funds to expenditures with little impact on poverty or the economy (Shantayanan, 1998). As in the domestic debate over social welfare, many have suggested that the agencies themselves should be restructured (International Financial Institutions Advisory Commission, 2000), and that aid might be better channeled through nongovernmental organizations, including faith-based organizations.

On the other hand, foreign aid is being rethought. Some have suggested that there is a way to increase the certainty that aid will be devoted to its intended purposes and be effective. They propose a new form of aid, called the Millennium Challenge Account (MCA), which the U.S. Congress commissioned early in 2004. The MCA is a commitment of the U.S. to raise its grant aid by a factor of 50% over the next three years and will result in a $5 billion annual increase over current foreign aid levels (Heyneman, 2003). Many other countries and multinational development assistance agencies are being asked to cofinance this new account, and their participation would augment the original proposal from the United States. The MCA offers the opportunity for a quantum change in the prospects for peace and stability. It will be allocated entirely to health and education. It will be targeted to nations that are poor and need it the most, and who have met the standards for macroeconomic policy accountability and reform on the grounds that a nation that cannot put effective economic development policies in place will not be likely to use aid effectively (Burnside & Dollar, 1998). If aid is nested within nations with supportive economic and social principles, it is expected to have its intended effect. But the purpose of aid is equally important.

Public aid is being targeted to support public functions and public goods in health and education on the grounds that it is morally right for children of all nations to have equal opportunity. Aid will support policies addressing health issues such as infectious disease, dangerous sexual practices, smoking, and the abuse of alcohol. In education, aid will lower (but hardly eliminate) the gap in per-pupil expenditures. It will increase educational opportunity for girls and the availability of simple educational goods and services such as textbooks (Heyneman, 2005).

Thus, the world is slowly but carefully edging toward a single minimum standard of education and social justice. It is also edging toward a change between philanthropy or charity to a regime of government policy to redistribute income in order to increase the opportunity for social justice. While there is no legal mandate to transfer resources from wealthy to poor nations, as there are to transfer resources from wealthy to poor school districts within the United States, the framework is in place to provide universal educational opportunity. This first step will likely lead to the consideration of a basic level of equality of opportunity across nations.

A broader question concerns the nature of charity: Is it possible to have a charitable relationship without at the same time having expectations of behavior? I think not. I believe that the relationship among nations is parallel to the relationship among individuals within countries. While the poor deserve assistance, that assistance obligates them. No nation nor individual has a right to misdirect philanthropy from a legitimate to an illegitimate purpose. The rights of the donor are important. They sacrifice on specific grounds—health, education, welfare, and the like—and would have the right to withdraw new funds if that charity were to be misused.

Withdrawal of public assistance does not necessarily solve the problem of poverty, however, and families—like nations—may soon request a new round of "debt relief," triggering questions from donors about how previous philanthropy was managed. It is a difficult question, and one that has no single response. There are rights and obligations on both sides. The key underpinning assumption, however, is the perception that children, whether in Michigan or Malawi, deserve the same opportunity to attend school and to learn what the world offers.

REFERENCES

Akhand, H. A., & Gupta, K. L. (2002). *Foreign aid in the twenty-first century.* Boston: Kluwer Academic.

Baicker, K., & Gordon, N. (2004). *The state giveth, the state taketh away? School finance equalizations and net redistribution.* Washington, DC: National Bureau of Economic Research.

Bane, M. J. (1975). Economic justice: Controversies and policies. In A. M. Levine and M. J. Bane (Eds.), *The inequality controversy: Schooling and distributive justice* (pp. 304–326). New York: Basic Books.

Bell, W., & Robinson, R. V. (1978). Equality, success, and social justice in England and the United States. *American Sociological Review, 43*(2), 125–148.

Bendix, R. (1964). *Nation-building and citizenship.* New York: Wiley.

Berne, R., & Stiefel, L. (1984). *Measurement and equity in school finance: Conceptual, methodological, and empirical dimensions.* Baltimore: Johns Hopkins University Press.

Berne, R., & Stiefel, L. (1999). Concepts of school finance equity: 1970–present. In H. F. Ladd, R. Chalk, & J. S. Hansen (Eds.), *Equity and adequacy in education finance: Issues and perspectives* (pp. 7–33). Washington DC: National Academy Press.

Beynon, J. (2002). Policy implications for aid allocations of recent research on aid effectiveness and selectivity. in B. M. Arvin (Ed.), *New perspectives on foreign aid and economic development* (pp. 265–291). Westport, CT: Praeger.

Brainard, L., Graham, C., Purvis, N., Radelet, S., and Smith, G. E. (2003). *The other war: Global poverty and the Millennium Challenge Account.* Washington, DC: Brookings Institution Press.

Burnside, C., & Dollar, D. (1998). *Aid: The incentive regime and poverty reduction.* Washington, DC: World Bank.

Carr, M. C., & Furman, S. H. (1999). The politics of school finance in the 1990s. In H. F. Ladd, R. Chalk, & J. S. Hansen (Eds.), *Equity and adequacy in education finance: Issues and perspectives* (pp. 136–174). Washington DC: National Academy Press.

Coleman, J. S. (1973). The equality of opportunity and the equality of results. *Harvard Educational Review, 43* No. 2 124–137.

Coleman, J. S. (1974). Inequality, sociology and moral philosophy. *American Journal of Sociology, 80*(3) 739–764.

Corcoran, S., Evans, W. N., Godwin, J, Murray, S. E., & Schwab, R. M. (2003). *The changing distribution of education finance: 1972-1997.* College Park: Maryland Population Research Center.

Dollar, D., & Pritchett, L. (1998). *Assessing aid: What works, what doesn't and why.* Washington, DC: World Bank.

Heyneman, S. P. (1982). Resource availability, equality, and educational opportunity among nations. In L. Anderson and D. M. Windham (Eds.), *Educational development issues in the analysis and planning of post-colonial societies* (pp. 129–144). Lexington, MA: Lexington Books.

Heyneman, S. P. (1997). Economic development and the international trade in education reform, *Prospects, 27*(4), 501–531.

Heyneman, S. P. (1999). The sad story of UNESCO's statistics. *International Journal of Educational Development, 19*(3), 65–74.

Heyneman, S. P. (2000). From the party/state to multi-ethnic democracy: Education and social cohesion in Europe and the Central Asia Region. *Education Evaluation and Policy Analysis, 22*(2), 173–193.

Heyneman, S. P. (2003). The social aspects of the Millennium Challenge Account: Risks and prospects. *Economic Prospects, 8*(2), pp.23–27.

Heyneman, S. P. (2004). International education quality. *Economics of Education Review, 23* no. 2, 441–52.

Heyneman, S. P. (2005). *The role of textbooks in a modern education system.* Geneva: International Bureau of Education.

Heyneman, S. P., & Loxley, W. A. (1983). The effect of primary school quality on academic achievement across twenty-nine high- and low-income countries. *American Journal of Sociology, 88*(6), 1162–1194.

International Financial Institutions Advisory Commission (2000). *The Meltzer Commission report.* Washington, DC: U.S. Government Printing Office.

Lauren, P. G. (2000). *The evolution of international human rights.* Philadelphia: University of Pennsylvania Press.

Martens, B., Mummert, U., Murell, P., & Seabright, P. (2002). *The institutional economics of foreign aid.* Cambridge: Cambridge University Press.

McGillivray, M., Leavy, J., and White, H. (2002). Aid principles and policy: An operational base for the assessment of donor performance. In B. M. Arvin (Ed.), *New perspectives on foreign aid and economic development* (pp. 57–91).Westport, CT: Praeger.

Melchiorre, A. (2002). *At what age are school children employed, married and taken to court?* Report for the Right to Education Project. Stockholm: Swedish International Cooperation Agency.

National Education Association (2005). Rankings and estimates: Rankings of the states, 2004 and estimates of school statistics, 2005. Retrieved July 12, 2006 from http://www.nea.org/edstats/images/05rankings.pdf.

New York State Education Department, Fiscal Analysis and Services Unit (NYSED). (2004). *New York, the state of learning: A report to the governor and the legislature on the educational stratus of the state's schools.* Albany, NY: Author. Retrieved January 27, 2006 from http://www.emsx.nysed.gov/irt/655report/2004/volume1/combined_report.pdf.

Nozik, R. (1975). Distributive justice. In A. M. Levine & M. J. Bane (Eds.), *The inequality controversy: Schooling and distributive justice* (pp. 252–276). New York: Basic Books.

Organization for Economic Cooperation and Development (2002). *Aid at a Glance.* Paris: Author.

Pritchett, L. (2004). Access to education. In B. Lomborg (Ed.), *Global crises, global solutions* (pp. 175–234). Cambridge: Cambridge University Press.

Rawls, J. (1958). Justice as fairness. *Philosophical Review, 67*(2), 164–94.

Rawls, J. (1971) A Theory of Justice Cambridge (Mass.): Harvard University Press

Rice, J. K. (2004). Equity and efficiency in school finance reform: Competing or complementary goals? *Peabody Journal of Education, 79*(3), 134–151.

Shantayanan, S. (1998). *The implications of financial aid fungibility for development assistance.* Washington, DC: World Bank.

Sogge, D. (1988). *Give and take: What is the matter with foreign aid?* Dhaka, Bangladesh: The University Press.

Tarnoff, C., & Nowels, L. (2002). *Foreign aid: An introductory overview of U.S. programs and policy.* Washington, DC: Congressional Research Service.

UNESCO. (2002). *Education for all: Is the world on track?* Global Monitoring Report 2002. Paris: Author.

United Nations Development Programme. (2004). *Cultural liberty in today's diverse world.* Human Development Report. New York: Author.

World Bank. (2001). *Global development finance 2001.* Washington, DC: Author.

World Bank. (2002). *Achieving education for all by 2015: Simulation results for 47 low-income countries.* Washington, DC: Author

World Bank. (2004). *World development indicators.* Washington, DC: Author.

TOWARD A VISION OF SOCIAL JUSTICE
FRAMEWORKS IN SCHOOL FINANCE

R. Anthony Rolle

Texas A&M University

Gloria M. Rodriguez

University of California–Davis

Julie López Figueroa

California State University–Sacramento

PUBLIC EDUCATION HAS BEEN UNDER SERIOUS SCRUTINY during the past two decades for failing to provide all of the nation's children—regardless of economic, ethnic-racial, or geographic distinctions—with the level of education needed to be productive citizens in an increasingly multicultural and global society. This lack of a general pursuit of social justice objectives has generated speculations among academics about how increases in levels of diversity will affect the popular culture of the United States, and what it means for future educational aspirations, economic objectives, and sociopolitical characteristics of the emerging population. In fact, the U.S. Bureau of the Census released a working paper projecting a national population of approximately 575 million people by the end of the 21st century (Hollman, Mulder, & Kallan, 2000). These projections reveal that not only will a larger American population exist, but also one that is increasingly more ethnically and racially diverse. Specifically, by the year 2100, it is estimated that the U.S. population will be 1% Native American, 13% Asian–Pacific Islander, 13% African-American, 33% Latino/Hispanic, and 40% white.

In light of these changing demographics, public policy reformers have offered various approaches to educational improvement and accountability: (1) whole school reforms; (2) schools within schools; (3) accelerated and decelerated schools; (4) single sex or single race schools; and (5) multiple school choice options from magnet schools to voucher plans. Despite these numerous efforts, the most widely implemented—and accepted—strategy for focusing education systems on student performance may be standards-based accountability reform (Fuhrman, 1999). At the national level, from *A Nation at Risk* (National Commission on Excellence in Education, 1983) to the Improving America's Schools Act of 1994 to the No Child Left Behind Act of 2001, there have been calls for high academic standards for all students, including those in poverty and in special populations, while stressing the importance of organizational accountability. In addition to national efforts, over 45 states have established school accountability systems to report on or rate school performance, with test scores as the most frequently cited primary outcome measure (Education Week, 2001, pp. 80–81). Consequently, the challenge for 21st-century education systems—posed by political demands for improvements in school performance—is to finance and manage schools equitably and efficiently in their provision of high quality educational services (Hansen, 2001).

Despite this research activity around education reform efforts, noticeably absent from education policy debates—beyond the general acceptance that the average low-income or minority student will compare unfavorably with the rest of the nation in terms of student achievement—are discussions of the appropriate role that social justice principles should play in the development of education policy finance policy. The present volume has addressed this policy discussion avoidance by initiating a discussion on the nexus of social justice principles and education finance theory and policy. The voices heard here have attempted to provide initial comment on important social justice principles in the hopes that researchers from all fields will begin to investigate the theoretical and practical issues raised.

This book begins with Bull's theory of social justice for education that critiques the underlying normative philosophical structure that legitimizes the current organization of school finance systems. In essence, equality is a central concern of traditional normative theory in that equal liberties and opportunities are to be among the social results to which the school system contributes. However, Bull asserts that simple equality of school resources between schools or school districts—often referred to as *horizontal equity*—is insufficient to provide an acceptable measure of the system's contribution to individual liberty. Thus, Bull concludes, social justice in school finance is "significantly a matter of vertical equity—that is, of providing the unequal distribution of resources to enable schools to meet these varying conditions of children and their families." He further supports these ideas with four principles:

1. *Liberty:* Conduct public schooling in way that allows children to develop personally meaningful conceptions of the good and to acquire the reasonable capacities to pursue them.
2. *Democracy:* Conduct public schooling in a way that fosters children's ability and willingness to participate in public decision-making processes and make constructive contributions to, learn from, and act on the results of those processes.
3. *Equal opportunity:* Conduct public schooling so that children have an equal chance to develop the differential abilities required for success under their emerging individual and collective conceptions of the good.
4. *Economic growth:* Conduct public schooling in a way that allows children to understand the role that economically valued capabilities may have in formulating and pursuing their emerging personal and social conceptions of the good and that helps them develop the economic capabilities included in their life plans.

As such, Bull challenges the social justice relevance of *horizontal equity* as defined in the school finance literature historically. Ultimately, he calls for an expansion of the meanings and applications of vertical equity in an attempt to improve student learning objectives.

Next, Alemán examines the legitimacy of human capital theory applications to discuss the merits of issues such as equalized state funding, high stakes testing or accountability systems, or performance incentives in teacher pay prior to examining social justice considerations. His aim is not to refute the legitimacy of human capital theory nor to abandon economic and productivity analyses in education. Instead, Alemán's purpose is to delineate a supplementary theoretical framework—critical race theory—from which to evaluate, analyze, and discuss educational finance in the quest for socially just educational opportunities. Ultimately, Alemán questions how the use of human capital theory discourses in the political arena precludes legitimate challenges to the assumptions, beliefs, and principles at the heart of the theory. In essence, its "unquestioned prevalence" detracts and disparages arguments of those attempting to achieve measurable social justice objectives.

Following Alemán's contribution, R. Anthony Rolle and Arthur X. Fuller assert that trends in education seem to be exemplified by continued increases in organizational size and fiscal resources and decreases in organizational and student learning outcomes—both with an abundance of compromise over how much to preference the pursuit of certain social justice values. Given these differentiated efforts and disparate pursuits of certain educational and social justice goals, Rolle and Fuller state that normative economic theories seem inappropriate for a public school's level of productivity to be measured as a pursuit of what could be the unattainable: an absolute mathematical representation of a sociopolitical process that determines and distributes resources to school administrators who may or may not direct resources toward desired organizational goals. As such, they explore new linkages between educational productivity and social justice by providing evidence that supports two assertions:

1. Given the differential social justice climates existing within various educational contexts, levels of school productivity should be reconceptualized as the amount of technical efficiency generated by combinations of financial and human resources, sociopolitical influences, instructional and management strategies, and levels of student effort that maximize educational outcomes.

2. Given the differential pursuits of social justice objectives within various educational contexts, the measurement of efficiency in public schools should be re-conceptualized to focus on what the *highest* student learners achieve compared to the lowest student learners—not the best average performances predicted by traditional production function analyses. Accordingly, the measures used should focus on relative comparisons of the best performers to the worst.

Ultimately, Rolle and Fuller conclude that without such exploration of alternative educational productivity frameworks, the true relationship between educational expenditures and student outcomes will remain coupled loosely at best by analyses utilized within the normative production function framework.

Alexander proceeds with her assertion that adequacy is a socially derived concept—not a mathematically or statistically derived one—that encompasses socially derived notions of what it means to have a just society and equitable schooling. Specifically, she notes

Current definitions of adequacy do not necessarily address the different social contexts faced by various student groups, including students of color, English-language learners, and immigrant students. While statistical models often include variables measuring percentages of poor, percentages of minorities, and so on, they exclude more qualitative factors like institutional racism, cultural incompetence, and the like.

Alexander begins by exploring different conceptualizations of social justice and usages of adequacy concepts as a vehicle in education finance programs. She continues her chapter by questioning the conceptualization of adequacy as expressed by the results of a traditionally adequate school system. Ultimately, she argues that adequacy should be considered based on the standards set by policy makers because they act as official representatives of the community. "Accepting the existing standards, however, does not excuse us from an explicit examination on the institutional and cultural implications of these standards."

The persistence of "cultural deficit model" thinking in the field of school finance is the subject of critique in Rodriguez's analysis of the California school finance system. She employs here an exploratory strategy derived from conventional and critical frameworks in education and public policy studies to consider new avenues for both creating and assessing policy in school finance. A key dilemma that arises from her analysis is that the eradication of cultural deficit thinking in school finance could lead to a reversal of longstanding practice aimed at deficit-based allocations in favor of pursuing a strategy that identifies and invests resources in student and community assets.

Gonzales and Rodriguez investigate the desirability of educational organizations to allocate extra resources to support high-quality English-learning instruction. This chapter is further framed by the view that educational responsiveness is enacted in the professional practices of teachers who are attuned to—and engaged in—the cultural, social, and linguistic diversity of their students as they promote learning and high achievement. Through the use of several examples, Gonzales and Rodriguez examine the different types of educational environments where low-income children and children of color are able to perform well academically. Ultimately, they attempt to explore the resource needs of English-learning students and their teachers through the lens of educational responsiveness.

Berliner proceeds with his argument that public education is used as "the mechanism of choice" to reduce poverty among all Americans, yet this choice represents a misunderstanding of what schooling can ordinarily accomplish. He states that "we sometimes forget that schooling is a relatively weak treatment, often limited in its accomplishments by the poverty that exists outside the classroom." Consequently, Berliner's chapter discusses the importance of outside-of-school factors that mitigate the impact of school finance policy. He contends that the occasional outlier school will "beat the odds," and be heralded for its success; but, the vast majority of schools educating poor and minority students can also be assisted by addressing community and family issues (e.g., lack of access to health care) that are important to parents and students. Berliner urges us to consider our investments in education in tandem with much broader considerations of social policy that increase the likelihood for improved life chances among low-income and minority children.

In a similar vein, Heyneman calls upon us to extend the argument of the broad policy view even further to explore the current (and changing) international context. He presents his analysis of the global context and identifies the current and potential leadership role the United States can play, particularly through how it structures its international investments in education. While education is not guaranteed through our own federal constitution, Heyneman's analysis reminds us of the critical social justice role that access to education has played in the international scene thus compelling us to ponder how we might proceed with local educational investments, guided by the view of education as a human right.

Given that this volume is designed to be a beginning, there still is a need to investigate the three primary educational finance and human-resources-management challenges from a variety of social justice perspectives. Further analyses are warranted to determine the crucial interrelationship—conceptual and practical—among educational accountability, human/financial resource distribution, efficiency, and the social factors (wealth, race/ethnicity, geography) that differentiate our communities.

Accordingly, there must be efforts to apply social justice frameworks to the use of expenditures from state legislatures to state departments of education to district financial offices; and when possible, to individual schools and classrooms. Legislators, superintendents, principals, teachers, parents, and the public need to know where and how money is spent in attempts to improve the quality of education provided to students—not just that more dollars or fewer dollars were spent on their children's education.

To the degree that the social justice goals we have introduced with this volume are desirable, shared, or even just intellectually intriguing, we view the work of our contributors as reflecting the potential means by which such ends might be accomplished through the field of school finance. We are also compelled to state that while we strive to advance the social justice aims of education in our society, our intention is to participate in a scholarly dialogue. Furthermore, we hope that this scholarly passion can be grounded in a sense of humanity, as the practice of social justice is in other arenas. Certainly none of our contributors can lay claim to the oft-sought educational "magic bullet" or the even more elusive "magic dollar amount" that would guarantee socially just outcomes. In this spirit, we consider this volume an invitation to colleagues—the supportive, curious, and skeptical alike—to engage with us in this dialogue and demystification process. We seek to locate the problems of school finance (and education) within the policy contexts that are more likely to yield advancement toward broader social change, thereby interrupting decades-long cycles of disappointing results despite public investments and well-intended policy efforts. In this regard, we welcome the opportunity to continue to grapple with the challenging theoretical puzzles we have introduced in this volume, and to engage with colleagues in pushing for even greater clarity in the parameters and indicators of social justice in educational and school finance theory and policy.

REFERENCES

Education Week (2001, January 11). Quality Counts: A Better Balance—Standards, Tests, and the Tools to Succeed. Volume 20, Number 17.

Fuhrman, S. H. (1999). The New Accountability. CPRE Policy Briefs. Philadelphia, PA: Consortium for Policy Research in Education.

Hansen, J. S. (2001). 21st Century School Finance: How is the context changing? ECS Issue Paper: Education Finance in the States—Its Past, Present, and Future. Denver, CO: Education Commission of the States.

National Commission on Excellence in Education (1983). A nation at risk: The imperative for educational reform. Washington, D.C.: U.S. Government Printing Office.

EDITORS AND CONTRIBUTORS

ENRIQUE ALEMÁN, JR., is an assistant professor of educational leadership and policy at the University of Utah. Utilizing critical race theory and Latina/o critical race theory frameworks, he studies educational policy and politics. Dr. Alemán's research has been published in *Educational Administration Quarterly* and *Educational Policy*.

NICOLA A. ALEXANDER is an associate professor in the Department of Educational Policy and Administration at the University of Minnesota. She focuses on issues of equity and adequacy surrounding educational policy for PreK–12 schools. Recent publications on these issues include, "Being on Track for NCLB: Examining the Capacity of Massachusetts Public 8th Grade Programs," published in *Educational Policy*, "The Changing Face of Adequacy," published in the *Peabody Journal of Education*, and "Race, Poverty, and the Student Curriculum: Implications for Standards Policy," published in the *American Educational Research Journal*.

DAVID C. BERLINER is Regents' Professor of Education at Arizona State University. He co-authored *The Manufactured Crisis* (1995, with B. J. Biddle) and the textbook *Educational Psychology* (1998, with N. L. Gage), and co-edited *The Handbook of Educational Psychology* (1996, with R.C. Calfee). He is a past president of the American Educational Research Association and a member of the National Academy of Education.

BARRY L. BULL is a professor of philosophy of education and education policy studies at Indiana University–Bloomington. His research is concerned primarily with the ethical and political justification of a variety of education policies. Recently, he has conducted research and published on standards-based school reform, civic and moral education, education for the gifted, school finance, national standards for education, and local control of schools. He is the coauthor, with V. Chattergy and R. Fruehling, of *The Ethics of Multicultural and Bilingual Education* (1992).

JULIE LÓPEZ FIGUEROA is an assistant professor in the Department of Ethnic Studies at California State University–Sacramento. Dr. Figueroa continues to work in the areas of higher education, qualitative research, and academic success to identify the processes that mediate and shape the Latina/o experience in higher education. She has also engaged in research on urban schooling and teaching in cultural contexts and has published on topics related to institutional racism, the Latina/o educational pipeline, and methodological issues in studying the educational experiences of Latina/o students.

ARTHUR X. FULLER is a doctoral student at Vanderbilt University's College of Education and Human Development. He is the executive assistant to the director, and fiscal budget officer, of the Tennessee State Board of Education. In this capacity, he serves as policy adviser on education accountability, charter schools, finance, and college access issues.

PATRICIA GÁNDARA is a professor of education in the Graduate School of Education and Information Studies at the University of California–Los Angeles. She has directed education research in the California legislature (1985–87), and has been a commissioner for postsecondary education in California (1981–86). During her recent service as a professor of education at the University of California–Davis, she directed the Center for Applied Policy in Education and was associate director of the UC Linguistic Minority Research Institute. Dr. Gándara also served on a statewide, multi-sponsored adequacy/cost study of California public schools, contributing her expertise on teaching and learning support for English-language learners.

SARAH A. GONZALES has spent the last three decades in urban public education as a teacher and administrator. She was on the faculty in the Department of Educational Leadership at California State University–East Bay, where she mentored administrative credential candidates who sought to develop social justice leadership in primarily urban schools in diverse communities. Her research interests include educational equity and the professional role of classroom teachers, with a focus on instructional leadership in support of teaching and learning. Dr. Gonzales is also the current president of the Board of Trustees for the Hayward Unified School District.

STEPHEN P. HEYNEMAN received his PhD in comparative education from the University of Chicago in 1976. He served the World Bank for 22 years. Between 1976 and 1984 he helped research education quality and design policies to support educational effectiveness. Between 1984 and 1989 he was in charge of external training for senior officials worldwide in education policy. And between 1989 and 1998, he was responsible for education policy and lending strategy, first for the Middle East and North Africa and later for the 27 countries of Europe and Central Asia. In July 2000 he was appointed as a professor of international education policy at Vanderbilt University. Current interests include the effect of higher education on social cohesion, the international trade in education services, and the economic and social cost of higher education corruption.

GLORIA M. RODRIGUEZ is an assistant professor in the School of Education at the University of California–Davis. She specializes in school finance and educational leadership from a critical, social justice perspective, as well as finance and policy issues affecting Latina/os and other communities of color. Prior to pursuing her graduate studies, she worked in various capacities in state and local government, including a position as a fiscal and policy analyst with the California Legislative Analyst's Office. Dr. Rodriguez has served as a member of the Board of Directors for the American Education Finance Association (AEFA) and is a recipient of the AEFA Jean Flanigan Outstanding Dissertation Award for her study of the California school finance system and the equity status of the state's Latina/o students.

JAMES L. RODRIGUEZ is an associate professor of education at San Diego State University. Dr. Rodriguez is an educational psychologist and a specialist in early childhood development and the academic achievement of culturally and linguistically diverse students. His publications have appeared in educational and psychological journals including *Applied Developmental Science, Child Development, Early Childhood Research Quarterly,* the *High School Journal,* the *Hispanic Journal of Behavioral Sciences,* the *Review of Educational Research,* and *Theory into Practice.*

R. ANTHONY ROLLE is an associate professor in the Department of Educational Administration and Human Resource Development at Texas A&M University's College of Education and Human Development.

Dr. Rolle has conducted K–12 education finance and policy research for such organizations as the University of Washington Institute for Public Policy and Management, the Washington State Legislature, the Indiana Education Policy Center, and the National Education Association. His professional interests include educational productivity and public school finance equity. Dr. Rolle is a recipient of the AEFA Jean Flanigan Outstanding Dissertation Award for his empirical work that modified budget-maximizing theory and questioned traditional notions of efficiency in public education. He is also a current member of the AEFA Board of Directors.

INDEX

S

T

teachers
  academic needs, 147
  education distribution, 63
  linguistic needs, 147
  professional development, 183
third generation equity issues, 64
total economic efficiency, 60
Tunisia, 192

U

uniform system, 94
United Nations Convention, 195
United States
  budget outlays, 197
  Bureau of the Census, 207
  children population, 165
  children poverty, 162
  Department of Education, 153
  Department of Health and Human
    Services, 180
  educational finance, 191
  education concerns, 198
  eighth grade test scores, 168
  ethnic group differences, 42
  financial disparities, 193
  foreign aid, 198
  foreign aid budget, 197
  foreign aid economy, 196
  fourth grade test scores, 168
  GDP, 196
  history of racism, 50
  inequality, 172

  literacy problem, 169
  literacy scores, 170
  mathematics problem, 169
  national populations, 207
  PISA science scores, 171
  poverty, 167
  poverty problem, 163–167
  public schools, 1
  qualified teacher, 153
  racial discrimination, 39
  science problem, 169
  seventh grade mathematics scores, 172
  universal educational opportunity, 202
  World War II, 196
urban language learning needs, 152

V

vertical equity, 122
violating equality
  personal liberty, 23
  political liberty, 23
vision, childhood poverty, 174

W

wealth, black community, 126
Williams v. California, 110
  California school finance policy, 114
  settlement, 113–114
workers' capabilities economic growth,
  28
World War II, 192
  US GDP, 196